STATE AND WELFARE

STATE AND WELFARE
Tawney, Galbraith and Adam Smith

David Reisman

First published 1982 by
THE MACMILLAN PRESS LTD
London and Basingstoke
Companies and representatives
throughout the world

ISBN 0 333 31917 6

Printed in Hong Kong

Contents

PART IV: CONCLUSION

Acknowledgements

The author and publishers wish to thank the following, who have kindly given permission for the use of copyright material: George Allen & Unwin Ltd for the extracts from *Equality* and *Attack* by R. H. Tawney, and Pantheon Books (a division of Random House Inc.) for the extracts from *The Radical Tradition* by R. H. Tawney; Bell & Hyman Ltd for the extracts from *The Acquisitive Society* by R. H. Tawney; Cambridge University Press for the extract from *Structure System and Economic Policy* (1977) by W. W. Leontief, and for the extracts from *Commonplace Book* by R. H. Tawney; André Deutsch Ltd and Houghton Mifflin Company for the extracts from *Annals of an Abiding Liberal*, copyright © 1979, and *Economics and the Public Purpose*, copyright © 1973 by John Kenneth Galbraith; and Routledge & Kegan Paul Ltd for the extracts from *History and Society* by R. H. Tawney. The author and publishers also wish to express their gratitude to the following for assistance at various stages in the preparation of this book: the British Library of Political and Economic Science, J. K. Galbraith, Margaret Gowing, the John F. Kennedy Library, Ann Oakley, Ross Terrill and Michael Vyvyan.

PART I

INTRODUCTION

1 The Market Mechanism

This book is concerned with the place and interaction in social theory of two key concepts, political intervention in social processes on the one hand, the well-being of the community and its members on the other. It does not argue that market is superior to command. Nor does it call for a mix of public and private. This book is a series of essays in the history of ideas and seeks simply to understand what, in terms of theoretical justifications and empirical evidence, has led sensitive and intelligent thinkers to conclude that society is most successful in attaining its shared objectives when it attempts to do so consciously and collectively.

This book has eight chapters. The first – the present chapter – explains what the market is, upon what assumptions its effective operation reposes, and why it might have its opponents as well as its advocates. The second, third and fourth chapters deal with Richard Henry Tawney and investigate why he, a committed democratic socialist of Christian persuasion and the heir to traditional British concern with a common culture, rejected any measures to cope with the alleged niggardliness of nature which abstracted from morality of intent, compassion toward one's fellow-men, and deliberate action to shape a common destiny. The fifth, sixth and seventh chapters examine the views on voluntary exchanges and stranger gifts of John Kenneth Galbraith, whose confidence and optimism regarding the ultimate and inevitable convergence of economic and social systems on the mixed economy reflect principally his economic and technological determinism.

The eighth and last chapter in this book is about Adam Smith; and it might from that fact be inferred that the book ends as it begins, with a simple exposition of how the pure market mechanism, as if guided by an invisible hand, solves the central economic problems of what to produce, how much to produce and for whom to produce. Such an inference would be a false one. It would suggest that this book offers at the end of the journey at least the prospect of a safe harbour; and that, unfortunately, is not the case.

The economic problem is widely thought to be one of perceived scarcities of goods and services and hence the need rationally and efficiently to deploy those limited resources that we have. The market mechanism is one proposed solution to this problem. Suppose that there are only two goods in the economy, guns and butter; and specifically that there are 200 guns and 200 pounds of butter. And suppose that people want to purchase precisely 200 guns and 200 pounds of butter. Then clearly the economy is in stable equilibrium, since the quantity demanded of guns is equal to the quantity supplied of guns and the quantity demanded of butter is equal to the quantity supplied of butter.

Suppose now that the country is threatened by an enemy from abroad; and that as a result people want more guns (and, by implication, less butter, since there is no reason to anticipate, other things being equal, that incomes rise in the very instant that preferences alter). Then, via the free market mechanism, the price of guns will rise until only 200 guns are demanded, while the price of butter will fall until at last the 200 pounds of butter that has been produced can also be sold.

Naturally, there are other ways in which the sudden rush on guns could have been met. There could, for instance, have been a policy of constant prices and distribution on the basis of first come, first served. Thus, where people previously wanted 200 guns and now desire 250, would-be consumers assemble in an orderly queue outside shops in the hope – a hope doomed in many cases to disappointment and frustration – that they will be given the opportunity to buy into the supply of 200 guns in stock. Such a system, however, is somewhat arbitrary (allocation by queueing might deny guns both to workers on night shifts and to soldiers on duty, and thus serve individual at the expense of social purpose) and may be widely perceived to be unfair (as where the old and the infirm might be unable to queue up all night for a gun and yet still be able to shoot it).

In order to overcome these difficulties, the government might decide to print ration-books and in that way to allocate the 200 guns on the basis of some more rational criterion than the willingness and ability of the shopper to sleep on the pavement. Yet rationing would impose a tremendous administrative burden if it were extended to the allocation of all goods and services in the community; and, quite apart from that, it also presupposes for its successful operation that all consumers want the commodity with more or less the same intensity of desire. Were this not the case, one man could buy the gun to which he is entitled by virtue of his ration book and then re-sell it to another man at a higher price (even where such a transaction is in contravention both of the law and of the rational criterion behind the law). As long as some people are willing to pay more than others for a commodity with a nominally fixed price, there is always the threat that rationing will break down and be circumvented by the workings of parallel, free ("black") markets.

Rationing is in any case problematic because of the difficulties associated with the formulation of socially acceptable rules (and the menace of coercion, sanctions and perceived other-directedness should criteria in practice turn out to be the will of a minority imposed on the majority, perhaps for the greatest good of the greatest number but still such as would be rejected by some hypothetical referendum). Sometimes the content of the rules is dictated by tradition (in a shipwreck, the rule is "women and children first, captain last", although there is probably more politeness than wisdom in an arrangement which ensures to some immediate physical survival in a freezing lifeboat without the skilled leadership which alone could eventually guide it to shore), while sometimes the rules emerge so naturally from the logic of the situation that no well-informed and impartial observer could possibly take issue with that which is obviously the optimal means for attaining a non-controversial end (in the rush hour, the rule on public transport is "let them off first, please", and this makes sense where it is clearly not possible to squeeze in the next generation before squeezing out its predecessors). Sometimes, however, the nature of the rules promulgated is a subject of debate and a cause of division, as where those rules involve a social value-consensus which either may not exist or may exist but not be easy to measure. Suppose, for instance, that the government wanted to allocate housing as a partial gift and thus at maximum rents below those which would have been set by higglers and bargainers. Here the quantity demanded will by definition exceed the quantity supplied and a conscious choice will have to be made from a lengthy list of candidates. The government might decide to allocate accommod-ation on the basis of size of family (but then some taxpayers will grumble all the way to the polling station that it is inequitable for me to subsidise your children), or on the basis of social utility of occupation (but he who is likely to favour the policeman is unlikely to favour the pop singer while the pacifist is likely to show as little warmth for the war hero who has committed murder in the name of the Fatherland as the war hero will show for the conscientious objector who opted for butter when the majority of his countrymen went for guns) or on the basis of political allegiance (but it is then open to discussion whether the elegant Hampstead flat with its fine views and its central heating should go to Socrates, Christ, Robespierre, Lenin or Hitler). The government might choose to allow rich and poor, black and white, Catholic and Protestant to live in separate areas, or it might insist that mixing is preferable to segregation; but whatever it does in so complex an area of social policy it does on the basis of a rule promulgated from above and not reflecting direct consultation with each member of the community involved.

The market mechanism at least has the advantage of securing that high degree of on-going democratic consultation, and of doing so with the minimum of administrative interference and cost. Returning to our previous example of guns and butter, we can see how this happens by disaggregating the magic of the market into first a "short-run allocation effect" and then a "long-run production effect".

The short-run allocation effect operates as follows: when the threat of invasion caused consumers previously satisfied with 200 guns and 200 pounds of butter to demand 250 guns and less than 200 pounds of butter, a scarcity of guns clearly developed and, simultaneously, a glut of butter. Suppose that at the previous point of equilibrium a gun cost £2 but that there is no (legal or conventional) reason for prices not to change with the times. Then the price of a gun will understandably rise (since the existing price is too low and shoppers at that price want more of the thing than is actually in existence); and at a price of, say, £3, perhaps ten people drop out of the auction, each one saying regretfully that he "just can't afford" to buy a gun at the new, higher price. There remain nonetheless people in the market with an effective demand for 240 guns and hence the price rises again to, say, £4, when a further thirty people fall by the wayside (each of whom would rather have liked one gun, but not at any price); and thence to £4.50, when the number of people left in the marketplace is such as to demand exactly 200 guns. Since the quantity supplied of guns is also 200, the bidding now ceases and the market is in equilibrium again. The invisible hand has, in short, automatically allocated the limited supply of guns, and has done so entirely without any intervention on the part of the State. Of course, the only question it asks of the purchaser is "Are you willing to put your money where your mouth is?" and that may be the wrong question; for the market mechanism has no way of ascertaining that the people just willing to pay the final price for the guns are also those people most prepared to use them in the social interest (they might thus be intending not to fight the enemy but to rob a bank). Nor is the market mechanism capable by itself of explaining why some people can permit themselves the luxury of paying more than others for the same commodity, particularly where differential desires are backed up by differential incomes, since differential incomes might be a market-determined measure of differential productivity and local scarcity (as where a skilled man is the source of more output than an unskilled one, or where a computer programmer earns more than a dustman because the latter category of employees is better stocked than the former) but they might also be a measure of something totally unconnected with supply and demand (as where one man is able to pay more than another while remaining himself unemployed because he is the beneficiary of unearned returns accruing to invested wealth inherited from rich parents, or where I am able to buy more guns to rob more banks because of the considerable profits derived from similar activity in the past). Such complexities lie beyond the remit of the invisible hand. All that the market mechanism does, at least as far as the short-run allocation effect is concerned, is to ensure that, although 250 guns were demanded at the start of bidding, only 200 were demanded at the end.

Inertia is short-lived, however, because of the long-run production effect. At the new price of £4.50, the sellers of guns are obviously pleased, for they had expected to supply their 200 guns at £2 each, i.e. at less than half the price that those guns ultimately came to command. Meanwhile, of course, a more depressing situation obtains in the butter industry: since incomes are in aggregate constant, and since there are in our model only two commodities, it is clear that if people are now choosing to spend more of their money on guns they must also be budgeting less for butter, and that butter-producers must consequently be experiencing lower prices and earning lower (perhaps negative) profits. The obvious thing for those producers to do, attracted by the carrot of high profits on guns and repelled by the stick of low profits in the butter industry, is to flee from butter to guns. The quantity supplied of guns then expands from 200 guns to more than 200 guns; the quantity supplied of butter falls from 200 pounds to less than 200 pounds; the price of guns falls as the quantity rises; the price of butter rises as the quantity falls; and the process of shifting and transferring continues until, at some equilibrium combination of prices and quantities, no producer remains tempted to move from one industry into the other.

It is by virtue of the short-run allocation effect and the long-run production effect that the market mechanism is able to present a viable solution to the central economic problems of what, how much and for whom. That solution reposes on four assumptions.

First, flexible prices – so that the desires of the consumer can make themselves felt. For a market to be an optimal conduit for the transmission of information, it must be such that no single buyer and no single seller can influence the price at which he trades, since only in that way will the market sensitively register a general change in tastes and preferences via a change in prices and quantities. Needless to say, this assumption reposes in turn on further assumptions concerning consumer sovereignty (that people act on the basis of authentic wants), consumer rationality (that people consciously attempt to satisfy their desires with the minimum expenditure of input per unit of output) and consumer enlightenment (that people possess adequate information about the alternatives open to them).

Second, the profit motive – so that private vices may become public virtues. The idea here is that each producer is exclusively interested in his own personal profit, not in serving the social interest; but that, as our example of guns and butter indicated, each is nonetheless led by his rational quest for a maximum rate of return to do that which the community demonstrably most highly values. A producer of butter with a traditional attachment to his village and a moral conviction that "thou shalt not kill" will, in a society which craves guns and has enough of butter, be as unwelcome and as unpopular as an oarsman who stubbornly rows upstream towards Jerusalem while his team-mates desperately row downstream towards the finishing line.

Third, *laissez-faire* – so that government intervention (with inescapable exceptions made for law and order and selected other essential public services) does not come between the sovereign consumer and his faithful producer, or distort a relationship so obviously bordering on the idyllic.

Fourth, free entry and exit – so that resources can move from industry to industry at the drop of a price.

This is the concept of the market mechanism, a concept so simple in its essentials that it was once said concerning it that "you can make even a parrot into a learned political economist – all he must learn are the two words 'supply' and 'demand' ".
No one has ever taught a parrot to be an economist. Many people, however, have taught economists to be parrots; and by so doing have caused them to confuse a simple idea with a complex ideology by means of a lemming-like leap to certainty of which the haunted intellectuality of Adam Smith (whose name is so often invoked in defence of propositions so naive that a critic without personal knowledge of *The Wealth of Nations* might with complete propriety reject it out of hand as "Adam's Myth") would never have approved. It is, after all, without doubt conceptually possible that the magic of the market, like most other forms of magic, is today as out of place as a sow in a drawing room. It will be useful to examine this possibility under three headings: competition, motivation and relevance.

(a) Competition

The theory of the pure market mechanism presupposes that prices are completely flexible and that the quantity supplied by each individual producer is so small relative to the total quantity of his product on the market that he is in practice a passive price-taker, able to sell as much as he likes at the going market price but unable by himself to have any effect on it. It may, however, happen in the real world that prices are not quite so flexible nor firms quite so passive as the theory would lead us to expect. Suppose, for instance, that there exists an industry inhabited not by a large number of small firms but rather by a single giant firm, a monopolist who is the only supplier of his product. Even the monopolist must *ceteris paribus* operate through the market mechanism and even he would find it difficult to force customers simultaneously to buy more and to pay more; but he at least (unlike the passive perfect competitor) has the option of reducing his price (so as to sell more of his product) or of raising it (so as to sell less, but at a higher price per unit sold). His choice will depend on how intensely people desire what he has to sell. If, say, the commodity is a necessity rather than a luxury, it is likely that a small decrease in quantity supplied will generate much competition among purchasers of the good and permit a more than proportionate rise in price on the part of the producer (a highly lucrative course of action, and one against which – in the absence of competition – the consumer has no defence). If a monopolist could control the quantity supplied of air, for example, then could raise the price of his product to a dramatically high level and still retain his customers: air is a necessity and people would not buy substantially less of it no matter how much it cost, so long as they had any money at all to spend. It is in this way that the monopolist holds the community for ransom.

It is, fortunately, difficult to think of genuine monopolies in the modern economy; for even if I had a monopoly of coffee-production at home, you could always import coffee from abroad or else drink tea, while if I had a monopoly of rail transport you would remain free to travel by car or bus. There are in any case few areas of production where there is room for only one firm, and precisely because of the limited numbers involved these natural monopolies are not impossible to supervise and regulate (on occasion they have also been nationalised in an attempt to prevent them from employing purely commercial criteria in fields where they have such vast potential power). Yet, just as pure monopoly is rare, so oligopoly is common; and these markets too are imperfectly competitive, for there are here a small number of large firms. Such a situation typically develops where there are economies of large scale, where large amounts of capital must be committed for long periods in production lines and research and development divisions in order to produce in an efficient manner. These expensive overheads are a considerable barrier to entry, and one should in addition remember that the need to produce large quantities, if it is to be economical to produce at all, carries with it the further entry barrier of potential market saturation: should but one more giant move in, he could easily convert the windfall profits of existing producers into spectacular losses not simply for existing producers but for himself as well.

In industries characterised by oligopolistic market structures, firms are interdependent and aware of their interdependence: clearly, if I raise my prices and you do not raise yours, then I am likely to lose some of my customers to you, while if I reduce my prices and you immediately follow suit, then you and I will enjoy the same relative price levels as before while having mutually beggared one another in terms of absolute levels. The key problem is uncertainty concerning the market strategies of a handful of powerful competitors; the obvious solution is collusion and cartel so as to give each other security by putting our cards on the table and continuing the game as allies rather than opponents; the government's reply is restrictive practices legislation to make illegal those intimate dinner parties at which we talk turkey, carve up markets, and agree to behave as the monopoly which we – collectively – are; and the key problem thus remains uncertainty (accompanied no doubt by a modest amount of industrial espionage, but recognising at the same time that it is not easy to spy into the future) as to competitors' actions, reactions and attitudes.

Because of this uncertainty, the oligopolist dares not let his prices fluctuate with fluctuations in supply and demand and tends to compete not so much via changes in prices as via the quality and image of the product he offers. Because of the need to compete via the perceived differentiation of his product, in short, the oligopolist comes to rely heavily on advertising.

Advertising is, of course, more than just an aspect of the firm's competitive strategy. It also has an important role to play in the forward planning of the organisation. Understandably, if a corporation commits large sums of money to the construction of plant designed to produce a new commodity which will not finally be marketed until a gestation period of many years has elapsed, it wants to be reasonably certain of success in disposing of the targeted quantity of output at some targeted price. It cannot afford to wait and see what price the forces of the market will at some time in the distant future decide to assign to its planned output (or, alternatively, what quantity the market will absorb at the price the firm sets) and seeks instead, by means both of careful market research and of experimentation with demand manipulation, to avoid expensive failures and to score resounding successes. Yet what is good for the producer need not be good for the consumer; for whereas in the traditional theory of the market mechanism the consumer communicated his desires through the market to the producer, it may be that today in the real world the consumer, having satisfied his basic needs for food, clothing and shelter, is confused as to what he wants and open to the blandishments of persuaders who play upon his psychological instincts and aspirations in an attempt to cause him to buy something he would not have wanted on its own merits. While it is by no means clear how far desires can in fact be manufactured out of nothing, it is nonetheless important to distinguish the informative from the manipulative function of advertising and to bear in mind that the welfare-furthering properties of the market mechanism are seriously called into question where producer replaces consumer sovereignty.

(b) Motivation

The pioneers of the theory of the pure market mechanism couched their approach in terms of an owner–entrepreneur who invested his own savings and ran his own business in such a way as to maximise the rate of profit on his own capital. Yet one feature of modern business life is the separation of ownership from control in the large joint-stock corporation. The decision makers in the modern corporation, it is argued, are increasingly not the capitalist owners, the shareholders, but rather a new élite of salaried meritocrats, the managers. These managers, it is maintained, have no particular incentive to maximise the profits of the firm (since any surplus remaining after some funds have been reinvested and some siphoned off in the form of corporation tax goes not to the decision-makers but to the anonymous, amorphous and ever-silent mass of dividend-takers) but they do have the power to run the firm so as to attain their own occupational objectives. An executive's remuneration, it is pointed out, does not depend on the rate of profit of his firm so much as on its absolute size and rate of growth; while the executive's prestige (derived as it is from the prestige of his firm) may more effectively be boosted by an extensive if not particularly cost-effective advertising campaign or by the launching of a new product principally in order to give the firm the image of being "go-ahead" than it would have been by a high rate of return on the capital invested. In the era of the managerial revolution, it is concluded, large firms are simply no longer profit-motivated; and for that reason may no longer have the beneficent philosophical property of serving the social interest by serving their own.

Some observers go further and argue that, not only has power in the large corporate organisation devolved from capitalists to managers, but it is now devolving still further – to the specialists, experts and technocrats (men such as highly trained economic forecasters or research chemists) who alone possess the requisite skill and information to make highly sophisticated technical decisions and on whose knowledge and advice the more generalist managers have no choice but to depend. Naturally, since the technocrats have no share in the ownership of the firm, the question then arises as to what, precisely, they desire to maximise; as to how far their private and personal goals might conflict with those of the capitalists and those of the managers (as might be the case where a group of civil engineers all with training at post-doctoral level proposed a massive research and development programme purely in order to have the satisfaction of carrying it through); and as to where the ultimate locus of power in the modern corporation is in fact to be found. Should power truly have devolved to organisation men similar in personality and objectives to State bureaucrats in the civil service, then it could be maintained that functionless capitalists should now be bought out and the private sector bureaucracy be made directly responsible to the democratically elected representatives of the members of the community. Citizen-sovereignty might, in other words, be preferable to consumer-sovereignty where the invisible hand is invisible for the simple reason that it is not there.

(c) Relevance

Even if it could be demonstrated that the market mechanism still functions – possibly because, although prices may not fluctuate freely, they do fluctuate; because new entry might be difficult but it nonetheless occurs; because advertising is more successful when appealing to existing wants than it is when attempting to create totally new ones; because even if the profit-motive is no longer the unique goal of the firm, it remains a goal nonetheless (it is, after all, out of internally generated funds that many corporate executives seek to finance expansion; and in that way they do, at the level of reputation even if not of dividend, obtain a share in profits) – it could all the same be suggested that the market is not acceptable in terms of the sort of society in which we as a group wish to live.

First, the market mechanism does not solve the problem of externalities, since when a firm calculates its costs, it has no economic reason to include those costs which it does not itself pay but imposes on society as a whole (costs such as, for instance, river pollution, road congestion and aircraft noise). Naturally, some of those externalities could be internalised (as where a high-risk employer is compelled to cover the full economic cost of treating an industrial disease frequently contracted by workers in a particular trade) and others could be prevented (as where legislation is introduced to ban advertising hoardings which uglify the countryside). Not all externalities, however, are susceptible to such directives and guide-lines, as is the case with, say, stress-linked complaints that are brought on by the rat race to win success in acquisitive societies dominated by values of emulation, rivalry, aggression, the unbridled greed for a fuller trough and the clear perception that one's neighbour is not one's brother but one's competitor or one's customer. The costs of mental illness (together with those imposed by the flowering of crime and the withering away of the gift relationship) can to some extent be calculated, but it is nonetheless not easy to locate the tort feasors and guilty parties so as to charge them the market price for these expensive consumer durables with a high-income elasticity. Recognising that economic exchange cannot cope with these externalities (not least because it may itself be the cause of diswelfares in its own right), social welfare schemes are often introduced to prevent the costs from lying where they fall.

Second, there exist some commodities which are on administrative grounds difficult efficiently to provide via the market mechanism (it is possible to price entry into theatres on the basis of supply and demand, thereby relating private cost directly to private benefit with a sensitivity which anyone who has ever been placed in an uncomfortable position because he did not have a penny will readily understand; but the same cannot be said of user charges for roads in the city centre or for the services of the police, and in such cases the choice is normally between free provision to all consumers or no provision at all to any). There are, moreover, things which the market is incapable of supplying in a manner which satisfies consensual notions of justice (the case against private schooling is that it, like nepotism in appointments, perpetuates the ascribed status derived from inherited wealth and in that way goes against popularly held preferences for a society based on ability, mobility, achievement and merit not distorted by the ability of the rich to buy a better start in life for their offspring; the case for State provision of relatively standardised education is that all children should not only be given an equal opportunity to become unequal but also encouraged to mix on equal terms with children from different backgrounds so as thereby to develop perceptions of common condition, shared situation, humanity, community and belonging which will stand them in good stead as they in future wrestle with the terror of interest and the loneliness of individualism). There are, finally, things which the market can supply but not in the optimum quantity (if the social exceed the private benefits of education, then State intervention is needed to prevent under-investment in human capital, a resource from which all citizens ultimately derive benefit in the form of more rapid economic growth; while as an economy becomes more oligopolised it may, being less capable of co-ordination through the market than when prices were more flexible, require some extension of national economic planning to help make consistent the network of voluntary contracts). In cases such as these, market and welfare are complements, not alternatives.

Third, the market mechanism places emphasis on results, not on motivation; and, indeed, the private vices/public virtues argument would even seem to eulogise attitudes which most of us would regard as highly unethical if they were to be adopted towards ourselves by our wives, our children, our parents and our friends. Yet if it is morally wrong to charge all that the traffic will bear (plus expenses and Value Added Tax) for the visits we make to an uncle in hospital, it must also be morally wrong to adopt a similar orientation towards strangers in the street or customers in the shop.

What is morally wrong might, of course, be economically right (as where we all enjoy higher standards of living precisely because each of us acts exclusively as considerations of enlightened self-interest would rationally dictate). It is, however, possible nonetheless to think of cases where that which is economically right is also morally right (as where a craftsman refuses, because of absolute commitment and professional pride, to sell a watch or a table which he knows to be genuinely sub-standard; or where a surgeon, even in a private enterprise system of medical care, is less interested in the patient's wallet than in the symptoms buried beneath it) and of mixed cases where men do that which is widely regarded as morally right because what they desire most of all in life is the esteem and approbation of their fellows (and may even seek money to purchase commodities primarily because of the status-communicating function those commodities fulfill as tokens in the social game, and only secondarily because of the intrinsic utility yielded by the things in their own right). It is certainly encouraging to think that men can be good and comforting to believe that by some combination of moral intent and conscious action they can directly shape their future without relying in hopeful passivity on invisible hands and unintended outcomes; but, obviously, little progress can be made in any serious discussion of design versus mechanism without a theory of human nature. In so far, therefore, as the essays in this book are about State and Welfare, they are also inescapably about man in situation as well.

PART II

R. H. TAWNEY

Biographical Note

Richard Henry Tawney was born in Calcutta on 30 November 1880 and died in London on 16 January 1962, and was thus the child of an age in which traditional institutions (the aristocracy, the House of Lords, the public schools, the Church of England, the BBC of Lord Reith, the class culture, the *done thing*) were important. It was, however, also an age which experienced a new consciousness of sin (resulting partly from the discoveries of Charles Booth and Seebohm Rowntree concerning the epidemic dimensions of poverty, discoveries made more dramatic by the poor quality of recruits in the Boer War and the two world wars and magnified by the rapidly expanding mass media), witnessed the impact of socialist argumentation through empirical documentation of the Webbs and other Fabians, recorded the relative decline of the Liberal Party, saw the birth and adolescence of the Labour Party (and ultimately the Attlee Government of 1945–51, which among other things – including the establishment of the National Health Service and the taking of similar steps towards the welfare state – used its new political power to validate an old intellectual victory by nationalising the coal mines, as the Royal Commission on the Coal Mines of 1919 under Mr Justice Sankey, a commission on which Tawney himself represented the union side, had recommended). Tawney was at his zenith in the early inter-war years (particularly the years up to 1931), a period in which Britain was in desperate search of new ideas to fill an intellectual vacuum and when the only antidote to the unemployment and depression associated with individualistic free enterprise appeared to many to be the totalitarian regimentation of Mussolini, Hitler and Stalin; and it is to his credit that he continued even then to plead for a middle way – unlike, increasingly, more extreme Leftists such as John Strachey and Harold Laski who did indeed "go red" – and to stress that social justice and political liberty are not incompatible. It is ironical that he is buried at Highgate, a stone's throw from the grave of Karl Marx.

Tawney's father was Principal of Presidency College, Calcutta, an eminent Sanskrit scholar and educationalist (curiously though, India, and more generally the problems of Empire, were not topics on which Tawney himself chose to write – which is not, of course, to say that Tawney totally neglected Asian affairs, since he twice visited China in the early 1930s in order to study agricultural, industrial and later educational issues). Tawney was given a typically gentlemanly upbringing in Weybridge. He was educated at Rugby (where a contemporary was his life-long friend, William Temple, later Archbishop of Canterbury; and where he imbibed at first hand the public school ethos of service, obligation and duty) and then, like Adam Smith, at Balliol College, Oxford (where a contemporary was another life-long friend, William Beveridge, whose sister, Annette Jeanie – Jeannette – Tawney married in 1909; and where a major intellectual influence on him was Canon Charles Gore, later Bishop of Birmingham, a man firmly convinced that the Church had an important social and political as well as religious mission on earth). He achieved a BA in Greats (with Second Class Honours) in 1903; never paid the fee for a bought MA (a transaction which he regarded as immorally commercial); and then turned his back on respectability (in the form of a post in the Indian Civil Service or some equivalent at home) by going, with Beveridge, into educational social work at Toynbee Hall where, in the East End of London, Canon Samuel Barnett was trying to bring university culture and Christian ethics to the poorest of the people.

At Toynbee Hall, Tawney gave classes on literary and religious topics, but also more and more involving political and economic themes; and, since no payment was received for these courses, he simultaneously took a paid job as Secretary to the Children's Country Holiday Fund (a charity which arranged country holidays for ailing children from deprived backgrounds). Meanwhile, increasingly of the opinion that education rather than philanthropy was primarily instrumental in giving the masses both the will and the power to reform the nation, he adopted the class-conscious approach of linking learning with the new labour movement by joining in 1905 what was to become the executive of the Workers Educational Association, which had been founded two years earlier by Albert Mansbridge. He was to serve on the executive of the WEA for 45 years (from 1928 to 1943 as President). He also joined the Fabian Society (1906) and the Independent Labour Party (1909) and made himself useful in electoral campaigns, as speaker and canvasser, as the principal author of several Party manifestos, and also, on four occasions, as a candidate for parliament (never, as it turned out, a successful one, even in a working-class constituency such as Rochdale).

In 1906 Tawney moved from Toynbee Hall to Glasgow University where, as Assistant in Economics in a Department headed by Professor William Smart, he was evidently pleased to be lecturing in a socially relevant discipline (even if also one which too often degenerated into a disillusioningly abstract "body of occasionally useful truisms") in an industrial town (one on which he had an additional impact through the controversial occasional pieces which he provided for the *Glasgow Herald*, articles which anticipate the massive journalistic contribution he was later to make to the *Manchester Guardian*). From 1908 to 1914 he was a full-time teacher in the Manchester area for the Tutorial Classes Committee of Oxford University (his most famous student from this period is A. P. Wadsworth, destined to become editor of the *Manchester Guardian* and a distinguished economic historian in his own right), learned from as well as taught his almost exclusively working-class students (thereby distinguishing himself from many academic socialists who have no personal knowledge of the groups whose interests they purport to represent), found time from 1912 to serve as Director of the Ratan Tata Foundation (a Foundation endowed by an Indian iron and steel magnate and affiliated to the London School of Economics which sought to study the socio-economic origins of poverty and produced several valuable studies on the effects of minimum pay rates under the Trade Boards Act of 1909, including those set by the Chain Trade Board, of which Tawney himself was later to be a member, from 1919 to 1922); and it was in this period that he began to carry out historical research into problems such as inequality and acquisitiveness which he felt to be of use to our understanding of social life now as well as then. The distinction of that research led to his appointment in 1920 (after war service from December 1914 until July 1916 when he, refusing a commission, went as a private to the front and was seriously wounded at Fricourt, on the Somme) to a Readership in Economic History at the LSE. He was promoted to a Chair in 1931 when he was over 50 (later perhaps than would have been the case had he had less extensive outside political interests, or if his academic work had been less open to the charge that he blurred the lines between historical investigation and moral philosophy in the unconscious attempt to provide factual support for his own personal brand of socialism) and remained at the LSE, with absences (as when, in the

Second World War, he was briefly advisor on labour relations to the British Embassy in Washington and prepared for the Foreign Office an interesting memorandum on the nature of the AFL and the future of the CIO which may be found in *The American Labour Movement and Other Essays*, 1979) until his retirement in 1949 (after 1946, with reduced duties).

Tawney helped found the Economic History Society in 1926, from 1927 to 1934 co-edited (with Ephraim Lipson) its journal, the *Economic History Review*, and was instrumental in making the economic approach to the study of the past academically respectable. He was, however, far more than simply an economic historian of the Tudor and Stuart period (the epoch when modern capitalism was born), the author of important works on the Elizabethan enclosure movement (*The Agrarian Problem in the Sixteenth Century*, 1912), the relationship postulated by Weber and others between the Protestant ethic and early modern capitalism (*Religion and the Rise of Capitalism*, 1926), the role of social classes in the English Civil War ("The Rise of the Gentry, 1558–1640" and "Harrington's Interpretation of His Age", both 1941) and the linkages between government, finance and social structure in Jacobean England (*Business and Politics under James I: Lionel Cranfield as Merchant and Minister*, 1958). Tawney was also the author of two seminal and inspiring contributions to that tradition of common culture in British social philosophy which embraces thinkers as diverse as John Ruskin, Matthew Arnold and William Morris, namely *The Acquisitive Society* (1920) and *Equality* (1931); and of numerous influential papers and essays on a range of topics concerned with social justice, education, democratic socialism, Christian ethics and social reform, of which the most important have since been reprinted in two collections, *The Attack and Other Papers* (1953) and *The Radical Tradition* (1964) and which demonstrate, there as elsewhere, that Tawney was not only a distinguished scholar and an important social critic but a master of the English language as well. Tawney was for good reasons widely admired, and *The Times*, commenting on Tawney's eightieth birthday in November 1960 at the same time as an important dinner was held at the House of Commons to mark the event, truly had cause to write as follows: "No man alive has put more people into his spiritual and intellectual debt than has Richard Henry Tawney. . . . He is more of a saint than a socialist."

2 Culture and Condition

Culture refers to the way in which we think and live and to the nature of the relationships that we form when we interact; and a common culture refers to that which we share with the other members of our social team. Tawney was convinced that a healthy society was one in which no individual or class of individuals spoke a social dialect so divergent from the norm that it could not easily be understood. He also believed that, not only should the quantity of overlap in life-experiences be extended, but the quality of relationships should in addition be improved through a remoralisation of our social usages and our attitudes to one another.

Condition refers to geographical location on a social map; and common condition refers to a material environment in which inequalities of income and property, opportunity, power and status are not so great as to reflect social distances so vast that fellow citizens cannot enjoy the vital sensation of participating with equal human beings in a shared enterprise which serves each first and foremost because it also serves all. In this chapter we shall be concerned, in two successive sections, with these two key concepts in the thought of Richard Henry Tawney.

I. THE COMMON CULTURE

The *first* thing to remember about Tawney is that he regarded material prosperity as of secondary and instrumental importance, not as an end in itself but as the means to some higher end: "If the Kingdom of Heaven is not eating and drinking, but righteousness and peace, neither is civilization the multiplication of motor-cars and cinemas, or of any other of the innumerable devices by which men accumulate means of ever-increasing intricacy to the attainment of ends which are not worth attaining".[1] Obviously a reasonable level of material affluence is an important goal. Beyond that point, however, a society is not to be judged by its success in the accumulation of wealth and the diffusion of comfort, but in terms of a more qualitative and less quantitative index: "What matters to a society is less what it owns than what it is and how it uses its possessions. It is civilized in so far as its conduct is guided by a just appreciation of spiritual ends, in so far as it uses its material resources to promote the dignity and refinement of the individual human beings who compose it."[2]

Tawney hence advised the members of the lower classes not to "pay salaams of exaggerated amplitude to established proprieties" or to "accept the moral premises of their masters", lest the "working-class movement", by seeking to wriggle into an existing Elysium rather than founding a new one, forget its true mission: "When it does so, what it is apt to desire is not a social order of a different kind, in which money and economic power will no longer be the criterion of achievement, but a social order of the same kind, in which money and economic power will be somewhat differently distributed."[3] Socialism, in other words, stands for a society in which a higher value is put on people and a lower value on things for their own sake: "What the working-class movement stands for is obviously the ideal of social justice and solidarity, as a corrective to the exaggerated emphasis on individual advancement through the acquisition of wealth".[4] Socialism stands for humanism, not the acquisitive society or pecuniary self-love, and humanism is to be defined as follows: "It is the belief that the machinery of existence – property and material wealth and industrial organization, and the whole fabric and mechanism of social institutions – is to be regarded as means to an end, and that this end is the growth towards perfection of individual human beings."[5]

The *second* thing to remember about Tawney is that, despite his talk of individual fulfilment, his proper focus was on the individual as a member of the group, and his true fear that men might become so separated from their fellow-citizens that they might no longer be able to enjoy that warm feeling of integration that comes from the perception of belonging together. An agglomeration, after all, is not a family:

> Social well-being does not only depend upon intelligent leadership; it also depends upon cohesion and solidarity. It implies the existence, not merely of opportunities to ascend, but of a high level of general culture, and a strong sense of common interests, and a diffusion throughout society of a conviction that

civilization is not the business of an élite alone, but a common enterprise which is the concern of all.[6]

We are obviously dealing here with something far more ambitious and cosmic than mere equality of opportunity or the recognition of exceptional talent, namely equality in relationships between full participants in a shared activity who accept each other's common humanity: "Individual happiness does not only require that men should be free to rise to new positions of comfort and distinction; it also requires that they should be able to lead a life of dignity and culture, whether they rise or not, and that, whatever their position on the economic scale may be, it shall be such as if fit to be occupied by men."[7]

Whether or not they rise, all citizens should be given access to the "means of civilization", for atomism and fragmentation will only be transcended by cohesion and fraternity where men are able to communicate with one another on the basis of a shared way of life: "What a community requires, as the word itself suggests, is a common culture, because, without it, it is not a community at all."[8] Mobility by itself is not enough to break down what are principally class barriers, for a man's outlook is normally more determined by the class he enters than the one he leaves.

The *third* thing to remember about Tawney is his conviction that people (albeit within limits) have the freedom creatively to shape material conditions in accordance with ideal conceptions, his rejection of deterministic theories of inevitable patterns in historical evolution (and his praise of Marx for having been "as saturated with ethics as a Hebrew prophet": "He was not so naïf as to fall into the vulgar error of supposing that historical statements are either a substitute for judgements of value, or can be directly converted into them"[9]), and his belief that principles must be accompanied by a good measure of practical socialism if right relationships between men are to obtain:

A common culture cannot be created merely by desiring it. It must rest upon practical foundations of social organization. It is incompatible with the existence of sharp contrasts between the economic standards and educational opportunities of different classes, for such contrasts have as their result, not a common culture, but servility or resentment, on the one hand, and patronage or arrogance, on the other.[10]

In order to make men regard each other as brothers, in other words, a good measure of social and economic equality is essential – "not necessarily in the sense of an identical level of pecuniary incomes, but of equality of environment, of access to education and the means of civilization, of security and independence, and of the social consideration which equality in these matters usually carries with it."[11] What matters is not that some men earn more than others (for where there is a common purpose and "a common tradition of respect and consideration, these details of the counting-house are forgotten or ignored"[12]); "What is repulsive . . . is that some classes should be excluded from the heritage of civilization which others enjoy, and that the fact of human fellowship, which is ultimate and profound, should be obscured by economic contrasts, which are trivial and superficial."[13]

The case for socialism was hence to Tawney a moral one, namely the will to assist "common humanity" to triumph over artificial inequalities and class differences which permitted some men to regard others as means rather than ends (this latter abuse being "the ultimate and unforgivable wrong"[14]):

The revolt against capitalism has its source, not merely in material miseries, but in resentment against an economic system which dehumanizes existence by treating the mass of mankind, not as responsible partners in the co-operative enterprise of subduing nature to the service of man, but an instruments to be manipulated for the pecuniary advantage of a minority of property-owners, who themselves, in proportion as their aims are achieved, are too often degraded by the attainment of them.[15]

The case for socialism was not to Tawney primarily a scientific and technocratic one, and here he parted company with utilitarian socialists such as the Webbs, who were more preoccupied with order, organisation, material well-being and efficiency of mechanisms than with questions of common culture and social values.

The *fourth* thing to remember about Tawney is the Christian nature (more often implicit than explicit, and always with reference to structured relationships, not simply to individual belief) of his social theory. Put bluntly, capitalist institutions today are "not so much un-Christian as anti-Christian";[16] for capitalist virtues (the emphasis on material riches, acquisitive appetites, and economic power; the subordination of the majority to an exploitative economic system which yields disproportionate financial benefits to a minority of property-owners) are Christian vices, and Christian values (community service, self-sacrifice, the dignity of all men and their essential equality in the sight of God irrespective of economic, social or biological differences, sharing rather than hoarding of advantages and privileges, the obligation to love one's neighbour as oneself if one is truly to be capable of loving God) the direct antithesis of capitalist ones. Because "the necessary corollary . . . of the Christian conception of man is a strong sense of equality",[17] because that "economic egotism which snatches private gains at the cost of neighbours or the community"[18] is a poisonous evil which prevents the nation from acting as a family and sharing fairly whatever income is available to be divided, because the idolatry of property "leaves little room for any more genuine forms of religion",[19] the Christian must also be a socialist:

> The Churches . . . should assert that class privilege, and the gross inequalities of wealth on which it rests, are not only a hideously uncivilised business, but an odious outrage on the image of God. While recognising that change must necessarily take time, they should state frankly that the only objective which can satisfy the Christian conscience is the removal of *all* adventitious advantages and disabilities which have their source in social institutions. They should throw their whole weight into the support of measures calculated to lead to that end.[20]

Given that the nature of the Churches is primarily sacred rather than profane, social reform is nonetheless a fully Christian activity. It is Christian in a narrow sense:

> The Churches are not a humanitarian association or a social reform movement. But, granted that their function is to convert the world to Christianity, the fact remains that the conduct of man in society forms a large part of human life, and that to resign it to the forces of self-interest and greed is to de-Christianise both it and the individual souls whose attitude and outlook are necessarily in large measure determined by the nature of their social environment.[21]

It is, however, also Christian in a broader sense, in so far as Christians (who are not fatalists and see that, while there are limits to action based on ideals – "Christian principles will not put coal where there is none, or cause wheat to grow in a swamp"[22] – nonetheless man still has many very real alternatives open to him in the field of social organisation) regard it as irresponsible to delegate their choices to impersonal forces following non-existently unique paths as prescribed by fictitious laws of motion. Christians *qua* Christians must concern themselves with the problems of illness among children, poor nutrition, bad school buildings and staff; and should also learn to regard snobbery and class disabilities as "an essay in blasphemy" which "ought to be particularly detestable to Christians".[23] A Christian who seeks to draw a sharp line between things of the Spirit and things of the world is not simply constructing a false duality; he is also renouncing his Christian duty to build truly Christian bridges between the ideal and the material. Of this crime the Church of England has in the past (at least "till recently"[24]) unfortunately not always been entirely innocent: "For a long period, lasting almost into our own day, that Church, in spite of distinguished examples to the contrary, was so closely identified in sympathy and outlook with the upper strata of society as to create the impression that it was a class institution, committed to the defence of the existing social order".[25]

The *fifth* thing to remember about Tawney is that to him the common culture was a classless culture, a universal brotherhood based on a shared manner of existence which has more in common with the all-embracing national Church than with the more narrow proletarian solidarity posited by Marxism or the still smaller-scale model communities developed by Robert Owen. Because it is a classless culture, of course, the common culture is not to be identified with contemporaneous working-class culture (with which Tawney had come into contact through the WEA and at the front) nor, indeed, with contemporaneous upper-class culture (which Tawney knew from Rugby and Oxford). It is an as yet not fully observable body of beliefs and behaviour-patterns in which all classes and persons will be able to share regardless of individual differences, and which will ripen only when citizens are no longer forced into class-roles.

Although the common culture is a classless culture, it would be wrong to imply that Tawney had no respect for the working classes. Rather the contrary is the case, as Tawney's admiration for the common man (whom he christened Henry Dubb and described affectionately as "the common, courageous, good-hearted, patient, proletarian fool – who is worth, except to his modest self, nine-tenths of the gentilities, notabilities, intellectual, cultural and ethical eminences put together"[26]) clearly demonstrates. Hence Tawney was critical of all social systems and moral philosophies which sought to lead Dubb rather than follow him: "In the interminable case of *Dubb v. Superior Persons and Co.*, whether Christians, Capitalists or Communists, I am an unrepentant Dubbite."[27] After all, the Bible ("a neglected classic") says quite unambiguously that " 'He hath put down the mighty from their seat and hath exalted the humble and meek' ".[28]

Because of its élitist paternalism, because it "puts Dubb on a chain and prevents him from teaching manners to his exalted governors",[29] Tawney had little patience with Soviet-type socialism (although he followed the Webbs in admiring the collective purpose of the Soviets and accepted that Stalinism had increased national wealth and improved social services). Arguing in defence of the common working man and against the party bosses and the bureaucrats, Tawney stressed that a society has still more than half its battles before it which has one dimension of democracy without the other:

A conception of Socialism which views it as involving the nationalisation of everything except political power, on which all else depends, is not, to speak with moderation, according to light. The question is not merely whether the State owns and controls the means of production. It is also who owns and controls the State.[30]

Tawney thus believed that socialism ought to be democratic, and this belief in democracy extended to its conception as well as to its mode of operation: "It is not certain, though it is probable, that Socialism can in England be achieved by the methods proper to democracy. It is certain that it cannot be achieved by any other; nor, even if it could, should the supreme goods of civil and political liberty, in whose absence no Socialism worthy of the name can breathe, be part of the price."[31] The achievement of socialism in England presupposes not a violent revolution led by a vanguard of activists but rather a peaceful and democratic revolution radiating out from polity to economy, finding its inspiration not in inexorable evolutionary laws of political economy but in the evaluation and rejection "of a system which stunts personality and corrupts human relations by permitting the use of man by man as an instrument of pecuniary gain"[32] and reflecting the aspirations of men like Henry Dubb. As Tawney says: "I consider it not impossible that he may one day wake up; make an angry noise like a man, instead of bleating like a sheep; and in England, at any rate, in spite of scales weighted against him, use such rights as he possesses . . . to win economic freedom".[33]

Although the revolt against capitalism had to Tawney to reflect the aspirations of the common man, the very fact that it had to work its way through the machinery of parliamentary democracy meant that a popular party capable of mobilising committed socialists was indispensable. Such a party was the Labour Party, whose members and supporters are united by intellectual convictions rather than educational background or economic status to a greater degree than is true of other major parties. Tawney also believed, however, that the Labour Party had failed to rise to the challenge of the day. Its weakness, apart from the venality of certain of its leaders with respect to Establishment institutions such as the Honours system ("Who will believe that the Labour Party means business as long as some of its stalwarts sit up and beg for social sugar-plums, like poodles in a drawing-room?"[34]), is its tendency to provide programmes which are "less programmes than miscellanies": although it "requires an army", it nonetheless "collects a mob", and this is to be expected, since it provides no "ordered conception of the task", no "scheme of priorities", no "stable standard of political values, such as would teach it to discriminate between the relative urgency of different objectives".[35] Rather than dispersing its energies in so many directions, rather than seeking to offer "the largest possible number of carrots to the largest possible number of donkeys"[36], the Labour Party would be well advised to focus on a unique central objective capable of stimulating the enthusiasm and faith of its adherents; for "the finest individuals are nothing till mastered by a cause".[37] The clear-cut cause must be socialism, partly because the keeping of detailed promises presupposes a peaceful revolution and nothing less ("Onions can be eaten leaf by leaf, but you cannot skin a live tiger paw by paw"[38]), and partly too because the electorate will be lukewarm towards a socialism which is capitalist in all but name: would it be surprising "if they concluded that, since capitalism was the order of the day, it had better continue to be administered by capitalists, who, at any rate – so, poor innocents, they supposed – knew how to make the thing work?"[39]

In this section we have thus far considered five aspects of Tawney's case concerning the common culture; and have shown that that case is in essence dependent on ethical judgements and political strategies. It may now prove interesting to consider some implications and extensions of the argument under both these headings.

(a) Ethical judgements

Concerning the central role assigned in Tawney's work to choices made in accordance with values, it is useful to recall that Tawney's own ultimate value is the desirability of applying the Christian perspective not just in matters of personal morality but to questions of society and its structure as well. Yet the difficulty inherent in pouring "the new wine of socialism into the existing bottles of Christian conscience" [40] is precisely that, as Ross Terrill points out, a secularised world which no longer takes for granted that all men are equal in the sight of God will find quaintly antiquated a legitimation of fellowship and dignity in terms of the Gospels. Tawney's declaration that "in order to believe in human equality it is *necessary* to believe in God"[41] then becomes a hostage to fortune, as indeed he himself recognised: "What is wrong with the modern world is that having ceased to believe in the greatness of God, and therefore the infinite smallness (or greatness – the same thing!) of *man*, it has to invent or emphasize distinctions between *men*."[42] Given that "it is *only* when we realize that each individual soul is related to a power above other men, that we are able to regard each as an end in itself",[43] the confession that "modern society is sick through the absence of a moral ideal"[44] would seem to anticipate rather the failure than the triumph of an altruistic socialism centring on problematic notions of mutual obligation, collective purposiveness and voluntary co-operation: such a socialism, after all, only can, in Tawney's view, truly command conviction if one is prepared to accept, on the recommendation of absolute and transcendental authority, that, when it comes to the man next door, "one can't look a gift cherub in the mouth".[45]

Should one refuse that authority, of course, then the picture becomes eminently depressing: "Since man is, of his nature, a religious animal, the alternative to religion is rarely irreligion; it is a counter-religion",[46] and here the leading candidates for the vacant throne turn out to be "worship of riches" (capitalism) and "worship

of power" (totalitarianism). Both are "neuroses" and "morbid
perversions", and for the same reasons:

Both are disposed to judge achievements in terms of numbers,
quantity, and mass; find in expediency, so expressed, the chief or
sole criterion of conduct; are unmoral in the sense that, except as
restrained by law or custom, they tend to treat men as means, not
ends; and, in so far as they prevail, dehumanise the societies
dominated by them by subordinating the spontaneity of individual personality to the exigencies of the system.[47]

Fortunately, in European history, these false Gods have enjoyed
only limited success owing to the existence of substantial "spiritual
resisting-power in individuals and communities",[48] a form of
countervailing power which originates quite simply in "the conviction of the existence of a higher law than any represented by the
powers of this world"[49] and which can in no way be traced back to
the rational norm of efficiency: "The sacredness of personality, and
the truth that the most important attribute of human beings
consists, not in the external accidents of nationality, class, colour
and condition by which they are divided, but in the common
humanity which unites them, are articles of faith not susceptible of
proof by logic."[50]

Historically speaking, "the respectable atrocities of law, custom
and convention have not lacked an inner tribunal to condemn and
correct them",[51] and Tawney believed that that inner tribunal is
unambiguously religious in origin and essence. Not only religious,
moreover, but specifically Christian. Tawney admitted that "it is, of
course, perfectly true that we do not need Christianity to make us
aware that. God exists" and confirmed that "the knowledge that
God exists is a source of immense strength to man", but he also, and
more significantly, asserted that such awareness and knowledge "is
not by itself very helpful": "What we want to know is *what kind* of
God he is, and what he is like in ordinary human intercourse. This is
what Christianity tells us."[52] Western ideas (notably those involving personal freedoms, tolerance of diversity and human equality)
may indeed "be reduced to one – the Christian doctrine that
institutions exist for men, not men for institutions".[53] Thus the
Puritan, isolated from his fellow-men and lacking in a sense of social
solidarity, was in practice not fully a Christian: "A servant of
Jehovah more than of Christ, he revered God as a Judge rather than
loved him as a Father."[54]

Because Tawney's socialism is so explicitly legitimated by his interpretation of High Church Christianity, the question must inevitably be posed of how much the disciple can share the former without accepting the latter. The reference to Jehovah, after all, reminds the reader that the Old Testament God is not in essence an all-forgiving God of love but rather a patriarch and a constitution-maker (one, moreover, who, primarily a tribal God with a favourite people chosen from the universe of his creation, displays no particular interest in the brotherhood of man); while casual empiricism suggests how difficult it would be to convince a devout Hindu Brahmin that he ought to love as himself the Harijan in the semi-detached next door. Evidently all religions cannot be relied upon to lead the believer in the direction of the socialism of common humanity; and the problem of legitimation is made still more complex by the fact that many modern societies are characterised both by religious pluralism and by increasing secularisation. One might, of course, be able to derive fellowship in some other way than from Christian ethics (if all men are created in the image of God, for instance, then their very similarity might cause birds of a feather to flock together even in total ignorance of the Original Birdmaker; and there is also the possibility that the experience of the warmth born of *camaraderie* will itself, like all shared experiences that yield pleasure, stimulate banding and foster cohesion), or wish to argue that two thousand years of Christian culture have sufficiently internalised norms and set up resonances as happily to render further explicit reference to Scripture unnecessary. The point to remember, however, is that Tawney did not do so. He derived the recognition on the part of ordinary men and women that they have duties and responsibilities towards one another from their discovery of shared essential humanity; but then derived equality and fraternity from authority, and specifically from the notion that we are all children of the same father and have a common obligation to honour his values.

From values comes action. Tawney rejected theories of historical inevitability which postulated the end of ideology and he empha-sized the importance of principles. Ideas, he insisted, can be "a high explosive";[55] but only, he added, in so far as they interact with the material environment. There is, in other words, no reason to assert that causation "can work in only one direction":[56] "The civilisation of an age forms a connected whole the different elements of which interact, and . . . as a consequence, economic causation does not

work in a straight line which can be traced without reference to
other forces which twist and divert it."[57] What is true of economic
determinism is also true of ideational determinism; and the social
philosopher would thus be foolish to fall into the trap of polarised
positions and unidimensional explanations, no matter how much
emphasis he nonetheless wishes to place on principles.

A good illustration of interdependent causality is the relationship
between the Protestant Reformation and early modern capitalism:

> There was action and reaction, and, while Puritanism helped to
> mould the social order, it was, in its turn, moulded by it. It is
> instructive to trace, with Weber, the influence of religious ideas
> on economic development. It is not less important to grasp the
> effect of the economic arrangements accepted by an age on the
> opinion which it holds of the province of religion.[58]

Capitalism (and particularly that of new commercial centres such
as Amsterdam, Antwerp and London) was undoubtedly "the social
counterpart of Calvinist theology"[59] (with its absolute emphasis on
labour, acquisition and inner-worldly asceticism), but most of all of
the Calvinism of a later age. Clearly, "the Calvinism which fought
the English Civil War . . . was not that of its founder";[60] for Calvin
himself in practice "made Geneva a city of glass",[61] a "giant
monastery",[62] and imposed collectivist discipline so anti-indi-
vidualist in nature that it punished usurers, monopolists and
engrossers (and as far as the other great figure of the Reformation is
concerned, the hostility to capitalistic attitudes – which he identified with the avarice of the Fuggers and the moral laxity of the
Catholics – is even more extreme: "For the arts by which men amass
wealth and power, as for the anxious provision which accumulates
for the future, Luther had all the distrust of a peasant and a
monk".[63]) Then, just as it would be wrong to exaggerate the extent
to which the Calvinism of Calvin opened the door to capitalism, so it
would be wrong to underestimate the extent to which latter-day
Calvinism was influenced by it – by, in other words, the new social
order that emerged from expanded overseas trade, the price
revolution consequent upon the influx of specie, the dislocation
caused by the dissolution of the monasteries and the Civil War, the
outburst of capitalistic activity and technological innovation in
mining and textiles, political centralisation and the associated need
for public finance, the growth of financial intermediation, the birth

of new classes. All of these changes on the side of matter reacted back on mind, and made certain religious and social philosophies thrive (notably those favourable to individualism, prosperity, improvement and acquisition) while they simultaneously doomed others to defeat (notably those that censured covetousness, unlimited interest and profits). Witness the failure of Richard Baxter's attempt in the seventeenth century to reformulate a collectivist and Calvinist casuistry of economic conduct such as had been acceptable only a century before. His rules "were subtle and sincere. But they were like seeds carried by birds from a distant and fertile plain, and dropped upon a glacier. They were at once embalmed and sterilized in a river of ice."[64] When it comes to new ideas, in short, demand as well as supply must be examined, and the observer should never forget that the questions asked by social science are eminently social in nature: "Individuals solve, or attempt to solve, its problems; but history poses them. The riddle must be stated before it can be answered; it can be stated only in the particular terms of a specific epoch".[65]

This is not to play down the important role of the intellect in the process of social change (no one would deny, for instance, that capitalism developed "in a country which was intellectually prepared to receive it . . . and there is a sense in which Locke and Blackstone were as truly its pioneers as Arkwright and Crompton"[66]), only to warn the reader against studying mind to the exclusion of matter: "Doctrines with sufficient iron in them to survive are more often the children of the market-place than of the study."[67] Nor, however, should one study matter to the exclusion of mind:

> The philosophy which sees the one constant dynamic in the pressure and pull of economic forces is a just nemesis on the facile sentimentalism of historical interpretations which idealise the flower to the neglect of roots and soil. But such forces are not automatic agents. They become a power, not directly, but at one remove, when passed through the transforming medium of human minds and wills, which are not passive, but impose, in reacting to them, a pattern of their own. . . . It is with the human response, not the material challenge, that the last word lies.[68]

At every cross-roads, after all, there are several paths to follow, and choice is in the circumstances unavoidable. The fact that men are

authors of as well as actors in their own drama then returns them to
the centre of the stage.

Men are not, of course, perfect beings. Far from it; and Tawney
believed that one of the least satisfying forms of matter is indeed
man's nature itself (a conclusion which might have been expected
from a Christian thinker imbued with ideas of Original Sin and the
Fall of Man). At the same time, however, Tawney also believed that
the more anti-social of the natural appetites (say, "the insistence
among men of pecuniary motives, the strength of economic egotism,
the appetite for gain", admittedly "commonplaces of every age"[69]
which demand no explanation), just as they were cultivated and
encouraged by the later Puritanism of the seventeenth century
"which converted a natural frailty into a resounding virtue",[70] both
can and must now be purified, restrained and tamed by moral
principles which, no less than the external and internal material
environment, can too set their stamp on man ("even when he is least
conscious of it"[71]):

> The conventional statement that human nature does not change
> is plausible only so long as attention is focused on those aspects of
> it which are least distinctively human. The wolf is today what he
> was when he was hunted by Nimrod. But, while men are born
> with many of the characteristics of wolves, man is a wolf
> domesticated, who both transmits the arts by which he has been
> partially tamed and improves upon them.[72]

Man, in other words, is both the legator and the legatee of a social
inheritance, and for this reason it would be wrong to discuss man's
acquisitive, possessive and selfish propensities as if they were
independent of time, place and, most of all, of the *Zeitgeist*: "In
reality, though inherited dispositions may be constant from generation to generation, the system of valuations, preferences, and
ideals – the social environment within which individual character
functions – is in process of continuous change."[73]

Precisely because of the two-way relationship between mind and
matter, therefore, man's natural imperfection can be tempered by
an awareness of ideals. Such an awareness serves at the very least to
make clear to him the error of his ways:

> It is true that, whatever its ostensible creed, no society lives up to
> it. It is one thing, however, to accept a system of ideas which gives

these values a high place, while failing to act with consistency upon it. It is quite another to affirm they are poison, not food. . . . Man is condemned to live in twilight; but darkness is darkness, and light is light. What matters is the direction in which his face is set.[74]

Such an awareness can lead, moreover, to positive action and thence to social reform. Whether at the level of enlightenment or of instigation, however, ethical judgements remain central in any discussion of the forces shaping man's conduct; and for this reason, because of the constraint of choice, "in the collective affairs of mankind, bad doctrines are always and everywhere more deadly than bad actions".[75]

(b) Political strategies

Tawney believed that social policies must not be things apart, but must simply represent the institutionalisation of a social consensus. Law in essence must not so much be imposed from above as bubble up from what each of us knows to be right and just: "A good law is a rule which makes binding objectively conduct which most individuals already recognize to be binding subjectively."[76] In a state of *anomie*, of moral normlessness, good laws are thus by definition impossible, since good laws can only emanate from moral valuations: "There *is* no creative force outside the ideas which control men in their ordinary actions."[77]

Fortunately, Tawney was convinced, we do not now live in a state of normlessness. Tawney believed that there both ought to be and is a certain body of principles which is "outside the sphere of party politics", representing as it does "matters agreed upon by the conscience of the nation" and "the attitude of all good men to social questions",[78] and gave the example of slavery: "Every one in England would feel that a man who got his income from slaves, was doing something disgraceful."[79] Such a sentiment is general today. It was not so in 1800, a fact which reminds us both that the collective consciousness can change over time and that even the economic problem is "a moral problem, a problem of learning as a community to reprobate certain courses of conduct and to approve others"[80] and which then leads us inevitably to the following question:

Why should not the same sentiment grow up towards the most

characteristic immoralities of modern industry? If an average decent Englishman feels that it is a disgraceful thing to buy and sell human beings to hold them as his property, why should he not feel that it is a disgraceful thing to exploit the labour of children, to take advantage of unorganized labour to beat down wages?"[81]

When considering the abuses and immoralities of modern industrial organisation, therefore, it is salutary to remember that "it is not only the employer who is to blame. It is all of us."[82] We must widen our sense of "moral abhorrence" from "property in human beings" to "property in the labour of human beings".[83] Once we have done so, then politicians – who, far from being a dynamic vanguard, ought to follow rather than lead the community – will respond by enacting on our behalf laws which do no more than express our unambiguous and shared beliefs.

Tawney stressed that common culture and the acknowledgement of common humanity were more than abstract intellectual constructs and had empirical significance (as the experience of Elizabethan England to some extent demonstrates). Tawney's ideal was that happy and contented society (whether rich or poor) which basks in the warm glow of cohesion, solidarity and, above all, ethical unity: "There are golden moments in the life of mankind when national aims seem to be bent for some noble purpose, and men live at peace in the harmony which springs from the possession of a common moral ideal."[84] Tawney's strategy for reform was indeed designed with the explicit objective of reducing the social distance between Englishmen and maximising the overlap of their life-experiences in such a way as to allow the light of popular culture to shine through, where popular culture is to be defined as follows: "Culture is popular, in the sense that it draws on a body of experience which is not the monopoly of a single class, but is, in some degree, a general possession. It voices the outlook on life, not of an elegant *élite*, but of the world of common men."[85]

The concept of national unity and purposive collectivism based on a shared manner of acting and thinking is an attractive one. It is, however, a utopia beset with difficulties, and the principal ones are as follows.

First, there is uncertainty as to the precise extent of present-day consensus. It is likely for instance, that there was greater cultural homogeneity in Tawney's day than there is in ours, at least in terms of widely-held assumptions. A culture of Shakespeare, the Bible and the BBC, in which most decent men accepted that it was right to wear a white shirt on Sundays and wrong to be a practising homosexual, is a viable social basis from which to project forth a political superstructure. In a more pluralistic culture, however, there is bound to be less agreement on social norms and ends, which in turn raises the question of how in practice to measure the collective consciousness: the occasional referendum on a major issue such as hanging might be a move in the right direction were it not for the fact that it is discrete rather than continous, and in a model concerned with common culture on a national rather than a local basis – although it naturally cannot be denied that "the local units are the primary cells of a larger organism, in Europe usually the nation-state"[86] – devolved parliaments and town meetings would stimulate men to situate themselves in the context of the particular rather than the general. In a pluralistic culture, Tawney's recommendations for collective action originating in consensus become problematic, precisely because without consensus behind it collective action by definition degenerates from authority to power.

Second, there is the point concerning the content of consensus that action in accordance with values might not generate an eternal Christmas but rather Oxford Street in the summer sales. This Tawney explicitly denies: "All experience seems to me to prove that people, or at any rate English people, will not accept efficiency as a substitute for liberty."[87] Thus, Tawney observes that "all decent people are against a creed which tries . . . things by the standard of 'utility' as though there were any end of life except life itself";[88] and, applying this result to the working classes in particular, he notes that "no political creed will ever capture their hearts which begins by saying simply 'we will give you a little more money. We will still measure success by the old standards. But we will let you have more of it'."[89] Yet it is in truth somewhat difficult to believe that Henry Dubb is more likely to opt for a vast community of the whole nation than he is for "motor-cars and cinemas", that consensus-thinking will lead the majority of citizens to reject colour televisions in favour of more adequate supplementary benefits, that freedom is more generally perceived as freedom *to* than as freedom *from*, and this presents a major obstacle to the conversion of socialist values into social institutions. In an increasingly secular and materialistic society where Henry Dubb, latching on to the *Zeitgeist* like the rest of his brothers and sisters, is greedy, self-seeking, anxious to buy cheap and sell dear, eager to vote in the market-place for inclusion and adaptive upgrading, it is simply not clear what cataclysmic upheaval may be expected to replace the values of the majority by those of a minority. Tawney, of course, would not have accepted that "the modern temper, which takes the destination for granted, and is thrilled by the hum of the engine"[90] represented a real threat or a serious challenge to the democratic socialism of universal brotherhood, and was on balance optimistic about the content of consensus and thus about the future of his society. Not every admirer of Tawney's socialism, however (and particularly not those unable to share his Christian ethics, because of which and "only" because of which, we stand under a moral obligation *ex machina* to regard our neighbour as an end rather than an instrument, or to know that he is our equal rather than a problem to be solved) will be able to share his optimism.

Third, Tawney envisaged a national government ruling a national family and taking instructions from it; but it is in practice often the case that the patriarch acquires a will of his own and becomes polity separated from society. Since God's will is greater than man's will, one would have anticipated that Tawney, a charismatic thinker anxious to effect change, would have been prepared to support a consortium of holy men in their attempt to guide Henry Dubb away from the worship of money and power. One would have been wrong, for Tawney unambiguously links reform to popular legitimation of philosophical ideals, not to the political machinery of the social engineer: "Politicians cannot rescue men from the vacuum which a false philosophy has created, for men cannot lift themselves by holding the soles of their boots."[91] Yet if men are today truly suffocating in a moral vacuum (or are, alternatively, the prisoners of a false philosophy), then it is hard to see why mind should ever change in advance of a change in matter, or why the vanguard should hesitate to defeat bad doctrines and institutions simply because goods ones lack the necessary support from public opinion and the democratic masses. Tawney's model, in other words, denying as it does that social change imposed paternalistically from above can ever prove a tolerable means of altering an intolerable consensus emerging from below, seems unable to reconcile the whole (socialism) with one of its parts (political democracy); and it also neglects the more mundane consideration that a minority, merely because it does not have the right to force reforms "down reluctant throats",[92] will not necess-arily refrain from doing so if it should happen to have the power.

Tawney in the late 1930s was naturally aware of the attempt on the part of foreign dictators to lead Dubb rather than follow him; and, deeply upset by the "strident self-advertisement of competing creeds",[93] the "hypnotism of infectious phrases"[94] and of insane ideologies masquerading as revelations",[95] warned of the danger that Europe might "truckle to hoary sophisms", "be swept off its feet by the glitter and swirl of pretentious novelties" or "be struck stupid with terror because some frantic dervish offers, not for the first time, conversion or the sword".[96] He did not choose, however, to provide any real explanation for the rise in Europe of totalitarianism (although this would surely have offered an ideal opportunity to study the linkages between legitimate authority and irresponsible power; between polity and economy; between civil and religious authority, particularly since in the dictatorships of Germany, Italy and Spain nationalism had not so much occupied the "vacant throne" of institutionalised piety as formed a holy alliance with it). Speaking of Germany, he recognised that leaders might "interpret unity in half-tribal terms of race and blood" and "conceive of it as consisting, not in a community of culture or in political homogeneity, but in the mere physical attributes of a human herd", but he was quick to add that it could not happen here and that the reason for such perversions is quite simply that the Germans do not have a common culture worthy of the name: "There is little in German history to remind them that there are loftier planes on which unity can be achieved."[97]

Undeniably, Britain is unique. Free of revolutionary upheavals in recent times, a relatively homogeneous people until (probably even despite) post-war immigration, ideas of self-help on the part of the lower classes (taking the form of chapels, co-operatives, friendly societies and the organic ties of the local community) have reinforced the public school ethos of service on the part of the upper classes and the more diffuse liberal ethos of respect for persons which teaches that there is no general will independent of the will of all, and have produced more of a caring community than can be found in virtually any other industrialised nation. It must also be noted that Parliamentary democracy has a longer history in Britain than, say, in Germany (where it "followed hard on the heels of absolute monarchy",[98] and well into the twentieth century), due in part to an early dispersion of economic power and the rise of the gentry: "In England the property of the Crown and of the monasteries was at a fairly early date distributed among the middle classes".[99] At the same time, however, there is no guarantee that Britain will never become like Germany, particularly when we recall that, because of the dynamic interaction between mind and matter, even national character is in flux. Noting the vested economic interest which is hostile to the march of socialism (the consumer culture of the television screen, for instance) and the threat of centralised abuse on the part of those leaders who obstinately confuse their own goals and beliefs with corporate moral purposes, the reader will no doubt regret that Tawney provided no analytical explanation of the circumstances in which power comes to be legitimated by a collective consciousness which it has itself engendered; or, worse still, by none at all.

Fourth, there is the question of divergence in life-styles. Here it must be noted that compulsory conformity (even where democratically legitimated by some widely shared perception of common humanity) can represent a definite threat to creative deviance; and that the awareness of being trapped in a situation where the individual actor cannot redefine his role might be regarded as the tyranny of the majority over members of minority groups forced not simply into unwanted fellowship but into a way of life which does not suit them (an awareness very often associated with questions arising in the field of education). There is, in other words, a definite sense in which encouragement should be extended rather to pluralism than to convergence in life-styles, even where pluralism proves somewhat of a threat to the common culture and to consensus thinking.

Tawney, as it happens, tended to minimise the extent of that threat. In his Manchester diaries (kept between 1912 and 1914), for instance, he noted and even welcomed a definite degree of diversity in the social arrangements and intellectual positions of the nation: "It is quite true that there must always be diverse groups and parties in a nation, that different traditions, mental aptitudes and experiences will result in different political doctrines, and that the existence of such variety, by offering a wide field of opinion from which to select, is the best guarantee of national wisdom".[100] Yet, while regarding such diversity as inevitable and desirable, Tawney also believed that national identity presupposes a substantial amount of agreement on common ground: "Variety in political opinion is beneficial. Variety in standards as to fundamental questions of conduct is not."[101] More specifically, the poison of social life is the profit-motive, about which no more than one view can be entertained:

Unity . . . is to be desired in all those matters which involve the everyday life of mankind, not in the sense that all must believe the same things or act in the same way, but in the sense that one man must not suppose that what another believes is dictated solely by selfish interests. While disapproving of his actions he may be able to see that it has a moral justification. It is just this moral justification which is lacking in the economic life of today. It is just the lack of it which turns disagreement into discord and bitterness.[102]

Consensus, in other words, is problematic only so long as capitalistic institutions and motivation exist; and hence, in a socialist society, frank intercourse between Englishmen will not necessitate any artificial convergence of life-styles, nor the desire to nurture a common culture prove a threat to social pluralism and that social experimentation which leads to innovation and change in place of stagnation linked with eternal perpetuation of rigid tradition. Tawney, here as elsewhere, was perhaps somewhat optimistic; for, to be fair, a perception of common humanity need not lead to agreement on common ends to be pursued. Where it does not, then social pluralism might still mean social conflict, even in a fully socialist Britain.

Fifth, there is the problem of the world common culture. Just as Tawney did not see any external obstacles to the institution of socialism in the United Kingdom, so he did not see any obstacles to peace in a world of multiple socialisms. At the same time, however, he was fully aware of the existence of "passionate particularisms",[103] "national idiosyncrasies"[104] and "localised loyalties";[105] and warned that it would not be easy, even within the framework of Europe itself, "to preserve both the common values and the national individualities by preventing attempts at a forced and artificial unity from crushing the diversities, and the diversities from degenerating into an anarchy which, since it leaves the weak at the mercy of the strong, leads by a longer road to the same ruinous end".[106] Looking at Europe, he noted on the eve of the Second World War, one "seeks a civilization, and finds a chaos of suspicious states".[107] Yet if selfish nationalisms were the order of the day in Europe (and noting that all European societies are principally Christian societies and thus share both a unique view "of the nature of man and the significance of human life"[108] and a social ethic "sufficiently comprehensive to provide a standard by which to judge the collective actions and institutions of mankind"[109]), then one would expect even greater selfishness at an international level as between nations of different persuasions. One could, of course, introduce here the notion of complementarity of interest and argue that peace results Spencer-like when I come to depend on your meat and you on my bread, so that I come to respect your sandcastle lest you demolish mine. Such a line of argumentation would, however, deriving justice as it does from expediency rather than morality, have had singularly little appeal to Tawney. The dilemma then is to say why the Israeli Jew should love the Palestinian Arab as himself, or why the Russian lion should lie down with the Czech lamb rather than acting as national interest and particular appetite would dictate; and it cannot but be conceded that we are here venturing into undiscovered territory which does not and may not appear on Tawney's map.

II. THE PROBLEM OF INEQUALITY

Tawney denied that all men were equal in their natural endowments and argued (relying in part on the evidence of Sir Cyril Burt) that the environmental determinists of the Enlightenment "greatly underestimated the significance of inherited qualities, and greatly over-estimated the plasticity of human nature".[110] Men are no more equally intelligent or equally talented than they are all of the same height, weight, race or religion. Yet the fact that some men are inferior in intellectual capacity does not imply "that such individuals or classes should receive less consideration than others, or should be treated as inferior in respect of such matters as legal status, or health, or economic arrangements, which are within the control of the community";[111] for although men are not equal in intellectual capacity, they are members of the same "human family"[112] and equal in value. The fact that a mother knows her children are not identical does not imply that she will favour the strong and neglect the weak. People have different requirements (and the reduction of a variety of character patterns to "a drab and monotonous uniformity"[113] is to be avoided rather than sought), but in a society based on the capital fact of common humanity differential provision will be made so as to supply privileges "equal in quality but different in kind":

> Equality of provision is not identity of provision. It is to be achieved, not by treating different needs in the same way, but by

devoting equal care to ensuring that they are met in the different ways most appropriate to them, as is done by a doctor who prescribes different regimens for different constitutions, or a teacher who develops different types of intelligence by different curricula.[114]

All men are not equal in their natural endowments. The real problem in England, however, is by no means entirely inequality based on inherent individual ability, nor even on older social divisions involving sex, race or religion. Rather, the real problem in England is the structured hierarchy of the class system, which via arbitrary and capricious distinctions such as those based on birth and family wealth rather than individual capacity prevents most citizens (all, indeed, save a privileged few) from growing "to their full stature".[115]

A class is not simply a social group (since "while classes are social groups, not all social groups, even when they have common economic interests, can be described as classes"[116]) nor to be defined simply in terms of occupational classification ("stockbrokers, barristers and doctors, miners, railwaymen and cotton-spinners represent half a dozen professions; but they are not normally regarded as constituting half a dozen classes"[117]). Rather the concept of class is a comprehensive one: "It relates not to this or that specific characteristic of a group, but to a totality of conditions by which several sides of life are affected."[118] At work, classes are economic groupings discharging different functions with respect to land, labour and capital (e.g. capitalist employer and wage-earning employee). At play, classes are social groupings "distinguished from each other by different standards of expenditure and consumption, and varying in their income, their environment, their education, their social status and family connections, their leisure and their amusements".[119]

The definition of class is a comprehensive one, and it would therefore be wrong to argue as if class emanated *solely* from economic basis: "The social fabric is stretched upon an economic framework, and its contours follow the outlines of the skeleton which supports it. But it is not strained so taut as to be free from superfluous folds and ornamental puckers."[120] Particularly in older traditional communities such as Britain, the class system is likely to contain vestigial elements "which, like the rudimentary organs of the human body, or the decorative appendages of the British Constitution, have survived after their function has disappeared and their meaning been forgotten".[121] Class in Britain must hence be looked at from a double perspective – the "crude plutocratic reality" ("as businesslike as Manchester") and the "sentimental aroma of an aristocratic legend" ("as gentlemanly as Eton")[122] – and we must also remember that even today, "though somewhat less regularly than in the past, class tends to determine occupation rather than occupation class".[123] One thing, however, is certain, namely that class-consciousness presupposes class and that matter is therefore in this instance primary: "The fact creates the consciousness, not the consciousness the fact".[124]

In Britain "the existence of divisions between the life and outlook of different classes" are "more profound than in almost any country of western Europe",[125] and the specific determinants of stratification are as follows.

(a) Property and income

In Britain the great majority of the population falls into the category of wage-earners and a small minority into the category of property-owners; and the two groups are quite distinct, for, while weekly wage-earners do own property via bank deposits and shares in building societies, the amounts involved are tiny compared to the quantity of property owned by other sectors of the population.

Quoting figures relating to the mid-1930s, Tawney noted that ownership was concentrated and that "this concentration of property gives a peculiar and distinctive stamp to the social structure of England. . . . Where conditions are such that two-thirds of the wealth is owned by approximately one per cent of the population, the ownership of the property is more properly regarded as the badge of a class than as the attribute of a society".[126] At least – and here Tawney disagrees with Marx – ownership is not becoming more concentrated. Rather the opposite: "So far from diminishing, as he seems to have anticipated would be the case, the number of property-owners in England has tended, if anything, to increase in the course of the last half-century. Though still astonishingly small, it is probably larger today than at any time since he wrote".[127] The improvement was evidently dramatic, for by 1952 the above-mentioned figure of two-thirds of wealth in the hands of 1 per cent of the population had apparently shrunk to one-half of wealth.[128]

Much property is inherited, and this reminds us that the recipients of income via ownership reap where they never sowed. Where ownership is passive rather than active, payment is a perfect sinecure, and a permanent one at that. Income as well as property is unequally distributed, but less unequally so than property: Tawney cites evidence relating to the early 1930s to show that 1½ per cent of the population received 23 per cent of personal incomes.[129] This shows that gross inequalities in pay do exist (partly reflecting an undemocratic educational system which leaves skill scarce and renders it expensive at the same time as untrained manpower is abundant and cheap). In general, exorbitant salaries "corrupt *morale* and ought to go".[130]

(b) Opportunity

In Britain all people have equal access to the services of the police, which are allocated on the basis of need rather than effective demand;[131] but that which can be said of law and order cannot be said of health and education. The incidence of disease and rates of mortality vary as between social classes (partly because of removeable evils such as unhealthy working environments and overcrowded and insanitary housing conditions among the poor), and so does schooling, whether in terms of duration ("it seems natural to those who slip into that mood of tranquil inhumanity that working-class children should go to the mill at an age when the children of the well-to-do are just beginning the serious business of education"[132]) or in terms of facilities (buildings, libraries, books, playing-fields, equipment, staffing ratios) or in terms of job prospects: "Even from 1924 to 1929, 64 per cent of the successful candidates for the administrative grade of the Civil Service still came . . . from 150 schools belonging to the Headmasters' Conference."[133] The public schools also appear to produce a majority of bishops and bank directors. Clearly, the existence of this parallel educational system means that those who complete State education do not stand an equal chance for employment when competing with middle and upper-class children who have attended the public schools. It also means that decision-makers in positions of responsibility will have had little personal experience "of the conditions of life and habits of thought of those for whose requirements in the matter of health, housing, education and economic well-being, they are engaged in providing. That deficiency is serious."[134]

Unequal opportunity with respect to health, education and security is in a sense incompatible with the utilitarian ideal of a career open to the talents and the equalisation of civil and political rights which followed the French Revolution. Estates collapsed into equality of legal status throughout Europe as the landed classes, fearing levelling pressures from below, "walked reluctantly backwards into the future, lest a worse thing should befall them".[135] The objective of the process of equalisation was to cause inequalities between classes to disappear, inequalities between individuals to come to depend on merit alone. In France the main inequalities were with respect to the law, while in England they tended to be based upon the economy; but even in England levelling of a legalistic nature came about in the form of the extension of the franchise, abolition of public sector sinecures and of many of the privileges enjoyed by the Church of England, termination of the disabilities experienced by Roman Catholics, the recruitment of civil servants by competitive examination. Nonetheless, obstacles to mobility remained in the form of, say, low wages (which prevented the workers from feeding their children properly or keeping them longer at school and thus perpetuated the vicious circle of poverty). And that is the essential irony in the doctrine of individual initiative and equality of opportunity. It serves as an outlet for tension (as a "lightning-conductor") but it is to some extent a fiction: "Its credit is good, as long as it does not venture to cash its cheques. Like other respectable principles, it is encouraged to reign, provided that it does not attempt to rule".[136]

The position today is hence beset with certain contradictions. On the one hand every man has been freed from legalistic disabilities which might prevent him from "using to the full his natural endowments of physique, of character, and of intelligence".[137] On the other hand, however, none is given the help he needs to escape from a stunting and sterilizing environment and to make the most of whatever natural endowments he may possess. There are not "equal opportunities of becoming unequal",[138] class succeeds to caste, and "economic realities make short work of legal abstractions"; for "the character of a society is determined less by abstract rights than by practical powers. It depends, not upon what its members *may* do, if they can, but upon what they *can* do, if they will."[139]

(c) **Power**

Power may be defined as "the capacity of an individual, or group of individuals, to modify the conduct of other individuals or groups in the manner which he desires, and to prevent his own conduct being modified in the manner in which he does not";[140] and the exercise of that capacity clearly extends to economy as well as polity. The power to make decisions that will affect the future of individual and collective life is, however, unequally distributed, both at the national level (where "the association of political leadership with birth and wealth is a commonplace of English history"[141]) and at the level of industry (where there is concentration of authority, initiative and control at the apex of the hierarchy and "the familiar division between the directed and the directors; between those who receive orders and those from whom orders proceed; between the privates and the non-commissioned officers of the industrial army and those who initiate its operations, determine its objective and methods, and are responsible for the strategy and tactics on which the economic destiny of the mass of mankind depends"[142]).

Some inequalities of power cannot be avoided. Irresponsible exercise of that power, however, can and must be; and here it is important to note that Western-type societies tend to have abundant checks against the abuse of political power (the principle of "one man/one vote", for example) and yet none at all against autocracy and oppression in the economic sphere (although, and "apart from the material evils which irresponsible power produces, it is alien to the political traditions of Englishmen that the livelihood of many should be dependent upon the arbitrary decision of a few, or that they should be governed in their daily lives by regulations in the making of which they have had no voice"[143]). This asymmetry is deplorable since the "business oligarchy" (and no longer the "aristrocracy of tradition and prestige") is in truth "the effective aristocracy of industrial nations"[144], and able to wield immense power over both consumption and production. Power over consumption because of business concentration:

> If a man eats bread made of flour produced to the extent of forty per cent by two milling combines and meat supplied by an international meat trust, and lives in a house built of materials of which twenty-five per cent are controlled by a ring, and buys his

tobacco from one amalgamation, and his matches from another, while his wife's sewing thread is provided by a third, which has added eight millionaires to the national roll of honour in the last twenty years, is he free as a consumer?[145]

Power over production because the worker has no influence over the decisions which most intimately affect his life:

Is he free as a worker, if he is liable to have his piece-rates cut at the discretion of his employer, and, on expressing his annoyance, to be dismissed as an agitator, and to be thrown on the scrap-heap without warning because his employer has decided to shut down a plant, or bankers to restrict credit, and to be told, when he points out that the industry on which his livelihood depends is being injured by mismanagement, that his job is to work, and that the management in question will do his thinking for him?[146]

Where economic democracy is so limited (where relationships nominally contractual are in practice quasi-feudal), a man's civic freedom is partial and circumscribed, no matter how much civil and political democracy also obtains; for whereas in the political sphere (itself hardly free of class considerations: witness "the possession by property of a second chamber to itself" and "the influence exercised by wealth in the choice of the first"[147]) at least all citizens have an equal vote for their decision-makers in the House of Commons, in the economic sphere the economically powerless remain at the mercy of the economically strong. This is a great injustice, and it also is socially divisive and spiritually injurious, as where it breeds dictatorial habits in the minority of rulers and a mixture of servile and hostile attitudes in the majority of the ruled.

We have previously seen that Tawney was aware of the increasing democratisation of property-ownership that took place in Britain in the 1930s and 1940s. It is important to remember, however, that he also associated this tendency with a parallel movement towards concentration of power:

It is sometimes suggested that the growth of joint-stock enterprise, by increasing the number of small investors, has broadened the basis of industrial government. But, if joint-stock enterprise has done something to diffuse ownership, it has centralized control. The growth in the size of the business unit necessarily accelerates the process by which ever larger bodies of wage-earners are brigaded under the direction of a comparatively small staff of entrepreneurs.[148]

Sometimes the owners of capital take decisions which the wage-earners then execute, while at other times the wage-earners are under the direction of managers acting as salaried agents for the proprietors; but whichever is the case, society is divided, economically and socially, into "classes which are ends, and classes which are instruments".[149] This abuse is incompatible with the objectives of a free society.

(d) Status

Not only are some men richer and more powerful than others, they are also more respected. Such inequality in status and its symbols (the mystifications of "Mumbo Jumbo") is, however, "out of tune with the realities of today",[150] in which no single Master Class either has or ought to have the right to behave as the natural repository of advantage. It is deplorable that the rich can exploit the poor "because, in their hearts, too many of the poor admire the rich",[151] but such indifference to inequality, such a two-nations state of mind, is nonetheless a national characteristic: "England, though politically a democracy, is still liable to be plagued, in her social and economic life, by the mischievous ghost of an obsolete tradition of class superiority and class subordination".[152] The English need co-operation based on a common culture, and yet "there is nothing, it seems, which they desire less. They spend their energies in making it impossible, in behaving like the public schoolboys of the universe. *Das Gentlemanideal* has them by the throat; they frisk politely into obsolescence on the playing-fields of Eton."[153]

Such "docility", such a "respect for their betters", such a "habit of submission"[154] does not obtain in the United States, despite undeniable differences in income and power; for, at least at the moment (and while noting that concentration of economic power may, as Tocqueville predicted, restore some sort of aristocratic social order), there is in that country a healthy "equality of manners and freedom from certain conventional restraints".[155] In America there is intermarriage between classes, a definite convergence in consumption-patterns, and no élite of public schoolboys trained to be leaders and accepted by the lower classes as such. Englishmen must come to recognise the advantages of a society where status may be associated with superior individuals but no longer with superior classes, for such a perception is the precondition for socialism: "To kick over an idol, you must first get off your knees".[156]

We have in this section examined four determinants of stratification in Britain, namely inequalities of income and property, opportunity, power and status, and have seen how closely they work together (as where wealth opens the door to a public-school education, to economic and social power, and to social status) to produce a divided community. They are collectively and individually the enemy of the common culture and the associated perception of mechanical solidarity; for, clearly, "obligations are only recognized where there [is] identity of nature. I have no duties to a tiger or to a fish."[157]

Men are men and nothing else; and it is this essential equality which makes the "violent inequalities of social condition and economic power"[158] that are indissolubly linked with capitalism so deplorable. Precisely because men are men and nothing else, moreover, precisely because even today no man is so far removed from the mean that he cannot perceive his fundamental similarity both with the greatest and with the least of his brothers, men are quite simply shocked by the injustices present in their society: "The problem of modern society is a problem of proportions, not of quantities; of justice, not of material well-being. Peace comes not when everyone has £3 a week, but when everyone recognizes that the material, objective, external arrangements of society are based on principles which they feel to correspond with their subjective ideas of justice."[159] Such a convergence of *what is* and *what ought to be* does not obtain today, and widespread social conflict is the result. Man is born free, is everywhere in chains, and no philosophical justification can be found to make acceptable to the human mind this insult to essential humanity: "What produces our social divisions is not mere poverty, but the consciousness of a moral wrong, an outrage on what is sacred in man".[160]

The problem of our day "is a philosophical rather than an economic one",[161] and one therefore which cannot be solved simply via economic growth (even where that growth is accompanied by marginal administrative measures such as modest redistribution of income towards lower-income groups). Where riches result from the fact that "a large part of modern society is engaged in the gentle pastime of buying gold too dear, and another part in that of selling other people's blood too cheaply",[162] nothing less is called for than the total restructuring of society according to popular ideas of right and wrong. Economic efficiency is not enough, not least because poverty in itself is simply not in all circumstances detestable ("Medieval poverty: the poverty of fishermen or crofters today – often is not"[163]). What is detestable about poverty is, first, that it is often the result of the exploitation of brother by brother ("The view of the causes of poverty to which I am coming is that they are to be sought in the existence of economic privileges which give those who enjoy them a lien or bond on the labour of those who do not"[164]); second, that it often constitutes the mirror-image of affluence within the bosom of one nation ("What thoughtful rich people call the problem of poverty, thoughtful poor people call with equal justice the problem of riches"[165]); and, third, that it is often associated with perceived economic oppression ("If men are free, in the sense of controlling, within the limits set by nature, the material conditions of their own lives, they may be poor, but they are not a problem"[166]). The focus, clearly, is on relative rather than absolute deprivation (although the latter undeniably remains an important problem).

The focus is also on deprivation as an industrial problem: "Half the thought and money spent on relieving existing evils would probably have prevented many of them from coming into existence at all".[167] Arguing that social policy ought to concern itself not only with the "submerged residuum" represented by derelicts on the Embankment but, more significantly, with "normal man in normal circumstances" (the underpaid mineworker, for example, who receives low wages while functionless shareholders receive high dividends), Tawney stressed that the key question is not why certain individuals fall into destitution but why certain classes are rich and powerful at the very time that others are not: "The problem of preventing poverty is not primarily to assist individuals who are exceptionally unfortunate. It is to make the normal conditions under which masses of men work and live such that they may lead a healthy, independent and self-respecting life when they are *not* exceptionally unfortunate."[168] In terms of methodology, the observer should look, in considering the poverty of a particular seamstress, beyond "the sufferings and merits of the individual to the economic environment which determines her position".[169] Having done that, he will see that improvement of individual character cannot be the solution, for "unemployment, short time, and low wages fall upon just and unjust alike": "The normal conditions of the normal worker are precarious" and "his economic prospects are to a great extent, except in a very few well organized industries, beyond the control of himself or of persons like himself".[170] Nor can the upgrading of a socially mobile and economically progressive society eliminate the incidence of poverty, "any more than tadpoles disappear from our ponds because a large number of them are annually converted into frogs": "The vision of an Elysium to be attained by continuing to play with marked cards and simply shuffling the pack . . . is, happily, as impracticable as it is sordid".[171]

Deprivation thus turns out to be inseparable from inequality, and inequality from the structural imperatives of capitalist institutions. This converts the war on poverty from its traditional concern with the relief of immediate distress and makes it into a crusade against a transitory economic and social system which is class-ridden, acquisitive, and committed to the perverted notion that men are means, wealth the end. This unhealthy system must be swept away, but the reason is not principally the material one of "restoration of booty" (for neither individual achievement nor social success can meaningfully be measured in terms of absolute income) but rather a spiritual one concerned with right and wrong: "Economic privileges must be abolished, not, primarily, because they hinder the production of wealth, but because they produce wickedness."[172]

Thus, in the last analysis, the case for common situation, like that for common culture, is bound up with ethical absolutes and moral imperatives. The idea of "the greatest good of the greatest number" might justify the enslavement of a small minority, but there is above utility a still higher standard of evaluation which teaches that social integration is better than national division and that justice must never be sacrificed to convenience: "There is a law higher than the well-being of the majority, and that law is the supreme value of every human personality as such."[173]

3 The Welfare Society

Perceived relative deprivation creates two nations and yet there is but one God. Such deprivation is the antithesis of common culture and situation and must be replaced by a welfare society in which one decent Englishman can communicate freely and equally with another. In the first part of this chapter we shall examine the techniques which Tawney felt would generate a more just, open and generous society, namely the progressive taxation of incomes and the punitive taxation of wealth, the extension of the social services (and in such a way as to treat absolute deprivation, upgrade potential meritocrats and help to encourage the values of common citizenship which are essential if equal creatures are to remain equal while enjoying unequal degrees of wordly success), and the socialisation of industry so as to deal once and for all with the inequities born of unearned incomes. Then, in the second part of this chapter, we shall extend our argument by examining the views on welfare of Tawney's most celebrated disciple, Richard Titmuss and, comparing them with those of Tawney himself, note a number of fundamental similarities between the two authors – similarities such as a conviction that the *I am* of welfareism is morally superior to the *I have* of possessive utilitarianism; that giving is better than taking; that consensus leads to kindness. We shall, however, also suggest a fundamental difference, that Titmuss's work was biased towards symptoms, treatment and repair while that of Tawney focused more ambitiously on the eradication of causes and the prevention of damage. Tawney's canvas was the broader one, but perhaps this is to be expected from a man whose theoretical synthesis matured in the shadow of his historical studies into the causes of the English Civil War. There he discovered that it was not the war that had destroyed the pre-existent social order but rather antecedent economico-social change (notably the growth of a land-market following the dissolution of the monasteries and the inflation, since "the article which it handles is not merely a commodity, but an instrument of social prestige and political

55

power"[1]) that had itself led to the war. He shared the view of Harrington that "the revolution of his day had been determined by changes in social organization"[2] and was undeniably convinced that the social reformer must reform much if he is successfully to reform at all.

I. THE STRATEGY FOR REFORM

Tawney believed that democracy "is unstable as a political system, so long as it remains a political system and nothing more"[3] and, regarding the atmosphere in Britain as "more sodden with a servile respect for money and position than exists in any other country of western Europe",[4] called for an extension of democratic attitudes (that the differences between men are of less significance than the similarities) and democratic principles (that all authority to be legitimate must rest upon the consent of the constituency) from the polity to embrace all aspects of social and economic organisation. Specifically, Tawney's proposals for the transcendence of unbridled capitalism by democratic socialism are along the following lines.

(a) Taxation

Socialism does not presuppose a complete equalisation of incomes, a total sharing-out or averaging such that each man has the same command over resources, but it does presuppose a rather more equal distribution than is at present the case: "If men are to respect each other for what they are, they must cease to respect each other for what they own. They must abolish, in short, the reverence for riches. . . . And, human nature being what it is, in order to abolish the reverence for riches, they must make impossible the existence of a class which is important merely because it is rich".[5] A society which is guided "by a just appreciation of spiritual ends" will hence avoid "violent contrasts of wealth and power, and an indiscriminating devotion to institutions by which such contrasts are maintained and heightened",[6] for "the extremes both of riches and poverty are degrading and anti-social".[7]

Progressive taxation should not be so steep as to deny the fundamental fact that "exceptional responsibilities should be compensated by exceptional rewards, as a recognition of the service performed and an inducement to perform it".[8] What is inequitable, after all, is not that a superior input should command a superior reward, but "that some classes should be excluded from the heritage of civilization which others enjoy, and that the fact of human fellowship, which is ultimate and profound, should be obscured by economic contrasts, which are trivial and superficial".[9]

Since the real enemy is not lack of parity in individual incomes *per se* but rather class differences in opportunity and circumstance irrespective of personal merit, moderation with respect to progressive income tax should be matched by severity with respect to death duties: "If the estate duties were increased, part of them required to be paid in land or securities, and a supplementary duty imposed, increasing with the number of times that a property passed at death . . . the social poison of inheritance would largely be neutralized."[10]

Equalisation via taxation is redistributive not merely of income but of expenditure, for it causes quite different goods to be demanded and supplied than is the case where distribution is less egalitarian:

> Since the demand of one income of £50,000 is as powerful a magnet as the demand of 500 incomes of £100, it diverts energy from the creation of wealth to the multiplication of luxuries, so that, for example, while one-tenth of the people of England are overcrowded, a considerable part of them are engaged, not in supplying that deficiency, but in making rich men's hotels, luxurious yachts, and motor cars.[11]

Such goods (to say nothing of grouse-moors, villas in the South of France, and armaments) are not wealth but waste and should not have been produced at all until more urgent social needs had been satisfied. These needs are neglected "because, while the effective demand of the mass of men is only too small, there is a small class which wears several men's clothes, eats several men's dinners, occupies several families' houses, and lives several men's lives".[12] Such a "misdirection of limited resources to the production or upkeep of costly futilities"[13] only demonstrates the dual mystification of modern economic life, namely that the quantity rather than the composition of production is taken as the index of achievement (whereas the purpose of industry is in truth an anthropocentric instead of a reiocentric one, and no less than "the conquest of nature for the service of man"[14]) and that market choices reflect social priorities (whereas they in fact only reflect the well-known proposition that "he who pays the piper calls the tune" in a world where not all men are equally able to pay).

Tawney is calling for a redistribution of purchasing power, but not fundamentally from the private consumption of the rich to the private consumption of the poor. Rather, he believes that the non-functional surplus appropriated by the State via taxation should be used to finance collective consumption in the form of social welfare programmes. Taxation is hence central to the strategy of reform not only because it negates the existing abuse of hereditary privilege but also because it positively promotes the social benefit of greater equality in life-chances.

(b) Social welfare

Tawney believed that the social services state was unambiguously redistributive in favour of the poorer classes: "The effect of an extension of social services, accompanied by progressive taxation, is to diminish inequality, since it involves, though at present on an extremely modest scale, the transference of wealth from large incomes to small".[15] And he may have been right, for the examples he gives suggest a lower-class Britain absolutely, as well as relatively, deprived: "It is not a small thing that certain diseases should have been virtually wiped out", that "some measure of educational provision, cramped and meagre though it is, should be made for all children up to fourteen", and that "the tragedies of sickness, of age and unemployment should have been somewhat mitigated".[16] Tawney was, after all, a witness to the tragedy of the inter-war years.

Social welfare measures benefit all classes, but the poor pro-portionately more; for money is taken "where it can most easily be spared" and spent "where it is most urgently needed"[17] as defined by social priorities. Conscious action dictates that "necessaries shall be provided before trivialities" and ensures that "doctors are set to work instead of gardeners, and the gamekeeper or chauffeur of the last generation becomes the teacher or the civil servant of the next".[18] Conscious action also dictates collective provision in the welfare field, and thus pooling rather than sharing out becomes the corner-stone of social equality:

It is not the division of the nation's income into eleven million fragments, to be distributed, without further ado, like cake at a school treat, among its eleven million families. It is, on the contrary, the pooling of its surplus funds by means of taxation, and the use of the funds thus obtained to make accessible to all, irrespective of their income, occupation, or social position, the conditions of civilization which, in the absence of such measures, can be enjoyed only by the rich.[19]

A joint-stock company with a capital of £10,000,000 is not "the precise equivalent of 10,000 tradesmen with a capital of £1,000",[20] and an army which divides the cost of an expeditionary force among the men participating in it is unlikely to stop the enemy advance. Society, like the joint-stock company or the expeditionary force, is an entity *sui generis*, conceptually more than the sum of its parts; and it too must often act collectively if it is to act effectively.

It is, of course, difficult to define the sphere of social welfare, for there is no permanent and universal line of demarcation which divides once and for all "needs which may properly be supplied by collective action from those which individuals should be required to meet by their personal exertions": "The boundaries between the spheres of communal provision and private initiative differ widely both from decade to decade, and from one community to another."[21] What we can say, however, is that perceptions of social obligation and public function are spreading, and that the range of requirements to be met by collective provision is steadily being widened: "Of the forms of such provision existing today, not only were the majority unknown half a century ago, but their establishment was resisted, as a menace alike to individual morality and to economic prosperity."[22] Even the United States, despite its much-vaunted reliance on "individual effort" and "pecuniary rewards",[23] has introduced free secondary education. The causes of what appears to be an inevitable movement towards increased social action are two in number – the first material (economic change), the second ideal (a revised perception of social justice) – and it will be useful to consider each in turn.

(1) Economic change
Economic development generates the means for providing elaborate social services, but also creates the necessity for them. For otherwise, in communities which interpret well-being as a commodity suitable for purchase and sale like tea and sugar, the result is

"the paradox of rising pecuniary incomes and deepening social misery":[24]

> No individual can create by his isolated action a healthy environment, or establish an educational system with a wide range of facilities, or organize an industry in such a manner as to diminish economic insecurity, or eliminate the causes of accidents in factories and streets. Yet these are all conditions which make the difference between happiness and misery, and sometimes, indeed, between life and death. In so far as they exist, they are the source of a social income, received in the form, not of money, but of increased well-being.[25]

This social income must be received collectively or not at all; for "high individual incomes will not purchase the mass of mankind immunity from cholera, typhus and ignorance, still less secure them the positive advantages of educational opportunity and economic security".[26] A competitive environment can deal with the atomic but not the organic, with the individual but not the collective or the common.

Despite his assertion that the principal benefits from the social services accrue in the form of "increased well-being" rather than "money", it would nonetheless be very wrong to argue that Tawney saw the welfare state entirely in terms of consumption as an end in itself: "The greater part of the expenditure upon the social services is not a liability, but an investment, the dividends of which are not the less substantial because they are paid, not in cash, but in strengthened individual energies and an increased capacity for co-operative effort."[27] The State, which via provision of the social services helps to ensure these two great social advantages, must come to play an important role in the profit-making process; and indeed, its contribution to the success of industrial activity is "at least as important"[28] as that of the capitalist.

Consider first the advantage of "strengthened individual energies". Tawney notes that tuberculosis (a "disease of poverty" but one which is completely preventable) "accounted recently for about 9 per cent of the deaths registered from all causes",[29] records that the number of working days lost in 1933 among the insured population is reported to have been equivalent to twelve months' work of 560,000 persons,[30] and makes clear that such drains on national potential can only be avoided by social intervention: "If health is purchasable, it is also expensive. For the mass of mankind its conditions must be created by collective action, or not at all."[31] Again, because health depends on accommodation and because overcrowding "is a form of under-consumption induced by poverty", therefore the same remedy as public provision of sewers to prevent cholera should be applied: "It is to make the provision of the indispensable minimum of housing a public obligation, borne, like other indispensable burdens, from public funds."[32] Similarly, State education ensures that the talents of the poor will not be left underdeveloped and enables a great pool of (often wasted) ability to be tapped: here industry benefits as well as society as a whole (via a faster rate of economic growth) and the child in particular (via a high flight from ignorance and misery), for "it is possible for the personnel, as well as for the material equipment of industry to be under-capitalized".[33] Finally, income maintenance in states of dependency not only compensates the recipient for uncertainty and social diswelfares borne on behalf of all, but also helps to stabilise purchasing power and mitigate fluctuations in total demand.[34]

Consider now the advantage of "an increased capacity for co-operative effort". Hunger can make men work, but it cannot compel them to work well, as the example of the coal industry reminds us, where the single greatest cause of economic waste and loss turns out to be employee-dissatisfaction: "If it is desired to increase the output of wealth, it is not a paradox, but the statement of an elementary economic truism to say that active and constructive co-operation on the part of the rank and file of workers would do more to contribute to that result than the discovery of a new coalfield or a generation of scientific invention."[35] The social services, fortunately, can help to breed that "goodwill and mutual confidence"[36] upon which efficiency and productivity depend. This is particularly the case with education: co-operation depends on mutual understanding, and "a common educational background fosters such understanding", while "an organization of education which treats different sections of the population as though they belonged to different species is an impediment to it".[37] The common culture is a precondition for a successful economic system,[38] for genuine commitment to work implies a career truly open to the talents in place of the resentments engendered by a "perpetual class-struggle".[39]

(2) A revised perception of social justice
The spread of the social services is to be explained not only in terms of economic expediency but in terms of collective goals that transcend profit and loss. Three such goals may in particular be distinguished.

First, genuine equalisation of life chances and of opportunities to make the most of one's innate ability. Tawney argued that the logical implication of the liberal conception of the career open to the talents was "complete environmental equality in respect of the external conditions of health, and education, and economic security"[40] (analogous to identical access to – although, obviously, not identical utilisation of – the services of the police and of sewers irrespective of ability to pay); and argued further that the attack must be on all three fronts at once since even the most intelligent slum-dweller will be impeded in his rise if he also has tuberculosis or no funds to fall back upon in case of unemployment. Tawney argued, in other words, that the liberal objective of "an open road" would only become truly meaningful when accompanied by a measure of socialism adequate to ensure "an equal start",[41] for the present system simply does not give an equal chance to all groups of players in life's game:

> Explanations which are relevant as a clue to differences between the incomes of individuals in the same group lose much of their validity when applied, as they often are, to interpret differences between those of individuals in different groups. It would be as reasonable to hold that the final position of competitors in a race were an accurate indication of their physical endowments, if, while some entered fit and carefully trained, others were half-starved, were exhausted by want of sleep, and were handicapped by the starters.[42]

Secondly, the humanitarian objective of assistance to those in need. Tawney was hostile to the "mere ambulance work for the victims of class privilege"[43] which he saw as one of the chief functions of isolated charitable activity, but he also appreciated that many of the poor need help on a more immediate basis than simply via the reform of the capitalist system; and he was expressing an attitude of unimpeachable pedigree when he proposed that not only the intelligent pauper (on grounds including economic interest) but also his "drowning companions"[44] (on grounds of ordinary humanity) should be made the object of public support. Moreover, since needs are spiritual as well as material, the crucial social service of education has the important function of providing countervailing power to "the spiritual crassness, the contempt for disinterested intellectual activity" of "those who would pick over the treasures of earth and heaven for a piece they can put in their purses".[45] Education is "a spiritual activity, much of which is not commercially profitable", while "the prevailing temperament of Englishmen is to regard as most important that which is commercially profitable, and as of only inferior importance that which is not".[46] The task of "those who believe in education" remains nonetheless to preach "that spiritual activity is of primary importance and worth any sacrifice of material goods"[47] and in particular to make clear to their fellow-citizens that "without education, rich men are really poor".[48] The excellence of an organisation such as the WEA lies precisely in the fact that it caters for humanistic – and particularly political – enlightenment rather than disseminating knowledge of purely occupational utility.

Thirdly, the perception of common humanity and thus the objective of cultivating the common culture. One of the main factors in engendering this sensation of a shared situation was war. In the First World War Tawney at the Front was impressed by the fellowship, solidarity and *esprit de corps* of all classes and, indeed, all nations; for even the German soldiers in the trenches opposite came to be regarded not as genuine devils but as "the victims of the same catastrophe as ourselves" and hence as "our comrades in misery".[49] He was further impressed by the extent to which the experience of being collectively at war against a common enemy led citizens in wartime to forget their divisions and seek together to attain a common goal: "We ought to perpetuate in peace the idealism of war, because that alone can deliver us from the selfish appetites that lie in wait for us in both."[50] Besides that, war showed up the irrationalities of the economic system in a dramatic way "when the nation found its soldiers and sailors threatened with a shortage of munitions and coal, because employers and employees could not agree as to the terms upon which their industries should be carried on":[51] this flash of lightning only illuminated an old abuse, namely the frequent failure of the social machine optimally to attain social objectives because of uncorrected flaws in its highly individualistic mode of operation. Then too, there is the fact that economic planning in wartime succeeded, and "by a *collective act of will*",[52] in rapidly transforming the economic mechanism from one which had sought to maximise personal profit and utility into one oriented towards the attainment of a clearly defined social purpose. Finally, war has an unexpectedly educational function in so far as it stimulates soldiers to ask intellectual question (such as why the war is being fought in the first place) and makes available to them a whole series of discussion-groups composed of a multitude of highly differentiated peers (discussion-groups, in other words, whose atmosphere is not all that different from that of the WEA tutorial).

Once men have begun to perceive their common situation and decided to opt for the promotion of a common culture, then education comes to play a central role in the resultant drama of nation-building: "Education, as I see it, though it is much else as well, is partly, at least, the process by which we transcend the barriers of our isolated personalities, and become partners in a universe of interests which we share with our fellow-men, living and dead alike."[53] Since this process of transcendence, moreover, has not only an ideal dimension (in the form of the lessons taught) but a material dimension as well (associated with the structure and composition of the school itself), positive measures should be taken to deal with the segregated one-class ghettoes represented by the expensive fee-paying public schools:

> A special system of schools, reserved for children whose parents have larger bank-accounts than their neighbours, exists in no other country on the same scale as in England. It is at once an educational monstrosity and a grave national misfortune. It is educationally vicious, since to mix with companions from homes of different types is an important part of the education of the young. It is socially disastrous, for it does more than any other single cause, except capitalism itself, to perpetuate the division of the nation into classes of which one is almost unintelligible to the other.[54]

Education ought to be the "symbol and cement of a spiritual unity transcending differences of birth and wealth".[55] The boarding school, however, inculcates the social poisons of arrogance, privilege, and social division, and causes its charges "to mistake the provincialisms of a class for the interests and manners of civilized mankind".[56] The boarding school is hence not simply the enemy of the career open to the talents but of social solidarity as well:

"Children learn from each other more than the most skilful of masters can teach them. Easy, natural and unselfconscious contacts between young people of varying traditions and different social background are not the least valuable part of their education. . . . An educational system which discourages them is, to that extent, not a good system, but a bad one."[57] Tawney says that "educational policy is always social policy"[58] and states categorically that "the English educational system will never be one worthy of a civilized society until the children of all classes in the nation attend the same schools".[59] Yet despite the grave nature of the inequality and snobbery which Tawney identifies in present-day institutions, he nonetheless does not propose socialisation of the boarding schools, and recommends that each private school should simply be required to obtain a special licence from a central authority which, because of its superior experience in comparing and evaluating schools, can "correct individual aberrations or laxities by reference to a range of knowledge which no single one of them can command":[60] "Such a licence should be granted to a school only on condition that its governing body is representative, that its endowments are administered in the general interest, and that it is equally accessible to all children qualified to profit by it, irrespective of the income or social position of their parents."[61] Tawney's objection is thus not to private schooling *per se* (the existence of which he admits is "favourable to initiative, experiment, and diversity of educational type"[62]), but rather to those academies "whose distinctive characteristic is that they are recruited almost exclusively from the children of parents with larger incomes than their neighbours".[63] Equality of provision need not mean identity of provision.

As well as a solution to the problem of the two-tier school system, other measures in the field of education are also called for. These range from the provision of adequate nursery schools and a school meals service to free schooling for all children up to age 16 and Tawney also seeks to put teeth into his recommendations by calling for "the creation of a system of maintenance allowances on a scale sufficiently ample to break the vicious circle which binds poverty in one generation to lack of educational opportunity in the next"[64] and "the general recognition that the provision of a liberal education for the future primary teacher is among the most vital of a university's functions".[65]

Alongside education, a sensible society should also provide for equality with respect to public health and income maintenance; and Tawney calls specifically for State-sponsored insurance schemes to replace the present dual system (whereby the rich have the comfort of private provision and the poor the stigmatisation of charity) in dealing with states of dependency related to sickness, old age and unemployment. Social security should be adequate in amount and a particular kind of abuse must be avoided – not abuse of the system by the individual (such malingering being "statistically unimportant") but abuse of the system by the State (as where it uses the availability of insurance against unemployment "as a lazy substitute for the attempt to prevent the contingency from occurring"[66]). Governments, in other words, must not simply "pay the unemployed to starve quietly"[67] (this may be termed "social malingering", which is to say "the disposition of the governing classes to rely on drugs, when the remedy needed is a drastic change of regimen"[68]) but must deal directly with the causes of unemployment (Tawney does not say how this should be done and was throughout his life surprisingly uninterested in questions of macroeconomic policy, including those associated with the Keynesian revolution, the very existence of which would appear from his writings virtually to have escaped him). Where they cannot do this, governments should at least acknowledge that unemployment allowances are not charity but compensation to the worker for the collective breakdown that prevents him from obtaining the job he deserves; ensure that this compensation is optimal rather than minimal (i.e. sufficient "not merely to keep him in physical existence, but for a self-respecting life"[69]); and guarantee that he receives his benefits as of right and without stigma.

(c) Socialisation of industry

Tawney defines capitalism as "the direction of economic activity by the owners of capital or their agents for the pecuniary gain of the owners of capital",[70] together with the social institutions, values, relationships and character patterns with which that mode of ownership of capital is habitually linked. He believes that it was a necessary evil in the early stages of modern industrialisation (possibly because, although he does not give his reasons, the collective consciousness of a poor country often assigns an inordinate weight to material growth, as opposed to cohesion and fellowship; and in such circumstances an appeal to greed may have a highly beneficial quick effect). He denies that it is in all cases necessary now. Capitalism today generates conflict between productive employee and passive employer and, via its adverse effect on *morale*, has detrimental consequences for economic efficiency; it is characterised by unnecessary duplication of as a result underutilised capacity and by the sacrifice of potential economies of large scale;[71] and it lacks co-ordination, both at the industrial level (the cobweb case of overproduction where each firm tries to win a game which by definition all cannot) and with respect to national objectives (as where profit-seeking organisations too rapidly deplete irreplaceable mineral resources while simultaneously neglecting alternative sources of energy which they regard as commercially uninteresting[72]). Capitalism, finally, generates vested interests so powerful and so articulate that radical reform inevitably presupposes some prior change in the balance of economic power: progress in the struggle against perceived social distance simply cannot take place "on the scale, or with the speed required, as long as the key positions of the economic system remain in private hands".[73]

Now to specifics:

> An intelligent policy will start from the centre, not nibble at the outworks. The first requirement is, clearly, to master the key positions of the economic world, whence the tune is piped to which the nation dances. Banking, evidently, is one, for it determines the economic weather more directly than any other; transport a second, and power a third; while the coal industry, in England the sole source of power, is a fourth, land and agriculture a fifth, and armaments a sixth.[74]

This is a long list, but Tawney adds, almost as an afterthought, that public control of the commanding heights may in some cases prove almost as satisfactory as public ownership: thus, with respect to the joint-stock banks, "the acquisition by public authorities of a controlling interest in private undertakings"[75] merits consideration, while, with respect to the railways, "the practical advantages of public ownership would be secured if their directorates were appointed by the State".[76] Once, of course, "the halo of mystery which at present surrounds capitalism, in the eyes of the simple" is shattered "by decisive and unmistakable victories at a few well-chosen points", then, as far as other industries are concerned, "the mopping up of the remainder will follow in good time".[77]

Tawney did not confine himself to the negative objective of the expropriation of the expropriator. Recognising as he did that socialisation by itself was no more than a first step in the direction of subordinating the particularistic to the general, he urged that it be accompanied by a number of complementary measures including an extension of participatory schemes designed to make industrial democracy a reality (and in doing this the State should use the industries in public ownership "as experimental stations"[78]). The clearest statement of Tawney's position on the manner in which a sensible socialist system ought to combine accountability, decentralisation and involvement in such a way as to produce fellowship and efficiency may be found in *The Acquisitive Society* in the form of a complex and sophisticated argument which we shall examine in detail in our chapter on "Production and Allocation". Meanwhile, one further comment is necessary in the present context, and it concerns those industries which remain in the private sector of the mixed economy. Even here, Tawney believed, the State should assist private enterprise to serve the public interest (say, by providing risk capital to finance modernisation of plant, or by stimulating rationalisation schemes through the good offices of a specially-created Planning Department) or, where necessary, should compel it to do so (via legislation governing hours of work, standards of health and safety, annual holidays; via import controls where appropriate to protect jobs; via the establishment of a National Investment Board which would – acting, of course, on the advice of "economists of unimpeachable propriety"[79] – then instruct firms as to the percentage of their profits above a minimum level which they ought to plough back rather than distribute, and sometimes also specify the direction of that investment). Even with respect to the private sector, Tawney believed, the Government should not hesitate to use economic policy as a form of social policy.

In this section we have examined the reforms which Tawney proposed (taxation, particularly of inherited wealth; an extension of the social services; the socialisation of the commanding heights of industry and trade and the restriction of the liberty of the remainder) to deal with the evils which he detected (the debility of the common culture and sense of national solidarity caused by inequalities of income and property, opportunity, power and status and the system which perpetuates them; the threat that "different classes of Englishmen" might become "almost as different from each other as though the minority were alien settlers established amid the rude civilization of a race of impoverished aborigines"[80]). It will be interesting to keep both the reforms and the evils in mind when we, in the following section, examine the contribution to the debate on the welfare society that was made, in Tawney's shadow, by Richard Titmuss.

II. FROM TAWNEY TO TITMUSS

No one, either before Richard Titmuss or since, has made such a comprehensive and influential attempt to integrate welfare and society; to study the dependent not as problems in essence but as citizens in situation; or to deploy the vast apparatus of sociological theory (showing, naturally, more familiarity with Durkheim and Weber than with the neo-utilitarianism of exchange theory or the massive system-building of Marxism) to isolate good questions, select relevant facts, and ultimately help to persuade the community to utilise social policy instrumentally in the service of the democratic socialist utopia of compassion, equality and integration that he so highly valued. As Professor of Social Administration at the London School of Economics from 1950 to 1973, through his provocative and stimulating books (notably *Problems of Social Policy, Essays on 'The Welfare State', Income Distribution and Social Change, Commitment to Welfare, The Gift Relationship, Social Policy*), through his activities (as adviser on population policy to the government of Mauritius, on health policy to the government of Tanzania, on pensions policy to the Labour Party; as member of Supplementary Benefits and Community Relations Commissions), Titmuss demonstrated his own integration in the collectivity and made himself widely respected.

Richard Titmuss believed that social policy cannot be value-free precisely because it is inextricably linked to the value-consensus of a particular society and is thus communitarian both in its origins (a manifestation "of society's will to survive as an organic whole") and in its function (reflecting "the expressed wish of all the people to assist the survival of some people").[81] Yet it is naive to expect a unique consensus to dictate unique choices in what is an increasingly pluralistic society; and the confusion which is bound to result when philosopher-rulers with power in their hands try to find out what we, the national family, regard as a "need" or a "collective responsibility" is anticipated by Titmuss's own reluctance to draw a clear distinction between a "trading commodity" (such as aspirins and private insurance) and a service "rendered by the community for the community" (such as blood transfusion and social insurance).[82] Even if an unambiguous collective consciousness does exist, moreover, socially-relevant policies will only emerge where that consensus can be measured; and in neglecting the case for consumer-participation (even via the consultation of representative lobbies and pressure groups), Titmuss was content to leave the power to decide in the hands of politicians, administrators and professionals, men with an inbred propensity to supply what the customer needs rather than what the customer wants and who are likely to have particularistic values and objectives of their own (own-values such as the moral superiority of the family and the "semi" over the unmarried mother and the council estate; own-goals such as security, promotion, self-importance, sense of achievement, which may give them a vested interest in the expansion of their own service and cause them to prefer the low-risk dependent to the hopeless case because of a confusion between their own success-indicators and those of the wider society). Finally, Titmuss was weak on causality: he believed that in Britain (unlike either America or Russia) the collective solidarity of a common condition and the altruism of the "spirit of Dunkirk" were becoming ever more characteristic of the value consensus but gave little proof to show how or why egoism is on the wane, and he seriously underestimated the extent to which the public regards services as social not because of generosity but because of inertia (as where citizens desperately defend the *status quo* since it forms part of an on-going way of life) or greed (as where citizens selfishly attempt, in the absence of a price-deterrent, to take as much and give as little as possible).

Because policy is communitarian, Titmuss was anxious to avoid the sense of stigma which he was convinced is intimately associated with a selectivist system based on the employment of a means-test as a gate-keeper to limit entry to the free welfare services. The means-test, he argued further, and apart from the fact that it is administratively unwieldy (since not even the best computer can process a multitude of discrete and ever-changing variables, particularly in that twilight land where facts are unavailable and needs urgent), promotes a dual standard of service and hence a sense of personal failure in those citizens condemned to enjoy residual and second-rate facilities clearly earmarked for inadequates. Here one may object that it is not the means-testing of the welfare sector that most stigmatises a poor man but rather the income-testing of the competitive market sector, where status is intimately linked to earning and consuming; and that if the psychological damage of spoiled identity is truly to be avoided, then the powerless must be made to feel first-rate citizens when at work or in the shops as well as when at school, in hospital or on the dole. One solution might be quotas to integrate the independent by applying the social-welfare principle of selective discrimination to the world of free enterprise. A second solution might be power-sharing at the place of work. A third solution might be the divorce of finance from provision (by means, say, of a negative income tax), since in the welfare sector men in reality often feel stigmatised by having no economic sanctions to apply: not only can they not demonstrate that they are responsible adults by shopping around for a differentiated product, but they cannot vote against being treated as passive takers rather than respected consumers by taking their business to a more courteous merchant. None of these solutions would have appealed to Titmuss, whose war on stigma focused on the shame and guilt he believed to be experienced when a man is compelled to prove he is poor in order to receive a free gift. Paradoxically, however, just as poverty itself (and not primarily the test of poverty) may be a fundamental source of shame and guilt to the poor man, so too may the receipt of the free gift itself be a cause of stigma: so strong is the pull of exchanging in the outside world, so rare the opportunity to take without giving, that the subjective perception of being a public burden rather than the holder of genuine citizenship rights not purchased through payment of taxes may arise and stimulate the recipient of welfare to attribute to himself some supposed dereliction. This will notably be the case where the dual standard of service survives in the form of private medicine and insurance (as Titmuss evidently believed it should) and housing and schooling (knotty problems about which Titmuss was strikingly reticent), buttressed not only by inequalities in occupational and fiscal welfare (which Titmuss noted but made no concrete proposals to reform) but by a socially-divisive system of income maintenance (and Titmuss himself favoured earnings-related superannuation benefits despite their much-deplored tendency to promote "two nations in old age").

Titmuss proposed universalism in social welfare provision so as to avoid stigma, but also so as to promote integration (since rich and poor, black and white, old and young enjoy equal access to the same facilities), cover social costs by social benefits (since many individuals, whether through the obsolescence of skills in a progressive economy or the incidence of industrial diseases brought on by unknown factors enshrouded forever in the mists of social time, are now asked personally to shoulder the diswelfares of social change), and to redistribute life-chances (particularly via a policy of selective discrimination in favour of deprived areas and under-privileged groups within the framework of a basically universalist structure of services, in contrast to the present system whereby the well-to-do benefit more than proportionately from the high-cost sectors of social welfare). Here again, however, even the most ardent disciple will wonder if integration is really to be promoted at the level of the dependent rather than the independent (boss and worker may be treated as of right on the basis of need alone in a public ward, potential meritocrat and potential dustman may start out together in the same classroom, but there is still no guarantee that fellowship will survive once equality of opportunity has collapsed into inequality of outcome and income); and will regard as flimsy Titmuss's evidence on solidarity (his key example of blood-donation is not "one of the most sensitive universal social indicators"[83] since it generalises on the basis of a sample of citizens *by definition* more community-spirited than, say, football hooligans, and falsely imputes "creative altruism" to the British national family on the basis of a gift which, unlike that of money, renews itself automatically). Then too, one is bound to wonder if Titmuss's attitude to social costs and social benefits does not demonstrate excessive defeatism concerning the extent to which guilty parties *can* be identified and *should* be made to compensate for the costs they impose on individuals and on the community: a social organism must be very harmonious indeed which is prepared to provide roads for cars, hospitals for smokers, programmers for computers without asking in return for a special levy on specific beneficiaries, and it must be blessed with the exceptional tolerance of the saint or the functionalist if it does not allow at least some costs to lie where they fall (for while it is humane to be non-judgemental and to eschew the punitive conception of guilt, it is still difficult to accept that people have minimal responsibility for themselves and their families or to dismiss phenomena such as alcoholism, addiction, voluntary un-employment or mass procreation by saying that "the devil in this particular piece seems to have more of the character of Bentham than of Freud''[84]). Finally, even the ardent disciple will challenge Titmuss's assertion that redistribution of life-chances can be effected without stigma being inflicted: those included in an Educational Priority Area may feel collectively insulted at being branded as subnormal problem children, while those included out may feel rejected and resentful when denied equal opportunity. Impersonal classification in any case only picks up a small percentage of the needy for the simple reason that the broad category into which most fall is not most significantly age, sex or geographical location but rather lack of money; and hence, if the means-test is not in fact a major source of stigma and if common facilities for the dependent do not in fact generate a sensation of national cohesion and collective brotherhood, then there is a theoretical implication that the State should curtail free services provided to those best able to purchase them in order to concentrate its help on those citizens whose need is greatest and ability to pay least.

Titmuss would not have accepted that the welfare state should confine itself to its safety-net function of serving as the refuge of last resort, and this because of economic efficiency as well as social justice: not only, he believed, was the utilitarian *quid pro quo* of economic exchange morally inferior to the unilateral stranger-gifts of social welfare, but market provision of services properly social is wasteful of scarce resources and in that respect too inferior to public provision. Free enterprise reduces the quantity of welfare available (consider, for example, the lack of blood for transfusion in America which, being bought to a great extent from a "blood proletariat" of mercenary donors facing a low-price elasticity of supply, is inadequate to meet demand; or the lack of long-term, low-cost hospital beds in that country); it raises the price of welfare (due to the absence of preventive medicine in the private sector, the cost of malpractice insurance and litigation, the wasteful duplication and underutilisation of computer and adiministrative facilities, the lack of co-ordination); it threatens the quality of welfare (witness the conflict of interest experienced by a doctor tempted by the cash nexus to remove a healthy appendix despite his professional ethic of disinterested service; or the soul-searching of the ooze-for-booze merchant debating whether to conceal a history of malaria or syphillis prior to selling his blood at the risk of passing on the stranger-gift of hepatitis); and it restricts consumer choice (as in the world of private insurance where the product is increasingly standardised in such a way that the consumer with special needs is often denied cover, at least at normal rates; where there is insufficient transferability of occupational benefits and frequent loss of survivor's rights; where funds are invested without either consumer or shareholder consultation). Here Titmuss may justly be criticised for substituting polemic for proof. Even if private systems do display the shortcomings he suggests, they could be reformed (say, by better screening of commercial blood banks or greater public control over the policies offered and investments made by institutional investors); and State systems themselves are hardly free of abuse (both blood and hospital beds are in short supply even in the United Kingdom; the general practitioner is not always a sympathetic family friend but often an overworked technocrat with a crowded waiting-room full of frustrated strangers and with a tendency to prescribe so as to treat individual symptoms rather than social disease; the service provided is not infrequently impersonal, administered by apathetic and arrogant officials on guaranteed incomes, and deliberately standardised so as to place a premium on conformity rather than choice). Titmuss gave no practical advice on the criteria which ought to be applied in the welfare sector (while simultaneously disparaging the uni-dimensionality of cost–benefit analysis and warning against excessive reliance on quantifiable indices which measure facts not feelings); and he apparently underestimated the financial constraint limiting the supply of gifts that can be provided by the community to itself while still avoiding regressive redistribution through inflation (the financial constraint being particularly important since many citizens resent paying taxes to help others, and since many welfare professionals demand eminently generous remuneration despite Titmuss's conviction that men integrated in the national family would come to regard their duties as highly cherished rights). It is not, in short, easy to accept without question all of Titmuss's views on welfare and society. But one thing is certain: his optimistic, multidisciplinary, original and unstintingly sociological contribution has raised both the academic level and the moral tone of the debate on dependency. Most important of all, Richard Titmuss was a good man.

Ross Terrill notes that it was Richard Titmuss "whom Tawney thought more highly of than anyone else at the LSE at the time he left it"[85] and pays tribute to Titmuss and "his own admirable work which finely expresses Tawney's spirit today".[86] It is through the Tawney–Titmuss relationship that the British tradition of common culture became translated into a demand for social welfare firmly rooted in shared social values. Recognising that in the history of ideas association is no proof of causation, we shall nonetheless now venture to suggest some similarities between Tawney and Titmuss, looking at the matter under two headings: first, the purpose of scientific investigation; second, the nature of the welfare society.

(a) Scientific investigation

The first point to note here is that both Tawney and Titmuss adopted an interdisciplinary perspective clearly formulated by Tawney as follows:

A student who is more interested in wild life than in museum specimens must be prepared to annoy gamekeepers by following it across country . . . It would be convenient if the question, Where is wisdom to be found? could be answered by referring the inquirer to the appropriate university department. But she appears to prefer the debatable land where titles are ambiguous and boundaries intersect; nor is her business much advanced by what in humbler spheres are known as demarcation disputes.[87]

The "majestic isolation" of "subjects" must be overcome – for, as Adam Smith's synthesis proved, "the best fish are caught when poaching".[88]

Precisely because of this search for an interdisciplinary method, each man integrated into his system elements of sociology, economics, political science, history, and Titmuss added medicine and social anthropology as well. Neither was reluctant to make use of economic argumentation but both warned that the economy is not a thing apart. Because of a belief in induction in place of deduction, Tawney was thus able to chide the utilitarian economists for adopting an a-social approach to the study of the social sciences ("English economic speculation had a distinguished history, but rigour in verifying its hypotheses had not been its strongest suit"[89]) and for compounding their narrowness of vision with a neglect of the extent to which matter is in motion (although "the study of economics is, after all, one branch of contemporary history"[90]). Translating theory into practice, both Tawney and Titmuss carried on a running battle with the economists at the LSE (of whom Lionel Robbins was for them perhaps the archetype, although it must also be recorded that Tawney in 1938 generously wrote an enthusiastic reference for a scholar with whose "doctrinaire individualism" he personally did not agree – "Robbins is unquestionably a very able and distinguished man. In his own field he is quite first-class, and whatever may be thought of his conception of economics or of the conclusions which he draws, there can be no doubt at all of his ability. He has a vigorous and agreeable personality and is a good administrator"[91] – and Titmuss in 1968 made common cause with him in fighting off the student threat). As Titmuss later wrote of Tawney: "He warned me when I came to the School in 1950 and had to sit on the Appointments Committee that 'the economists can get away with murder'. The Webbs had not foreseen the problem of the balance of power in the allocation of scarce resources at the School".[92]

A second point to note is that both Tawney and Titmuss were systematisers and organisers who believed that experience is only intelligible when interpreted in the light of general theoretical principles. Both stressed that analysis is vital if the wood is to be visible as well as the trees and hence Tawney took historians to task for combining "scrupulousness as to facts" (indeed, "the student of works on the last century of economic history is apt to find himself buried beneath a mountain of inert facts"[93]) with "casualness as to categories": "With certain brilliant exceptions, they have preferred burrowing to climbing. They make a darkness, and call it research, while shrinking from the light of general ideas which alone can illumine it."[94] Among these "brilliant exceptions" Tawney would clearly have wished to rank Titmuss, whose important early work, *Problems of Social Policy*, he found "admirable in its combination of industry with critical power"[95]: "Dr. Titmuss is a humane scientist, who does not succumb to the temptation to 'measure the Universe by rule and line'. His subtlety and insight in interpreting his evidence are as impressive as the meticulous scrupulousness with which he has performed the heavy task of collecting and sifting it."[96]

Only when the historian has general principles can he categorise phenomena in terms of shared properties common to the genus (for the facts alone do not always speak intelligibly for themselves): "History is too subtle a business for the last word on any subject to be said by figures. They are valuable to those who know enough of the social background of an age to be able to interpret them; to others they are a snare."[97] Only when the historian has some sort of theoretical framework at his fingertips can he go beyond description and observation to attempt explanation of causation and thus prediction (for "the lamp of the historian should cast light forward as well as back"[98]): "History, as I understand it, is concerned with the study, not of a series of past events, but of the life of a society. . . . Time, and the order of occurrences in time, is a clue, but no more; part of the historian's business is to substitute more significant connections for those of chronology."[99] Evidently, therefore, Tawney saw the work of the historian as approaching more nearly that of the sociologist and even the philosopher than is normally the case, a point made with some force by Titmuss and others in their privately-printed, eightieth-birthday tribute: "In him the historian and social philosopher are so closely related that the discussion of the one has inevitably meant saying much about the other. . . . He is the greatest of modern economic historians partly because, by some definitions, he is not an economic historian at all."[100]

Given the need to go beyond mere aggregation of empiricisms, one useful means of teasing out truths to which our attention is drawn by principles is the comparative method – between countries (as in Titmuss's study of blood donorship patterns and his work on developing countries, or in Tawney's study of Chinese educational and economic conditions; although it must also be recorded that, despite Tawney's lavish praise for the way in which Chinese achievements "lend lustre to a humanity which is our own",[101] both men in practice demonstrated a certain insularity in their attitude to foreign cultures) or, indeed, within a single country at different stages in its development (a temporal rather than a spatial approach to human interaction in the face of upheavals and shocks such as those associated with capitalist industrialisation, land reform or war). Either way, whether by looking at other societies in the present or at our own in the past, we through the use of the comparative method acquire valuable materials "which are inaccessible to the intellectual villager who takes the fashion of his generation for the nature of mankind":[102] "It is the rôle of the historian, by observing social behaviour in different conditions and varying environments, to determine the characteristics of different types of civilisation, to discover the forces in which change has found its dynamic, and to criticise the doctrines accepted in each epoch as self-evident truths."[103]

A third point to note is that both Tawney and Titmuss would have agreed that the search for knowledge, although in the field to be governed by the most scrupulous standards of data-collection and induction from experience, should nonetheless be sensitive to social contingency and collective purposiveness. As Tawney put it:

> If society is to be master of its fate, reason conquer chance, and conscious decision deliver human life from the tyranny of nature and the follies of man, the first condition is a realistic grasp of the materials to be handled and the forces to be tamed. The historian serves, on his own humble plane, that not ignoble end. His object is to understand the world around him, a world whose cultural constituents and dynamic movements have taken their stamp and direction from conditions which the experience of no single life is adequate to interpret. . . . If he visits the cellars, it is not for love of the dust, but to estimate the stability of the edifice, and because, to grasp the meaning of the cracks, he must know the quality of its foundations. In this sense, there is truth in the paradox that all history is the history of the present; and for this reason each generation must write its history for itself. That of its predecessors may be true, but its truth may not be relevant. Different answers are required because different questions are asked.[104]

What Tawney is saying is that as circumstances change, so do our perceptions of circumstances, our doctrines, our questions, to such an extent indeed that one might reasonably conclude that what is supposed to be the past "is in reality the present".[105] More importantly, not only do our perceptions change, so do our needs; and it is in the light of those needs – in terms of involvement rather than detachment, in other words–that scientific research is to be conducted. Ideas have consequences when supported by the facts, as the case of the Webbs demonstrates: "They researched, wrote, agitated, administered and – since only the last stages of legislation take place in Parliament – were not the less legislators because, save for ten years when both of them were over sixty, County Hall and the British Museum saw more of them than the House of Commons."[106]

As parliamentary socialists with a deep commitment both to social reform and to political democracy, both Tawney and Titmuss sought to relate their academic and their practical–political concerns. Neither was prepared (as Titmuss and his colleagues said of Tawney) to "remain poised in the reflective attitude";[107] both saw research not simply as a means of identifying abuses but as the first step towards re-shaping the social organism; both harnessed the erudition of the study to the hurly-burly of the every-day by making their considerable expertise available to the Labour Party (as where, for instance, Titmuss's impact on pensions policy is matched and surpassed by Tawney's influence on education, to say nothing of Tawney's industriousness in drafting the bulk of two election manifestoes, *Labour and the Nation*, 1929, and *For Socialism and Peace*, 1934).

Both Tawney and Titmuss appreciated, of course, that knowledge by itself does not alter action. It may deprive society of its excuse for inaction or unwise action, but it is only powerful when backed up by a ground-swell of public opinion capable of ensuring the election of good men and the relegation of bad ones. As Tawney put it in 1913:

> Whilst progress was undoubtedly retarded in the nineteenth century through the contempt of our grandfathers for economic investigation, there seems some danger that it may be paralysed in the twentieth through a superstitious reverence for accumulated facts; and I should be very sorry to be thought to suppose that the future welfare of mankind depended principally upon the multiplication of sociologists. There are, it is true, a considerable number of matters where practical action is delayed by the absence of sufficient knowledge. There are more, perhaps, where our knowledge is sufficient to occupy us for the next twenty years, and where the continuance of social evils is not due to the fact that we do not know what is right, but to the fact that we prefer to continue doing what is wrong. Those who have the power to remove them have not the will, and those who have the will have not, as yet, the power.[108]

The failures of the Asquith government, Tawney believed, do not discredit the attempt to utilise detailed evidence and careful documentation in order to impress the general public with the significance and validity of socialist argumentation; they only suggest the need for an even more intensified campaign of reasoned appeal backed up by evidence as a viable means of altering the *status quo* without reliance on the non-democratic alternatives of coercion and violence associated with radical revolutionary upheaval. This optimism with respect to the powers of persuasion reveals a deep-seated conviction, on the part of both Tawney and Titmuss, that men are rational creatures who can clearly identify their own and society's best interests and who vote not on the basis of product-images such as the avuncular smile or the charisma of Camelot but on the basis of observation and experience. Tawney and Titmuss had no doubts that a rational man, when confronted with all the facts, cannot but be a democratic socialist; and for that reason regarded their own research as having something of the character of a moral crusade. Both men had a masterly literary style (although Tawney obviously had the edge when it came to classical and Biblical allusions or literary references in foreign languages); both wrote in tones at times reminiscent of the Old Testament prophet; both produced work eminently readable even if not always as clear as it at first appears. The balance between commitment and scholarship will in the case of both authors long be a subject of discussion and debate.

(b) The welfare society

Both Tawney and Titmuss wanted a welfare society symbiotically linked to a welfare state, and both approached the problem in the same general manner. It was with considerable justification that Titmuss was able to trace the history of the Department of Social Administration at the LSE (a Department in which he was appointed to the first Chair) back to the work into the social origins of poverty done on the eve of the First World War at the School by the Ratan Tata Foundation (a Foundation of which Tawney, of course, was the Director) and to write as follows about the evolution of the discipline: "Academically speaking, it was not perhaps a very respectable affair in those days. That it is more acceptable now is due to Professor Tawney and to many men and women who, like him, never ceased to demonstrate their belief in the possibility of social progress."[109]

The British approach to social welfare was developed most of all by Tawney and Titmuss, and the following points are central to the world-view which they shared.

First, a belief in the actual existence of a moral consensus. As Tawney put it: "The first step towards an improvement in social life is to judge our social conduct by strict moral standards. I venture to say – though it sounds a heresy – that there [are] certain sorts of behaviour which we know to be right, and certain others which we know to be wrong. Let us act on what we know."[110] When these moral principles "are stated in a general form, nobody in practice would venture to deny them";[111] and it is therefore the task of the committed social scientist not merely to collect new facts but "to show how these universally accepted principles may be applied to particular sets of social conditions",[112] while recognising that any attempt at manipulation and persuasion is doomed to failure which offends against "the established principles by [which] most men admit that their conduct should be controlled."[113] The bedrock of ethics is a constant, not a variable.

As for the origin of those ethical absolutes which render it morally wrong that men should "substitute inexpediency for sin and social welfare for conscience",[114] Tawney would have had no doubt that it is to be found in values and attitudes in effect "the common property of Christian nations."[115] Titmuss, on the other hand, and while like Tawney directing his appeal towards that which he was convinced most good men most value (namely, compassion, community, cohesion, citizenship, comradeship, co-operation, brotherhood, dignity, responsibility, humanity, as opposed to wickedness, selfishness, and the rational calculation of pecuniary gain and loss), saw no need for religious legitimation of the "right order of life" and remained a secular moralist, as his daughter, Ann Oakley, has recently explained:

My father was never open about his attitudes to religion but I can say quite confidently that he did not share the High Church Christianity espoused by Tawney. He found religious ritual showy and offensive and never personally went to church – so far as I remember, that is. (I myself was baptized belatedly at the age of six because I was about to attend a new private school where my parents assumed everyone would have been thus initiated and I would feel out of place if I hadn't).

As an adolescent going through all the usual identity crises etc (and having a Catholic boyfriend) I used to ask Richard about religion a lot. These conversations definitely indicated to me that he held no belief in any sort of God at all. On the other hand, he was a very *moral* person, and some of his moral values, being espoused with great rigidity at times, could have had the appearance to others of deriving from a religious faith. I believe it was this that led Trevor Huddleston, at Richard's memorial service in St. Martins-in-the-Fields, to describe him as a 'true christian'. I'm sure this would not have pleased him – as indeed he would have found it difficult to accept the whole idea of a church memorial service. (Barbara Wootton refused to attend the service even though she had been a close friend of his, for this reason.) I would add that he was remarkably tolerant of other people's beliefs in this respect, and described himself as an 'agnostic' rather than an 'atheist' – a distinction that seemed important to him.[116]

What matters most of all, however, is not that one man was Christian and the other agnostic, but rather that both stressed the extent to which welfareism springs from altruistic attitudes which each was proud to share with the mass of his fellow-citizens. That having been said, both may justly be criticised for having opened the door to benevolent paternalism (a criticism most likely to be made by sceptics unconvinced that Dubb really ranks the social above the economic, the collective above the individual, and fearful lest his authentic preference-patterns be altered over time by those very welfare insitutions which acquire legitimacy through the invocation of his name). Probably there was in Britain a greater degree of moral consensus in the twenties than in the antinomian sixties, and Titmuss had in addition to deal with the massive influx of foreigners (many of them coloured) in a way which Tawney did not; but the central point is that both, by tying their model of welfare to popular perceptions of common culture and situation, put themselves in the dangerous position of deriving all from an axiom which is really a hypothesis.

Second, the integration of polity with society. Because both Tawney and Titmuss believed so sincerely in the reality of the collective consciousness (one recalls, for instance, how Tawney, talking of the relationship in the China of the 1930s between peasant revolt and Communist propaganda, decisively brushed aside "the theory that agitation is produced by agitators, not agitators by agitation"[117]), neither feared collective action organised by recourse to political means, where the latter concept Tawney defines as follows: "Politics, it may be suggested, is, or ought to be, the art of achieving by collective action ends which cannot be attained with the same measure of success by individual effort, and often cannot be attained by it at all."[118] Both writers had immense confidence in the future of political democracy (a term which they probably took as encompassing the rule of law, the multi-party system, elected chambers, freedom of expression, security of individual rights against arbitrary executive action, the tolerance of minorities and dissenters) and both deeply regretted that it had been sacrificed on the altar of productive efficiency by Soviet collectivism ("Dams, bridges, power-plants and steel-works, however admirable, are not a substitute for human rights",[119] Tawney noted); both adopted a quasi-Hegelian view of the State which abstracted from the vested interests of bureaucrats (in attaining organisational objectives) and of political leaders (in winning power); and both were able so confidently to deny that the road to socialism is also the road to serfdom because of their clear propensity to identify political culture as forming part of popular culture.

It was in part for its confidence in the good sense of the common man that Tawney praised Titmuss's *Problems of Social Policy* so highly: "His question 'were not the experts too remote from the ordinary people of Great Britain?' appears, in the light of the facts presented by him, to hit some nails on the head. It is a pity that he cannot hit some heads as well".[120] Titmuss was more cautious when speaking of Tawney: "His love of vigorous working-class commonsense has sometimes seemed to approach naïvety. 'I believe he thinks heaven will be populated exclusively by manual workers', an official of the WEA once remarked."[121] Certainly Titmuss is not on record as having asserted that it was the workers, "the obscure rank and file, who created the Labour movement",[122] nor as having stressed the high degree of internal democracy and popular consultation that obtains in the British (in contrast to the more autocratic and less accountable American) trade union:

> The British worker expects his union to secure him economic advantages but his relation to it is not adequately expressed in terms of a cash nexus. He is not a child to open his mouth and shut his eyes, and accept such plums as his officers are good enough to offer him. At lowest, he requires to be satisfied that the affairs of his society are conducted with reasonable efficiency. . . . At best, his union is to him the symbol of a cause – the emancipation of the workers – and, as such, commands, not only the formal adherence of self-interested egotism, but his loyalty, his self-sacrifice, and his pride.[123]

It may have been with passages such as these as well with Tawney's personal idiosyncrasies in mind that Titmuss and his colleagues said of Tawney that "he has . . . the innocence in worldly matters which has always been regarded as proper to philosophers".[124]

That the active component in democracy was more important to Tawney than it was to Titmuss is particularly apparent in those many places where Tawney, arguing in favour of a socialist society consisting not of "a herd of tame, well-nourished animals, with wise keepers in command" but rather of "a community of responsible men and women working without fear in comradeship for common ends",[125] seems to be convinced that ordinary people do actually value participation in "the control of the material conditions on which their lives depend"[126] as an end in its own right. Titmuss, in contrast, and probably closer to Crosland than to Tawney in this respect, would have found somewhat over-idealistic and even impractical the notion that ordinary people would, for example, accept that we ought "for two or three hours out of the 100 of our waking week to consider those issues of public and general importance with somewhat the same seriousness that we bring to our private affairs".[127] Titmuss, moreover, said nothing about the application of political democracy to economic phenomena in the form of worker self-direction; whereas employee initiative, autonomy and participation were vital concepts to Tawney (who prophesied, of course, that "either democracy . . . will extend its authority from the political to the economic system, and be established more firmly, because on broader foundations; or it will cease to exist, save in form, as a political institution"[128]). One searches in vain in Titmuss for passages such as the following, which demonstrate clearly the importance which Tawney chose to assign to representation and co-operation at all levels: "If the Government were proposing to determine the future organization of the medical profession or of the universities, it would pay attention to the views of the doctors and the university teachers. Our miners are a body of professional men, and they have the same right to be consulted in regard to their occupation."[129] It is, however, to be expected that Tawney, the Oxbridge Brahmin, the patrician, the gentleman, would have had more to say about the links between producer-involvement and common humanity than would Titmuss, the self-educated son of a small farmer whose background in insurance and the civil service is likely to have made clear to him at an early age the importance of doing as you are told.

It was, again, Tawney who called for councils to represent the interests of consumers in a post-market environment, while Titmuss makes no mention of such consultation. In fairness, however,

Titmuss is explicitly concerned solely with the welfare services; and in that limited area of activity even Tawney does not expressly mention bodies designed to represent the interests of patients, claimants, schoolchildren and their parents, and other consumer constituencies. Tawney, like Titmuss, did not see the multitude of ambiguities concealed by the fiction that professional standards imply a unique result rather than a wide spectrum of choices and options.

Third, the extension of institutionalised State welfare services as one among many structural alterations in the fabric of market capitalist society. Both Tawney and Titmuss were opposed to the philanthropy of church charity work (partly because of its restricted nature, partly because it failed to acknowledge the problem of *social* diswelfares); both saw that the problem of individual poverty would not automatically vanish through undirected economic growth (and believed that this was yet another instance where economic mechanisms could not be expected to serve social purposes); both identified poverty in terms of relative as well as absolute deprivation and thus related it to the perpetuation of class divisions and social inequalities which would not be made to vanish without reliance on stronger medicine than simply isolated relief and an appeal for personal reform. Both Tawney and Titmuss were anxious to use the social services as weapons in the battle for the equalisation of life-chances (as any theory of "fairness" – including that formulated in John Rawls' *A Theory of Justice*, which Titmuss described as "one of the most important books published in the field of social philosophy for the last twenty-five years"[130] – would in some measure dictate); but both – and this is absolutely central to the British approach to social welfare – also regarded the social services as means for fostering perceptions of common culture and situation through the integration of the dependent in a series of shared social experiences such as schooling and medical care.

Tawney, as it happens, went beyond Titmuss in so far as he extended the idea of the welfare society far beyond services aimed specifically at the dependent:

> One whole wing of social reformers has gone, it seems to me, altogether astray. They are preoccupied with relieving distress, patching up failures, reclaiming the broken down. All this is good and necessary. But it is not the social problem, and it is not the policy which would ever commend itself to the working classes.

What they want is security and opportunity, not assistance in the exceptional misfortunes of life, but a fair chance of leading an independent, fairly prosperous life, if they are not exceptionally unfortunate.[131]

Once social policy is defined in terms of "the daily regimen" of men not dependent, however, once the normal rather than only the pathological has been identified as reprehensible and unjust, then the door is obviously open to a whole series of measures – worker participation schemes, the minimum wage, public health and factory legislation, and even socialisation of passive property rights – which seek, in the name of solidarity and integration, to reform institutions traditionally regarded as more the preserve of the economist than that of the social administrator. Titmuss, on the other hand, was more cautious in his approach to plutocracy and a class-divided culture; and where he does bring himself to talk of reforms such as might make the independent regard each other as equals tends to focus on the taxation of surplus incomes (which is part but only part of Tawney's argument) without, indeed, making any explicit recommendations such as he might have done concerning, for instance, the introduction of high death duties. What Titmuss would probably have welcomed Tawney calls for in no uncertain terms: maintaining that "the transmission of more than a minimum of wealth from generation to generation has, in the conditions of today, little more to commend it than would have a right to travel in perpetuity in first-class coaches",[132] he then argues that a low minimum exemption level from death duties should be fixed (he mentioned in 1952 a figure of between £25,000 and £50,000[133]) and recommends that wealth above that level should in effect be confiscated. It is interesting that Titmuss, whose *Income Distribution and Social Change* shook the national consciousness in the 1950s by demonstrating the extent of continued inequalities in life-chances due to the transmission of inherited wealth and the manner in which untaxed money makes untaxed money (as with capital gains, then a loop-hole in the net), nonetheless preferred to let the abuses, once clarified, make their own plea for redress. Such caution was characteristic of the man; and it is almost certainly the reason why only in one place (significantly enough, in his introduction to the 1964 edition of Tawney's *Equality*) does he go beyond innuendo and hint expressly to demand the suppression of the public schools. Tawney was more explicit and more extreme in his proposals for a reduction in social distance and the creation of a unified society based on human fellowship; and for this reason he cannot be accused, as Titmuss can be, of designing a welfare society which might possibly succeed in ensuring equality of opportunity but which could not adequately guarantee lifetime equality of relationships.

Both Tawney and Titmuss highly valued the sense of integration in communities. As Tawney wrote: "All decent people are at heart conservatives, in the sense of desiring to conserve the human associations, loyalties, affections, pious bonds between man and man which express a man's personality and become at once a sheltering nest for his spirit and a kind of watch-tower from which he may see visions of a more spacious and bountiful land."[134] Both admired the solidarity and mutual support they identified as characteristic of the working-classes, and Tawney was particularly interested by Titmuss's account of how the seamless web of an organic way of life had caused people to weather out the Blitz in London in preference to evacuation: "In reality, the unbroken contact with familiar things and faces, in an environment charged with a life-time of memories, was a source of inner peace and strength. It preserved intact a thread of spiritual continuity which, but for it, might have snapped."[135] Both were impressed by the extent to which war in Britain had had the unexpectedly socialist functions of spotlighting social abuses (e.g. malnutrition), generating an atmosphere of conscious planning on the part of visible rather than invisible hands and, most of all, fostering a sense of national unity based on a shared objective and a common enemy:

> The most important aspect of human beings is not the differences of circumstance, income and race, or even of character and intelligence, by which they are divided, but the common humanity which unites them. The book of Dr. Titmuss on the social consequences of the war is not without some lessons for peace.[136]

It was this sense of a war on deprivation and division which lay at the root of the theories of welfare of both authors and which explains in addition why both were so hostile to the market mechanism: even if private enterprise is efficient in delivering the goods (and both, referring specifically in the case of Titmuss to the social services, denied that it was), it remains amoral in its motivation (and "no amount of cleverness will get figs of thistles"[137]). Good results, both believed, cannot come of bad motives (motives such as unbridled acquisitiveness and rational calculation of purely personal pleasures and pains); right relationships are called for (including those which encourage the altruism of stranger-gifts ranging from blood donation to income tax enthusiastically rather than grudgingly paid); and this once again brings the argument back to the sense of integration in communities.

In conclusion, a group of similarities of a more personal nature as between the two Richards. Both were highly sensitive men (and this despite the fact that Titmuss, as Margaret Gowing has put it, "had administration in his blood"[138]) who because of their eagerness to empathise also had a willingness to accept imagery where others would have demanded analysis. Thus Ross Terrill reports a conversation concerning Tawney with Pearl Buck as follows: "She said she thinks he was a thin-skinned man, tremendously sensitive, who felt the outrages of the world very directly. And she said this is the way he learned, not so much through his intellect as through his skin."[139] Both men were pillars of the LSE and happy to be working in an institution characterised by service to the community (one which exists not for itself and its own corporate egotism "but for the public"[140]) and by what Tawney described as an "unlaboured egalitarianism" ("the best atmosphere both for work and for young people"): "There is a natural and easy give and take between students and staff and different members of the staff with each other. People stand on their merits, not on their dignity, and do not, as at some Universities, acquire a status of undeserved inflation from the . . . prestige of the institution to which they belong."[141] Both men sought to use the LSE as an instrument in the struggle for socialism, as where both attempted to find ways of increasing the numbers of working-class students at the School (this was a particular concern of Tawney's once he discovered that WEA classes were more and more being orientated towards the leisure-time interest market and less and less towards the production of a politically conscious, socialist citizenry) and both opposed the schemes of economists and statisticians to substitute training in the service of the *status quo* for education as to *why* as well as *how*.

Both men were curiously reticent about foreign affairs, including economic affairs such as those involving speculators, multinationals and brain drains. Both were quintessentially English, parochial in their shared anxiety about the Common Market, concerned about ascribed more than achieved status in a society where the snobbery of birth has traditionally been of greater concern than the snobbery of Veblen's *nouveaux riches*, able to argue in that typically British fashion born of the marriage of Lady Bountiful with the Lord of the Manor which has rendered the country that give the utilitarianism of the classical economists to the world also on balance one of the more generous places on earth. Both saw British socialism as steering a middle course between the regimentation of Russian Communism (which, Tawney reminds us, is coloured by the national character and historical experience of the Russians) and the "traditional individualism of American life" (one of the many conditions "peculiar to America"[142] and which indeed render it culturally polyglot – "less a country than a continent"[143]) and thus in some considerable measure an emanation from the mainstream of British culture. Both Tawney and Titmuss were understandably weak on countercultures, self-help schemes, joyous experimentation with life styles and the do-it-yourself guruism of the beardy-weirdie; and it must be recorded how often towards the end of his life Titmuss was being outflanked on the left by critics who described him as a pillar of an Establishment way of life which his form of welfareism would actually reinforce rather than challenge.

Both Tawney and Titmuss were secular saints each of whom turned down the offer of a peerage (and regarded it as a genuinely socialist gesture to reject man-made inequalities of this kind). Each lived a life strikingly non-acquisitive and moderate in nature which represented, as Titmuss said of Tawney, "a realisation in action of his own high principles. . . . The severest criticism of *Equality* as a social theory is that it would be easier to realise in practice if all men were Tawneys"[144]: "Few men in the 20th century whose life was unplanned ('like that terrible thing, an unplanned economy') have combined so superbly – and so tidily – thought and action, personal integrity and political ideals".[145] Richard Titmuss was a good man. Hugh Gaitskell said the same of Tawney and more: "Looking back quite objectively, I think he was the best man I have ever known'.[146]

4 Production and Allocation

Production and allocation were matters of secondary rather than primary importance to Tawney, believing as he did that right relationships far more than material affluence were the hallmark of the good society. More specifically, Tawney was hostile for two reasons to the methodology of orthodox neo-classical economics. First, on normative grounds, Tawney dismissed traditional economic theory (with its stress on individualism, competition, acquisition, efficiency, progress, *laissez-faire* liberalism, natural harmony of interests, rational pursuit of self-advancement) as amoral if not actually immoral in its ethos. Secondly, on purely positive grounds, Tawney concluded that the study of economics is by definition abstract and incomplete since it attempts to isolate and examine one limb of a living organism as if that limb (namely, the sphere of production and allocation) were truly independent of others (spheres, for instance, such as politics, religion and law). Yet "the tension between human wants and the limited resources available for satisfying them takes place, not in a vaccum, but in a specific cultural environment, by which the character both of the wants and of the resources is determined".[1] Economic investigation, Tawney believed, "has close affinities with sociology";[2] and, indeed, he insisted, "there is no such thing as a science of economics, nor ever will be. It is just cant."[3]

Tawney had both normative and positive reasons for rejecting the methodology of orthodox neo-classical economics, but it would be very wrong to say that he ignored the key economic problems of making and exchanging in his theories of Christian socialism and social justice. It is with his attitudes to resources in the service of man that we shall be concerned in this chapter.

I. PRODUCTION

It was in the immediate aftermath of the First World War that Richard Henry Tawney, then at the half-way house of a long and productive life, chose to write (first as an article for the *Hibbert Journal*, then as a pamphlet for the Fabian Society, and ultimately in the form of his celebrated book *The Acquisitive Society*) of the need for a purposeful Christian community to opt firmly but democratically for socialised ownership and professionalised control in preference to the selfishness and inefficiency of modern capitalism. The conclusions reached in this section concerning that model – a section which, in four consecutive parts, initially examines Tawney's views on Principle and Purpose, the Acquisitive Society and the Functional Society, and then presents some Criticisms and Extensions – are that Tawney was a man of prescience and perception who in *The Acquisitive Society* raised questions which are in truth as much a challenge to our own times as to the, in so many ways, very different world of the 1920s.

(a) Principle and Purpose

Tawney said that "in the long run, it is the principles which men accept as the basis of their social organization which matter",[4] and sought to contrast the outdated principles which underlie *Gesellschaft* with the teleological and theological underpinnings of *Gemeinschaft*.

The Acquisitive Society is the heir to the Enlightenment, and thus lives intellectually in the past. For one thing, the individualism of the eighteenth century, like the socialism of the twentieth, was the enemy of privilege and the champion of equality of opportunity. Yet "the great individualists of the eighteenth century, Jefferson and Turgot and Condorcet and Adam Smith, shot their arrows against the abuses of their day, not of ours";[5] for their chief target was the functionless ownership of land (with the surplus profits of monopolistic trading corporations a close second), whereas the modern socialist is nowadays less concerned with "the spectre of agrarian feudalism" than with "the new ogre of industrial capitalism"[6] (which is today the form of property divorced from labour most likely to make "idleness the pensioner of industry"[7]). Then, secondly, while old-style individualism is praiseworthy in so far as it "had a high sense of human dignity, and desired that men should be free to become themselves",[8] it did seek to free the individual from collective constraints (admittedly not an unreasonable aspiration in a historical epoch when corrupt governments, despotic power and the relics of feudalism were still a problem) and to assign to him absolute and inviolable rights (some of them, significantly, implying the sanctity of private property), whereas the modern socialist argues that no rights can ever be absolute since all are merely held in trust for the whole society: "The State has no absolute rights; they are limited by its commission. The individual has no absolute rights; they are relative to the function which he performs in the community of which he is a member."[9] Finally, the classical liberal replaced purpose by self-adjusting mechanism, but also argued that complementarity of self-interest is nonetheless beneficent in outcome when allowed to operate in an atmosphere of *laissez-faire* such that the minimal State confines itself to the enforcement of contracts (the cement of society); whereas the modern socialist denies that the unintended outcome of selfishness is in reality either social harmony or economic efficiency, and points on the one hand to concentration of capital and the associated power, on the other to the divorce of rights from duties to such an extent that a multitude of payments today cannot be justified in terms of incentives to initiative precisely because they are independent of service rendered. Classical liberalism in that sense has now been left behind by the march of events, however logical it may once have been to defend private property in terms of the need to guarantee to each man the security that he would enjoy the fruits of his labours. Classical liberalism, in short, "though largely applicable to the age in which it was formulated, has undergone the fate of most political theories. It has been refuted not by the doctrines of rival philosophers, but by the prosaic course of economic development."[10]

The Functional Society is the heir to the socialist critique of possessive individualism, but its ideology goes beyond the simple recognition that the pursuit of self-interest does not (as if guided by an invisible hand) maximise individual felicity and social well-being, and seeks to introduce elements of teleology at once collectivist and organicist: "What gives meaning to economic activity, as to any other activity, is . . . the purpose to which it is directed. But the faith upon which our economic civilization reposes, the faith that riches are not a means but an end, implies that all economic activity is equally estimable, whether it is subordinated to a social purpose or not."[11] It is that faith which has given rise to the "superstitious veneration"[12] of economic life that characterises our present epoch, a period threatened by the prospect "that one aspect of human life may be so exaggerated as to overshadow, and in time to atrophy, every other".[13] This economic fetishism (this "confusion of one minor department of life with the whole of life"[14]) can and must be reversed by a simple recognition that industry exists for man and is social in purpose: "The purpose of industry is to provide the material foundation of a good social life."[15] If, however, the function of industry is truly social service (thus providing legitimation for increasing production and productivity) and the method association (since plenty presupposes co-operation and co-ordination), then every society, rich or poor, needs to act on principles and to seek out the desired goal of "a right order of life":[16] "Unless it is to move with the energetic futility of a squirrel in a revolving cage, it must have a clear apprehension both of the deficiency of what is, and of the character of what ought to be."[17] A decision concerning social objectives must be made, for even a refusal to deviate from the beaten path because of a temperamental antipathy to theoretical speculation is itself a decision (and a theoretical one at that, even if in so many cases men nonetheless "take their philosophy so much for granted as to be unconscious of its implications");[18] and Tawney's plea is that society in making that decision should reject the belief-system associated with mechanistic individualism in favour of the quasi-medieval notion that the significance of social institutions and economic activities is to be traced back to their instrumental function as means to the attainment of common, corporate and collective ends. Tawney believed, in other words, that men ought to define their social roles in terms of the service they render within the framework of the macrocosm as a whole, and then to orientate themselves to social duties rather than individual rights. Even the latter, after all, must themselves ultimately be derived from

> the end or purpose of the society in which they exist. They are conditional on being used to contribute to the attainment of that end, not to thwart it. And this means in practice that, if society is to be healthy, men must regard themselves, not primarily, as the owners of rights, but as trustees for the discharge of functions and the instruments of a social purpose.[19]

Teleology, moreover, presupposes theology, for Tawney was convinced that alone the social ethic of Christianity provides the moral foundations for the philosophy of the Functional Society: "Such a political philosophy implies that society is not an economic mechanism, but a community of wills which are often discordant, but which are capable of being inspired by devotion to common ends. It is, therefore, a religious one, and, if it is true, the proper bodies to propagate it are the Christian Churches."[20] Up to the mid-seventeenth century, indeed, individual rights were subordinated to collective ends precisely because up to that time "men had found the significance of their social order in its relation to the universal purposes of religion"[21] ("it stood as one rung in a ladder which stretched from hell to Paradise"[22]). Modern economic relations, accompanied by the Protestant Reformation, have unfortunately weakened men's attachment to that social purpose which is defined by responsibility to "some higher authority":[23]

> The conception of men as united to each other, and of all mankind as united to God, by mutual obligations arising from their relation to a common end, ceased to be impressed upon men's minds, when Church and State withdrew from the centre of social life to its circumference. Vaguely conceived and imperfectly realized, it had been the keystone holding together the social fabric. What remained when the keystone of the arch was removed was private rights and private interests, the materials of a society, rather than a society itself.[24]

True Christianity is valuable, for it imposes normative guidelines, sets limits, and ensures that combination of unity and diversity which is only possible where the parts are symbiotically united to the whole "by overmastering devotion to a common end".[25] True Christianity, in addition, defines (as the medieval Church chose to do) "the whole compass of human interests to be the province of religion";[26] imposes a transcendent moral standard superior to mere political expediency or the pursuit of riches; rejects "the unreasoning and morbid pursuit of pecuniary gain"[27] as merely indicative of the sin of avarice (and deplores "the prostitution of humanity and personal honour and the decencies of public life to the pursuit of money"[28]). True Christianity glorifies corporate unity rather than individual utility; and, "by affirming that all men are the children of God, it insists that the rights of all men are equal. By affirming that men are men and nothing more, it is a warning that those rights are conditional and derivative – a commission of service, not a property."[29] True Christianity, in sum, evidently extends its sphere of involvement far beyond the things of the spirit, and attributes "a certain sacramental significance"[30] to patterns of conduct which can only be described as socialist.

Societies nominally Christian have, of course, sometimes opted out of the battle for Christian virtues (as where they "make religion the ornament of leisure, instead of the banner of a Crusade",[31] or where they pretend that religion is an intimate man/maker dialogue with no relevance for the this-worldly social order) and have sometimes even used the Church as a means of providing spurious ethical legitimation for "that attempt to conduct human affairs in the light of no end other than the temporary appetites of individuals"[32] (as where unlimited greed or individual success are taken to be good in themselves and identified as worthy of esteem). Regrettably, the Church has not at all times and in all places acknowledged its duty to act as a Church militant and to exercise powerful moral discipline on its members (in the interests of social well-being, and quite separate from considerations of personal salvation). It must in future do so. Sunday Christians are clearly warned that "membership involves duties as well as privileges"[33] and are reminded that their religion is not compatible with every possible way of life but with one alone (so that an employer who underpays his workers, for example, is unambiguously defaulting on his obligation to love his brother as himself, however great his love for God). A revival of religious spirit and corporate constraint is needed, and the result of the process of remoralisation will be a welcome one, namely a truly Christian civilisation: "Its end is peace. It is to harmonize the discords of human society, by relating its activities to the spiritual process from which they derive their significance.[34]

(b) The Acquisitive Society

The primary and central evil in the Acquisitive Society is the existence of right to remuneration independent of performance of function; for functionless parasites are today given "a right of private taxation"[35] (in the form of mineral royalties, ground rents, monopoly profits, dividends on shares in joint stock companies) and are thereby entitled to "income irrespective of any personal service rendered".[36] Such private taxation is privilege ("for the definition of a privilege is a right to which no corresponding function is attached"[37]), and such privilege a "functionless perversion"[38] of private property. While some ownership-rights are active and defensible because closely associated with incentive to industry ("like the tools of the craftsman, or the holding of the peasant, or the personal possessions which contribute to a life of health and efficiency"[39]), the bulk by value of present-day rights are passive and unjustifiable (representing as they do cases where "there is no guarantee that gain bears any relation to service, or power to responsibility"[40]). In modern economic conditions, moreover, it is the passive right which advances, the active right which recedes, a process activated by "the insatiable expansion and aggregation of property itself, which menaces with absorption all property less than the greatest, the smaller master, the little shopkeeper, the country bank, and has turned the mass of mankind into a proletariat working under the agents and for the profit of those who own".[41] The ethical justification for private property cannot, of course, be extended from active to embrace passive property as well.

The primary and central evil in the Acquisitive Society is the existence of "predatory interests and functionless super-numeraries".[42] From this evil there then follows a whole series of economic deficiencies and social inequities.

To begin with, modern society is rent by class antagonisms based on conflict of interest: "Since the income available for distribution is limited, and since, therefore, when certain limits have been passed, what one group gains another group must lose, it is evident that if the relative incomes of different groups are not to be determined by their functions, there is no method other than mutual self-assertion which is left to determine them".[43] Social peace may come about (resulting from trial of strength, balance of power and market equilibrium) but it nonetheless remains "precarious, insincere and short",[44] since it is lacking in perceived moral legitimation; and social resentments remain endemic to an exploitative situation where the claimant to surplus is really only demanding a share in (levying a toll on) the work of another. The productive classes see through the ingenious rationalisations of those who wish "to continue to reap what another has sown";[45] and even economic growth, quite understandably, can do nothing to resolve a potential collision arising from a struggle for shares and proportions, not simply absolute levels of pay (which are in any case on the low side for all members of the labour-force, including scientists and managers). Social life, pivoting as it does on market power, becomes in consequence "a scene of fierce antagonisms" such that "a considerable part of industry is carried on in the intervals of a disguised social war".[46] That social war is caused not by a misunderstanding of interests but by a correct perception of their contradictory rather than complementary nature, and a perception in particular of the divorce of gain from effort. Social war is an enemy not only of social unity but of efficient work; for the worker experiences a disincentive to use his productive energies to the full where the result is simply to maximise profits not his own. More generally, society cannot blame the worker for demanding more and more money: "If the community pays anything at all to those who do not work, it can afford to pay more to those who do".[47]

Again, and turning to the nature of business decisions actually made, the employee is further alienated from the system by the wasteful manner in which quality is subordinated to marketability:

> He sees every day that efficiency is sacrificed to short-sighted financial interests; and while, as a man, he is outraged by the inhumanity of the industrial order, as a professional who knows the difference between good work and bad, he has a growing contempt at once for its misplaced parsimony and its misplaced extravagance, for, in short, the whole apparatus of adulteration, advertisement and quackery which seems inseparable from the pursuit of profit as the main standard of industrial success.[48]

The employee at present is not consulted, and is not prepared to do more than the minimum of work for a system which he does not respect and which cannot, precisely because of its poor results and its confusion of ends and means, enlist his good-will and his enthusiastic co-operation.

The wastes of the competitive system extend to production as well as marketing, as the present-day duplication of facilities in rail transport and mining abundantly demonstrates:

> Technical reasons are stated by railway managers to make desirable a unification of railway administration and by mining experts of mines. But, up to the war, business considerations maintained the expensive system under which each railway company was operated as a separate system, and still prevent collieries, even collieries in the same district, from being ad-ministered as parts of a single organization. Pits are drowned out by water, because companies cannot agree to apportion between them the costs of a common drainage system.[49]

The increasing concentration of property-rights does, of course, permit pooling (and also renders unnecessary some of the wastes associated with the competitive mode of salesmanship), but the undeniably lower costs to the firm are then unfortunately transformed into exploitatively higher prices to the consumer: clearly, "no one can argue that a monopolist is impelled by 'an invisible hand' to serve the public interest".[50] Whether or not competition was ever "an effective substitute for honesty"[51] is open to question, but one thing cannot be denied: it is not so today, since private interests need not correspond to public where greed colludes or combines with greed rather than countervails it. Cartels and mergers, it must be stressed, are not bad in themselves. They help to reduce the risks of business activity (thereby, incidentally, reducing the force of the argument that profits are an incentive to bear risk, although one notes at the same time how many of these risks are purely optional, associated with the excessively speculative nature of much of modern finance capitalism) and also alleviate via rational co-ordination of production-plans "the possibility of over-production followed by reckless price-cutting".[52] Yet, however beneficial they might be to the producer, the fact that "the principle of free competition . . . has clearly spent its force"[53] implies in turn both that the consumer is no longer "protected by the rivalry of competing producers"[54] and that our antiquated ideology must be brought up to date to take into account the emergence of non-competitive conditions.

The present economic order has neither the automaticity of the pure market mechanism nor the purposiveness of planning, for it is characterised by regulatory legislation (some of it to protect the consumer, some to defend the worker, some even to insure the capitalist against the multiplied insecurities of the competitive system by means of State-guaranteed profits minima in exchange for the entrepreneur's acceptance of maxima as well). Yet managed capitalism offers the worst of both worlds: "Hybrids are apt to be sterile. It may be questioned whether, in drawing the teeth of private capitalism, this type of compromise does not also extract most of its virtues as well."[55] Legislative intervention exists because "private ownership, by the admission of its defenders, can no longer be tolerated in the only form in which it is free to display the characteristic, and quite genuine, advantages for the sake of which it used to be defended";[56] but such controls on pay, profits, prices and hours (with controls on arbitrary dismissals in the offing) suggest that hiving off private power while still retaining private ownership falls in its incidence most heavily on the consumer. After all, in this limbo-land between two reasonably efficient systems, the capitalist, being less feared just at the time when he is also less respected, can now compel "neither the service of docile obedience, nor the service of intelligent co-operation".[57] In the regulated economy, the consumer is the victim of the vaccum that follows the death of old-style capitalism (whose discipline was "exercised through its instruments of unemployment and starvation") and precedes the birth of new-style socialism (where the norm becomes "the self-discipline of responsibility and professional pride"[58]).

We have up to now been concentrating on the wastes and inefficiencies of the Acquisitive Society, and have noted that these can be traced back to their origins in economic exploitation. It is important also to remember that differential ability to exploit is itself the source of still other forms of inequality no less difficult to reconcile with a commitment to social justice.

(1) Inequality of esteem
In the looking-glass world of the Acquisitive Society, those who produce enjoy less social standing than those who do not (the spectacle of the public school, the club, the hunt testifying to the fact that "when the criterion of function is forgotten, the only criterion which remains is that of wealth"[59]); admiration and applause are attracted not by those who give but by those who get; and, regrettably, it is those who create least who earn most and can in consequence spend most. Such consumption is conspicuous but frivolous, and the worker cannot be expected to seek enthusiastically to increase his productivity so long as effective demand is maldistributed towards "goods which no man can make with happiness, or indeed without loss of self-respect, because he knows that they had much better not be made, and that his life is wasted in making them".[60] The problem is that *morale* among producers is bound to be low when gardeners, chauffeurs, domestic servants are supplied in abundance to a small class of rich absentees and prestigious *rentiers* while simultaneously education, re-equipment of industry, and other necessary expenditures truly in the national interest are neglected. Evidently workers, in the building trades for example, will be inefficient and hostile where the result of their labours is merely the generation of "futilities" and "trivialities" to be consumed by the ruling class: "They must as a body be consulted

as to the purpose to which their energy is to be applied, and must not be expected to build fashionable houses, when what are required are six-roomed cottages to house families which are at present living three persons to a room".[61]

(2) Inequality of opportunity

Nowadays the class of rich men is self-perpetuating, and property is the sleeping partner. Not only does there exist a dramatic contrast between rich and poor, between squalor and luxury, but the functionless also appear able to hand on their privileged position to their children, and in particular to pass on the dispensation "from the common human necessity of labour".[62] To this must be added yet another inequity, namely the habitual nepotism of modern industry (for favouritism is traditional in the private sector – even where the leadership role in business goes as a result to sons "whom it would be economical to pay to keep out of it"[63] – while, more logically, a cause of scandal on the rare occasions when it is discovered in the State sector).

(3) Inequality with respect to security

The worker suffers from the perpetual threat of arbitrary lay-off in a period of slack trade, and may even deliberately (and wastefully) lower his productivity so as to prolong a job and thus to keep himself in work. Yet it is "odious and degrading" for a man to be "thrown aside, like unused material, whenever his services do not happen to be required",[64] particularly since neither the (macroeconomic) trade recession nor the (microeconomic) sacrifice of higher output and employment in order to obtain higher profits is the fault of the worker: he is prepared to supply his labour but, simply, there is no work for him to do. The worker is penalised for absenteeism, the property-owner is not similarly penalised for the inefficiencies of a system based on greed rather than ethics (indeed, even managers are treated as instruments of production to be scrapped if their views and actions diverge too sharply from those of the capitalists); and the latter is in any case better cushioned against the vicissitudes of modern life than is the former.

The Acquisitive Society is in Tawney's view wasteful, exploitative and unjust. It is also characterised by that psychological *malaise* of normlessness which Durkheim called *anomie*; for while the love of riches is "one of the most powerful of human instincts",[65] infinite aspirations bereft of guidelines and limitations are always morbid. What men need is the moral support of a corporate society within the collective and co-operative framework of which alone the function and purpose of their activity acquires significance:

> What gives its meaning to any activity which is not purely automatic is its purpose. It is because the purpose of industry, which is the conquest of nature for the service of man, is neither adequately expressed in its organization nor present to the minds of those engaged in it, because it is not regarded as a function but as an opportunity for personal gain or advancement or display, that the economic life of modern societies is in a perpetual state of morbid irritation.[66]

An individual sense of purpose simply cannot be supplied by the unique pursuit of individual happiness: "To say that the end of social institutions is happiness, is to say that they have no common end at all. For happiness is individual, and to make happiness the object of society is to resolve society itself into the ambitions of numberless individuals, each directed towards the attainment of some personal purpose."[67] Pity the man who does not see and accept his subordination to common social ends, for his single-minded lust for economic power "destroys the moral restraints which ought to condition the pursuit of riches, and therefore also makes the pursuit of riches meaningless".[68] Such a man is the *rentier*, for he lives in "the humiliating atmosphere of predatory enterprise which embarrasses to-day any man of honour who finds himself, when he has been paid for his services, in possession of a surplus for which there is no assignable reason".[69] The *rentiers* are not and cannot be truly happy,

> for in discarding the idea of function, which sets a limit to the acquisition of riches, they have also discarded the principle which alone gives riches their meaning. Hence unless they can persuade themselves that to be rich is in itself meritorious, they may bask in social admiration, but they are unable to esteem themselves. For they have abolished the principle which makes activity significant, and therefore estimable.[70]

That principle is function, the unique and socially-unifying "bond of service to a common purpose"[71] which reconciles the conflicting claims of different groups and alone "gives unity to any activity": "If men have no common goal it is no wonder that they should fall out by the way".[72] The same principle applies on an international scale ("in the long run the world reaps in war what it sows in peace"[73]); and this reminds us that an Acquisitive Society divided by a domestic struggle for relative shares and bereft of generally-accepted moral purpose is likely also to live in a bellicose world of rivalry, aggression and national aggrandisement.

(c) The Functional Society

The first step in establishing the Functional Society is to negate the negation and "to remove the dead hand of private ownership, when the private owner has ceased to perform any positive function".[74] The abolition of functionless ownership rights is essential, for such rights are "the magnetic pole which sets all the compasses wrong";[75] but it is vital to remember that expropriation "is a means to an end, not an end in itself ",[76] and that Tawney has no specific proposals to make concerning the precise structure of future socialized enterprise. Rather the opposite: "The administrative systems obtaining in a society which has nationalized its foundation industries will, in fact, be as various as in one that resigns them to private ownership."[77] Thus whereas some will no doubt be run as the Home Office is today run (by "civil servants controlled, or nominally controlled, by Cabinet Ministers"[78]), others will be run (on the model of the public docks and harbours) by "bodies representing the users of the service";[79] and Tawney also makes reference to self-managing co-operatives and to local authority participation in ownership and operation. Tawney, in short, excludes no future form of socialised activity (reminding the reader on more than one occasion that decentralisation is a viable alternative to bureaucratisation), and stresses that the particular method adopted in the course of removing industry "from the control of the property-owner . . . is a matter of expediency to be decided in each particular case".[80] But decided it must be; for while men will intensify their efforts if "the great body of their fellow-countrymen"[81] will in consequence benefit, they will not do so if their work will merely benefit classes whose reward is divorced from obligation and whose "payment without service is waste".[82]

While the Functional Society will abolish functionless property, it will not abolish the *rentier*. Interest will survive the demise of profit, for interest is a necessary cost of production: it is an incentive to the supplier of capital and hence functional, whereas the arrogation to the capitalist oligarch of a fluctuating share in earnings generated by others or a claim to authority in the organisation would not be (since the capitalist has no moral claim to a share in profits and no professional expertise such as might justify his right to a share in decision-making). The conversion of shares into fixed-interest debentures and the *de jure* separation of ownership from control will thus have two advantages. First, it will reduce the cost of hiring capital (for, in the case that "the capital needed to maintain and equip a modern industry could not be provided by any one group of workers"[83] and must in consequence be borrowed, a prudent enterprise will nonetheless "pay for service and for service only".[84] Second, it will "release those who do constructive work from the control of those whose sole interest is pecuniary gain".[85]

The negation of the negation is a necessary step in the direction of the Functional Society, but it is not by itself sufficient. A second step is also necessary if industry is to be carried on for the service of the public, namely professionalisation; for "the essence of a profession is . . . that its members organize themselves for the performance of function".[86] All professions impose collective discipline and constraint on members (whether rank and file or specialist élite), since all are morally obligated to discharge professional responsibilities – "as implied by the mere entry into the industry"[87] – with respect to conduct, standards of workmanship, quality of product; and this normative constraint (which is conceptually quite separate from the trade union role which professional bodies also play) turns out to preclude the very patterns of behaviour which the ideal of the competitive market both extols and presupposes. Clearly, when one is speaking of doctors, architects, consulting engineers and lawyers, the conduct one expects is "the exact opposite of the theory and practice which assume that the service of the public is best secured by the unrestricted pursuit on the part of rival traders of their pecuniary self-interest, within such limits as the law allows".[88]

The professional ethic (inculcated and enforced by the corporate solidarity of professional organisations not unlike the Church in their nature) differs from the commercial norm insofar as it presupposes the existence of an absolute objective superior to that of financial gain. In the professions, individual cupidity is subordinated to a sense of purpose (doctors may in practice grow rich; but the significance of their profession, both to themselves and to the outside community, is still "not that they make money but that they make health"[89]); and this is why doctors eschew perversions such as competitive publicity and do not typically exploit the public's ignorance for speculative profit, why judges do not deceitfully sell judgements to the highest bidder, why civil servants do not normally take bribes nor soldiers betray their country for money (or even bolt and run, thereby saving individual life at the cost of social purpose). In the sphere of the professions, in other words, the rule of *caveat emptor* no longer applies and disinterested service to the community has become the norm: "While a boot-manufacturer who retires with half a million is counted to have achieved success, whether the boots which he made were of leather or brown paper, a civil servant who did the same would, very properly, be prosecuted".[90] In the sphere of the professions, property-rights are with propriety held in trust for the whole community; and this sphere, which has expanded in the past, should expand still further in the future to embrace more and more of industry and trade. It is an illusion to pretend that "there is some mysterious difference between making munitions of war and firing them, between building schools and teaching in them when built, between providing food and providing health": "The work of making boots or building a house is in itself no more degrading than that of curing the sick or teaching the ignorant. It is as necessary and therefore as honourable. It should be at least equally bound by rules which have as their object to maintain the standards of professional service."[91]

The professionalisation of industry would enlist on the side of efficiency "the corporate pride of a profession which is responsible for maintaining and improving the character of its service".[92] This *esprit de corps* (so reminiscent of the Army and Navy, popularly but correctly called "the services"), together with the professional scrutiny of all over each and the collective commitment to reputation, in turn prescribes the normal degree of effort and ensures, via the conformity induced by peer-group pressures, that no one, regardless of remuneration, will lag too far behind the norm. This is not to say that professionals are indifferent to fees, only that their cupidity is constrained by their code of professional honour and by a large number of non-economic considerations:

> Among them are the character of the training received before and after entering the occupation, the customary standard of effort demanded by the public opinion of one's fellows, the desire for the esteem of the small circle in which the individual moves, the wish

to be recognized as having "made good" and not to have "failed", interest in one's work, ranging from devotion to a determination to "do justice" to it, the pride of the craftsman, the "tradition of the services".[93]

Evidently there are a multitude of factors that influence the degree of energy and proficiency displayed in economic activity, of which calculation of pecuniary costs and benefits represents only one (and, as we have seen, by no means a very effective one); and it is therefore desirable economically as well as morally to "create an environment in which . . . the egotism, greed, or quarrelsomeness of human nature"[94] are qualities repressed rather than qualities encouraged.

To some extent, the joint-stock company has itself already meant a transfer of power from (absentee) owners to (professional) managers; and this increasing "separation between property rights and constructive work"[95] is naturally to be welcomed in so far as it represents a devolution of decision-making from selfish speculators to men close to the "rough environment of economic life"[96] who, being of the craft, "have the feel of it in their fingers".[97] If anything, however, power must now devolve still further so as to enlist, in the service of the consuming public, the active participation (based on technical expertise, practical experience, proper training and, above all, internalised moral norms in place of the external constraints of law or bureaucratic direction) of each person ("from organizer and scientist to labourer"[98]) by whom the work is conducted and who has in consequence a vested interest in the maintenance of high professional standards.[99] Such a system of creative collective responsibility is, needless to say, impossible under capitalism (since there no standard of conduct can be rejected where it offends professional dignity if the profit potentially sacrificed is maximal); and for this reason professionalisation presupposes socialisation, so as "to release those who do constructive work from the control of those whose sole interest is pecuniary gain, in order that they may be free to apply their energies to the true purpose of industry, which is the provision of service, not the provision of dividends".[100] Such a partnership between producers and consumers without irritating interference either from shareholders or from civil servants is more than a utopian day-dream, as the success of the Co-operative Movement (with its fixed interest on capital, its profit-sharing, its popular control – and its economies of large-scale organisation) has already demonstrated.[101]

Industry is to be professionalised, but the devolution of power to professionals and their trade associations should nonetheless be "subject to rigorous public supervision"[102] in view of the fact that the professional spirit undeniably "has its sordid side":[103]

> Clearly, a profession should not have the final voice in deciding the charge to be made for its services. It ought not by itself to determine the conditions on which new members are to be admitted. It should not have so exclusive a control even of its own technique as to be in a position to meet proposals for improvement with the determined obstructiveness which the legal profession has offered, for example, to the registration of land.[104]

One check on the potential excesses of professionalism is joint consultation between (all grades of) producers, consumers, and the State, on controversial matters such as the amount of profits that should be held back as a contingency-reserve against the uncertainties of change.[105] A further check is full publicity concerning the costs and profits of enterprise: "Publicity ought to be the antiseptic both of economic and political abuses, and no man can have confidence in his neighbour unless both work in the light."[106] Publicity is a weapon particularly powerful when the producers in question are in the State sector, since there parliamentary criticism of waste and malversation (although it would naturally be self-defeating if too detailed or too continuous) is a powerful force on the side of the consumer, whose interests are all too often neglected by private enterprise (although even in the private sector publicity would in practice humiliate those firms thereby revealed to be of low cost-effectiveness): "If the railways were nationalized the Press would ring with protests against State incompetence and the sharp practice of officials. Since they are in private hands, not a murmur is heard. The explanation is simple. The policy of a public undertaking can be modified by criticism, that of a private business cannot."[107]

Joint consultation and full publicity go hand in hand, since a users' council in an industry can only make proposals for improvement of service if suppliers have previously placed all their cards on the table. Only when exact and detailed quarterly returns are published can it be known if an industry is being operated in a wasteful and extravagant manner or, more generally, precisely why the prices it sets are so high and the wages it pays so low: "The defence of secrecy in business resembles the defence of adulteration on the ground that it is a legitimate weapon of competition."[108]

The State, while recognising that not all property rights are equally defensible, should continue to enforce those that are functional. It is interesting to note, however, that the defence of private property is often in terms of security itself, and that here the notion of functional equivalence might be invoked. Small investors ("the majority of property-owners, though owning only an insignificant fraction of the property in existence"[109]), after all, hold wealth over and above personal possessions such as furniture and clothing not for power or even leisure from work but as a hedge against adversity. Such investors "are haunted by the nightmare of the future"[110] and hence defend all property (large because of small) "for fear lest the knife which trims dead matter should cut into the quick".[111] Their psychological need for perceived economic security is so fundamental to the human condition that it cannot legitimately be put in question. What must be questioned, however, is whether small holdings of property are the optimal means to the desired end. Shares, where they are held, fluctuate unpredictably in value; more property is held by powerful giants than is held by vulnerable dwarfs; and what is really needed is not so much a defence of investment income as an extension of insurance schemes of all kinds (particularly to the lower classes, who are today "miserably under-insured"[112] against the contingencies of illness, incapacity and old age) and also some sort of guaranteed income for the involuntarily unemployed (an expedient which, incidentally, also reduces the efficacy of the power to hire and fire as a weapon of economic discipline).

The State should also intervene to discourage the transmission by inheritance of wealth. And it should take into the public sector the ownership of mineral rights and of urban land;[113] for these privileges are not merely a-functional but anti-functional (as where urban land is "held from the market on the outskirts of cities in which human beings are living three to a room"[114]).

The professionalisation of industry would, in conclusion, breed an atmosphere of peace rather than one of strife; for both power and income would in consequence come to be allocated not on the basis of chance or birth but principle and role. In the Functional Society, "those who perform no function receive no payment, and those who contribute to the common end receive honourable payment for

honourable service".[115]) Each man will be guaranteed an income
sufficient "to enable him to perform his work"[116]), no man will
receive the surplus product of another man's labour, and the
economic basis will then be in place for the development of a
common culture characterised most of all by cohesion and
solidarity.

(d) Criticisms and Extensions

If the Functional Society is truly to stand to common culture in the
relationship of economic basis to social superstructure, then four
significant ambiguities central to the model must first be clarified.
These ambiguities concern the following four economic concepts.

(1) Success-indicators
The professional ethic in the Tawney model clearly refers to
technological rather than economic efficiency: "The technical and
managerial staff of industry is, of course, as amenable as other men
to economic incentives. But their special work is production, not
finance; and, provided that they are not smarting under a sense of
economic injustice, they want, like most workmen, to 'see the job
done properly'."[117] Yet the model thereby incorporates a false
dichotomy between the activity of producing (which, being creative
of value-added, is deemed to be good) and that of trading (which,
being geared to the pedlar principle of re-selling dear what one has
previously bought cheap, is indicative of a deplorable lust for what
the medieval schoolmen called *turpe lucrum*) and based on a picture
of businessmen (who, like most speculators and middlemen, "do not
themselves necessarily know anything of productive processes"[118])
which is, to be fair, a somewhat partial one:

> The businessmen who ultimately control industry are concerned
> with the promotion and capitalization of companies, with
> competitive selling and the advertisement of wares, the control of
> markets, the securing of special advantages, and the arrangement
> of pools, combines and monopolies. They are preoccupied, in
> fact, with financial results, and are interested in the actual
> making of goods only in so far as financial results accrue from
> it.[119]

Such a formulation is controversial; for not only does it focus exclusively on the more negative aspects of business activity, but it seems to disparage the perfectly normal division of labour between the man who produces the commodity and his brother who finds it a good home. Tawney's propensity to favour creating over exchanging no doubt reflects his sincere Christianity (for to love one's neighbour as oneself rather precludes aggressive marketing) and his overall judgement that there is (and ought to be) a "principle superior to the mechanical play of economic forces".[120] It does, however, leave the reader in the dark as to the transmission mechanism by means of which the instinct of workmanship is to be translated into priced goods in the shops.

Even if Tawney is justified, both on normative grounds (because "an economic system which takes as its premise that every group and individual shall be free to grab what they can get, and hold what they can grab"[121] is quite simply an offence to our moral sentiments) and on positive grounds (because competition among the few is not perfect competition, and because profit-making nowadays presupposes an attempt – he does not say whether or not that attempt is successful – to mould via advertising and salesmanship the desires of sovereign consumers), in rejecting our present-day modified version of the classical free-enterprise system, it must nonetheless be admitted that he has a somewhat over-optimistic view of the alacrity with which insiders will identify "fair standards",[122] hasten to "check offences against prices and quality",[123] or abstain from snatching "special advantages"[124] for the group at the expense of the nation. Such optimism is indeed somewhat surprising in view of Tawney's own illustrations concerning cases where the professional ethic in practice has clearly failed to serve the wider interest – cases such as conveyancing (a more expensive and less readily-available service because of arbitrary rules imposed by the legal profession[125]) and private medical care (for, after noting that doctors do not advertise their wares but charge for service and nothing else, Tawney then adds that "the fees which the more eminent among them charge for their professional services may often be excessive"[126]), to say nothing of the "corporate selfishness"[127] of Oxford and Cambridge. Tawney furthermore acknowledges the extent to which standards of professional conduct, being favourable to the rigidities of inertia and conservatism, almost by definition retard innovation and change ("The disposition of all occupations . . . is to relapse into well-worn ruts and to make an idol of good average mediocrity"[128]), but he is quick to add that the implicit threat of social stagnation can be averted by sound training such as to teach the young "not to avoid mistakes, but to show initiative and take responsibility, to make a tradition not to perpetuate one";[129] by the presence in and about the profession of outside experts and independent researchers, who would pioneer new ideas and "keep the profession intellectually alive by a fresh current of criticism and suggestion";[130] and (notably in the case of industry) by the existence of well-informed users' councils anxious to compel the employment of the very best technological innovations by appealing to "their results as evidence that a change of methods, which the profession might dislike, was justified by the increase in economy or efficiency which it would produce".[131]

Perhaps the pressure of consumers' councils in combination with "intellectual and moral training, professional pride, and organized knowledge"[132] would be more effective than the selfish calculation of costs and benefits in guaranteeing the consumer a good service at a reasonable price. Perhaps the spur to progress is on the other foot, however; for, where standards are prescribed, one might imagine that a worker who raises the norm, lengthens the working day, displaces surplus labour by means of a new discovery, or foregoes a wage-increase which he knows his employer cannot afford to pay without an inflationary rise in prices, would be stigmatised by his fellows to such an extent that a sensitive man would soon learn not to exert himself too much any more than too little, sensitive more to the corporate purposes of the small reference group which he inhabits than to those of the wider society outside and fully aware that the road to Coventry is paved with good intentions. Tawney himself notes that there today exists, alongside the "retail firm which pays wages incompatible with a self-respecting life", also the "trade union which sacrifices the public to its own professional interests"[133] via the exploitation to the full of a strong strategic position in the bargaining process; and thus, when he asserts that associations now primarily defensive in function will once liberated from the need to challenge the privileges of the functionless then begin "to advise, to initiate and to enforce upon their own members the obligations of the craft",[134] one cannot help but wonder whether this collective discipline will in the last analysis serve the general at the cost of the particular interest. Should it prove the case, of course, that professionals and their organisations do not ultimately think of themselves as the trustees of rights held conditionally on the discharge of social functions in the service of social ends, then the expropriation of predators and exploiters may not in practice prove a significant step towards enlisting the goodwill of the creative classes on the side of the community as a whole.

(2) Ownership

Tawney's idea of the Functional Society is first and foremost a negative utopia, focusing as it does so extensively on the expropriation of functionless ownership. One difficulty here, however, is that the shareholder is in reality not entirely functionless (Tawney indeed is himself happy that the *rentier* should survive, however self-stigmatised by the self-perception of being the only camel to pass through the needle's eye, in the form of the debenture-owner who provides capital at a fixed rather than a fluctuating rate of return) and the market for shares particularly functional (as where it, for instance, exerts discipline on inefficient managers when shares left undervalued as shareholders rush to abandon a sinking ship then become the object of a successful take-over bid on the part of a raider corporation). A more important difficulty in Tawney's idea of the Functional Society is this: his positive recommendations refer to control and decision making, but with respect to actual ownership do not go beyond the conversion of shareholders into bondholders to make fully explicit the future of rights to residual income.

Tawney does speak in places (and nowhere more so than in those lyrical passages in *The Agrarian Problem in the Sixteenth Century* which eulogize a wide dispersal of land among smallholders and the associated independence from landlords) as if he believes that the right to own should be vested directly in the hands of those who also work: "Whatever the future may contain, the past has shown no more excellent social order than that in which the mass of the people were the masters of the holdings which they ploughed and of the tools with which they worked."[135] Yet his plea for diversity in future modes of ownership shows that his model is in essence neither that of a property-owning democracy nor that of producers' co-operatives in which worker/owners decide collectively on ends (e.g. what kind of houses to build, and for what class of buyer), means (e.g. how many hours per day to labour, and what quality of materials to employ) and the goals of the firm (which might be job satisfaction, profit maximisation or direct social service, and thus at least potentially real alternatives). It is odd that administration is in the

Functional Society always to be vested in the industry, but not ownership-rights directly in the men on the spot.

Even if the question of ownership-rights were to be resolved in such a way as to win popular consent, there is still no guarantee that the consumer will reap the benefits promised. The confusion arises here because Tawney speaks of "the industry" where most economists speak of "the firm", and because Tawney does not recognize that the decision-making unit is the latter rather than the former. What Tawney seems to have believed is that one socialised enterprise should not tender against another: "There is to be publicity as to costs and profits, open dealing and honest work and mutual helpfulness, instead of the competition which the nineteenth century regarded as an efficient substitute for them."[136] Yet if costs and prices (and therefore profits) are not to be determined by competition, then it is not clear what economic meaning, in terms of opportunity-costs and decision-making criteria, is to be ascribed to them; while if firms are instructed not to compete for shares in their industry's total, then we remain in the dark as to how that total is to be allocated between producers. More generally, an altruistic orientation in the economic market would seem to remove from the producing unit any form of external discipline (the traditional examples of which are the spur of profit and the threat of bankruptcy) such as might compel it to supply the consumer with what he wants, not what he needs (as defined by the relevant professional); and even profits might be justified in terms of the stimulus they give to risky innovation and new technology where losses as well as gains might be made (since not all profits are the rotten fruits of collusion and combination). It must be noted, of course, that the nastiness of market rivalries is probably incompatible with the warmth of mechanical solidarity and the perception of a common culture and situation; but noted too that nastiness can still arise even in a world of capitalist-free production, within the organisation (where there might be disagreement as to what constitutes a "good" product or a "fair" price, and perhaps also some resentment of those members of the "intellectual proletariat"[137] who perversely continue to regard themselves as in some way superior to the rank-and-file) and particularly between trades (for whereas education may be regarded as a relatively homogeneous profession, the car industry is a mixed bag, within which computer experts might push for automation, designers for decoration, managers for expansion; whereas the unskilled, meanwhile, because of less training presumably less "imbued with the public obligations of their trade"[138] than are the specialists, push for job-security and better pay). Evidently even after the expropriation of the capitalist owner the socialised enterprise might not become merely a peaceful instrument acting purely "for the service of the public",[139] but might constitute a locus of conflict in its own right.

In the Tawney model, ownership-rights are not typically to be vested in the men on the spot; and if not, then one is bound to ask why Tawney is content to leave administration in the hands of the industry itself rather than in the hands of the democratically-elected representatives of Henry Dubb. Specifically, an ambitious national economic plan would not only (in the absence of market pricing) co-ordinate industries and ensure that inputs and outputs mesh (for if we in my firm all agree to work half-weeks for half-pay, you in your firm may have no choice but to produce half-quantities and go on half-time), but it would also give operative meaning to common ends and social purposes. Clearly, given that "it is the essence of a function that it should find the meaning in the satisfaction not of itself, but of the end which it serves",[140] there is much to be said for making industry directly subordinate to the general will by making it directly subordinate to the detailed instructions of the leaders of the community; and Tawney, in trying to steer a middle course between the guild socialism of Penty and Cole and the centralised collectivism of the Webbs and the Fabians, undeniably presented producers in his Functional Society with the immensely difficult task of having by themselves to estimate the common good of the whole society and to weigh at the margin the twin purposes of safety for miners and cheap fuel for pensioners unsuccoured by priest and congregation. Looked at in this light, Tawney's warning of "the danger of top-heavy bureaucracy and remote control"[141] acquires a slightly different significance from that which was intended.

(3) Scale
Tawney does not regard the size of the firm as a matter of particular importance or interest:

> The fundamental issue . . . is not between scales of ownership, but between ownership of different kinds; not between the large farmer or master and the small, but between property which is used for work and property which yields income without it . . . Once the issue of the character of ownership has been

settled, the question of the size of the economic unit can be left to settle itself.[142]

Yet here, in his habitual enthusiasm to bury parasitic property-rights, Tawney elides other but no less important questions. Do *all* large firms, for instance, enjoy genuine economies of large scale independent of the power to dominate? If so, what machinery is to be provided to ensure the day-to-day involvement and consultation of, say, coal-miners, in determining orders and influencing decisions? If not, what steps are to be taken to break up today's giants and impede future mergers aimed at domination rather than efficiency? And even if large firms were to prove both technologically and economically efficient, might not small still be beautiful in the interests of direct democratic participation (the model of kibbutz socialism suggesting itself in this connection)? None of these questions will be answered by the mere abolition of the capitalist class (even if that in practice proves a necessary precondition for the actualisation of industrial democracy); and it is hard to see that scale is less relevant than ownership to a form of socialism based on employee involvement in the establishment of both means and ends (although Tawney does at times suggest that the trade unions might be able to represent the producer interest, just as users' councils defend the consumer interest, making the implicit assumption that the union leadership is the passive instrument of the union membership and ignoring the fact that there is typically more than one union in an industry).

(4) Income differentials

Tawney argues that good work should be "honourably paid"[143] and that society should "proportion remuneration to service";[144] but, precisely because the "clear principle"[145] of function is in reality both nebulous and contentious, it is in practice extremely difficult to give operative meaning to these statements. What is clear nonetheless is a negative point, that free collective bargaining and the doctrine of payment according to marginal revenue productivity (and with them the liberal legitimation of market-determined pay differentials in terms of what the traffic will bear) are unacceptable: "When really important issues are at stake every one realizes that no decent man can stand out for his price. A general does not haggle with his government for the precise pecuniary equivalent of his contribution to victory."[146] Thus Tawney concedes that the manager of a great enterprise truly possesses a "special talent" such as would enable him without difficulty to command an income equal to that of no less than a hundred families. He then adds, however, that "economic considerations are not the only considerations. There is also 'the point of honour'. And the truth is that these hundred-family salaries are ungentlemanly."[147]

Payment, in Tawney's view, ought evidently not to be based on "what men can with good fortune snatch for themselves" but should be "appropriate to their function, no more and no less".[148] Yet Tawney nowhere spells out in practical terms how function is to be quantified, who is to determine shares and by what means, whether payment appropriate to function is necessarily the same as payment the incentive, to what extent a social consensus on the pecuniary ranking of occupations may be said to exist (and whether such consensus as does obtain actually reflects functional rather than traditional considerations), or how ordinary men can be expected to know what level of pay for a given job is popularly regarded as just (at least, in the absence of detailed incomes policies based on extensive attitude surveys); and he tends to assume, perhaps somewhat optimistically, both that consensus regarding function adequately corresponds to genuine role within macrocosm, and that honourable and decent men will demonstrate exemplary sensitivity to the collective consciousness by refusing to accept all that the employer is willing to pay (recognising quite rightly that such payment would be "an odious offence against good manners"[149]). One can, of course, imagine these assumptions proving realistic within a small society (say, a family) or in time of national emergency (the *esprit de corps* of the trenches and the Somme). One has some difficulty in extending the argument to embrace a whole nation, however, even one corporatised into the sub-groupings which professional units represent.

Tawney believes the Functional Society to be a more egalitarian society, but never makes fully clear why "the probable effect of turning an industry into a public service would be to reduce the size of the largest prizes at present offered. What is to be expected is that the lower and medium salaries would be raised, and the largest somewhat diminished."[150] Perhaps he was convinced that a more Stakhanovite nation would, simply because of its absolute ethical commitment to community and service, in some way decide to take from the rich and give to the poor; or perhaps he believed that a genuinely free labour market would work to the detriment of those who enjoy superior job satisfaction and prestige and thus do not require superior pay (to the detriment of the skilled teacher, for example, as opposed to the school porter). Perhaps the missing link in his argument, however, is some future expansion in the supply of meritocrats caused by greater equality of opportunity and the introduction of a system under which "every able man would 'carry a marshal's baton in his haversack' ".[151] Should this be the case, of course, then the reduction in differentials is evidently to be the free gift of the free market (purified of seniority and nepotism, and clearly capable of providing sufficient top jobs for top men); and the implication here is that the invisible hand itself in certain circumstances not only allocates differential inputs but does so in a manner which is not incompatible with consensual notions of freedom and equality. Besides that, the truly free market would ensure a pecuniary incentive to effort, at least for the lower paid: "If the pecuniary value of the largest prizes were reduced, the stimulus offered to the common man would be greatly increased, since he would know that it depended on himself to win them".[152] The narrowing of differentials will stimulate the have-nots without, presumably, discouraging the haves; and it is important to note the possibility that this desirable outcome can be brought about entirely by equality of opportunity and free market pricing without any reference at all to a Functional Society.

Tawney writes that "different sections of workers will exercise mutual restraint only when the termination of the struggle leaves them face to face with each other, and not, as now, with the common enemy";[153] but here again his views are controversial. Tawney is convinced that strikes and industrial conflict will cease once functionless men who plunder the common store without first having contributed to it are driven from "territory where they have no business to be".[154] Yet even if a united society truly presupposes a Functional Society, it would still be presumptuous to assert that every Functional Society is a united society; and casual inspection of our own imperfect world indeed reminds us how often in practice workers challenge not simply the class enemy but other workers as well (as where a union stubbornly fights a demarcation dispute or defends its traditional differential against all comers; or where it struggles with management for power in blissful ignorance of the fact that the manager is himself "a workman"[155]), to say nothing of the community as a whole (for much bitter conflict today involves teachers, nurses, coal-miners, railway workers, all of them in the United Kingdom in capitalist-free areas of life where there is no leakage from productive to non-productive classes, and some of them already bound by the professional ethic). These instances suggest that the buying out of passive shareholders might not prove sufficient (however necessary the strategy might be) to prevent the functional from continuing to quarrel, but now with each other, over relative shares in a cake which each has helped to bake, either because of need (which is not the same as function and may be far greater than service) or because of greed (for the functional are not also ascetics and may be sybarites). Tawney, naturally, would deny the possibility of such clashes between "particular and divergent interests" in a socialist society orientated most of all to "the provision of service".[156] Yet just as there can be a capitalism of grab, so there can be a socialism of grab; and Tawney's model is perhaps somewhat simplistic insofar as it attempts to link, by hoops of iron, the socialisation of ownership rights, the professionalisation of production processes, and the perception of each that he is bound by a moral consensus superior to all. The socialisation and the professionalisation might exist quite independently of the perception; and in such a case it is perfectly possible to have the cat without having the grin.

In this section we have sought to draw attention to four significant ambiguities in *The Acquisitive Society*. We have suggested that (despite Tawney's expressed wish to build bridges between mind and matter) it is stronger on conviction than on substance and implied that no firm conclusion can be reached on the crucial question of whether the edifice (like most, in need of some redecoration) may be regarded as structurally sound. *The Acquisitive Society* is no definitive textbook for the economics of the future (nor, indeed, was ever intended to be one). It is, however, a provocative and stimulating essay in social philosophy, the central contribution of which is perhaps as follows.

First, it compels a reappraisal of the case for private ownership. It is superficially clear that, if oil is discovered on my estate by another and exploited by a third man, then I need to back up my claim to a share in the product with reference to theoretical principles more elaborate than an appeal to tradition, the *done thing* and the *status quo*; for if my ground-rent truly is a "quaint historical survival"[157] serving no present-day purpose, then I must reconcile myself to the spoiled identity of the private-enterprise scrounger.

Second, it demands that we remove the intellectual blinkers of convention and reflect deeply both on our collective destination and on the road that we as a group wish to select; and thus marries abstract thinking to purposive acting by warning us against behaving like the man who, "when he finds that his shoddy boots wear badly, orders a pair two sizes larger instead of a pair of good leather".[158] Men, after all, are the masters, not the prisoners, of their fate.

Third, it stresses the importance of moral principles in the abstract and of popular perceptions of moral principles in particular: "An appeal to principles is the condition of any considerable reconstruction of society, because social institutions are the visible expression of the scale of moral values which rules the minds of individuals, and it is impossible to alter institutions without altering that valuation."[159] It thus assigns a unique role to internalised ethical norms that transcend self-interest and that may be expected to generate a sense of social purpose (even with respect to economic criteria and activity) which the isolation and independence of commercial exchanges cannot provide. It also, however, raises by implication the complex question of whether it is possible to retain teleology while rejecting theology, precisely because moral reformation is itself expressly the cause rather than the product of socialism.

Fourth, it calls for "active and constructive co-operation on the part of the rank and file"[160] and for worker involvement in the making of decisions and the sharing out of returns, both because attachment to social groups is a good thing in its own right (there are shades of Tocqueville and Durkheim in Tawney's recommendations for *corporations*, for intermediate groups serving as a bulwark against mass society and totalitarian *élites* while also providing a sense of belonging and the welcome moral discipline of all upon each which alone can check *anomie* by standing between the atom and the infinite) and because a more convivial form of industrial structure would boost efficiency as well as reduce alienation (at a negative level, because the worker will not wish to raise his productivity where he "has no guarantee that the result will be lower prices rather than higher dividends and larger royalties";[161] at a positive level, because it enables society to enlist for the first time in the running of industry "the latent forces of professional pride to which the present industrial order makes little appeal".[162]) It hence reintroduces into discussions concerning the goals of the firm the vital issues of job satisfaction, participation, creativity, duty, esteem, self-esteem, corporate solidarity, professional pride, technological optimality and social service; and emphasizes in particular that "it is idle to expect that men will give their best to any system which they do not trust, or that they will trust any system in the control of which they do not share".[163]

II. ALLOCATION

Tawney, as we have seen, was no great friend of economic homeostasis, and in case after case rejected the thermostatic approach to social systems – because allegedly self-regulating mechanisms had failed to ensure a common and classless culture; because they had not succeeded in guaranteeing reasonable equality with respect to property and income, opportunity, power and status, and were incapable of doing so unaccompanied by State intervention; because they introduced the perception and the reality of war rather than peace into economic life and simultaneously debased standards of workmanship. Tawney, in short, was the intellectual opposite of his celebrated colleague, Friedrich von Hayek; for, although both watched the events of the 1930s from the same haven of the London School of Economics, each came to dramatically different conclusions concerning the relationship between direction and democracy.

Tawney took *The Road to Serfdom* seriously: "Professor Hayek's book has been composed with genuine emotion and a sincerity which commands respect. He writes, as Burke was said to speak, with the expression of a man confronted by assassins. His honesty and competence are both beyond question, and I have no wish to treat his warnings lightly."[164] At the same time, however, Tawney recognised that the "nervous professor" who "on grounds of high theory" saw planning as a wolf rather than a sheep was, although resident in Britain, a foreigner, and thus prone to express a view clearly "the product of an authoritarian nightmare which, in countries so unfortunate as not yet to have taught their rulers that they are servants, not masters, has only too much justification, but which a mature democracy should have outgrown".[165] Conditions vary from country to country; and undeniably "there are nations with histories so tragic and environmental difficulties so immense that some form of authoritarian *régime* may well be the best of which for the time being they are capable".[166] Fortunately, Britain is mercifully free from the totalitarian menace: "British socialism has advanced on lines which not only are those alone possible in this country, but are superior in themselves to any alternative yet in view."[167]

Tawney accuses Hayek of mis-specifying the problem at issue by failing to stress that planning is a genus with several species, and in particular compatible with political institutions attractive (e.g. democratic socialism) as well as hideous (e.g. totalitarian despotism). Hayek, Tawney argues, misleads the reader by defining planning in a way which no "British socialist of standing" has ever accepted but from which exceptional model the desired conclusions must inevitably follow:

> Professor von Hayek, it would appear, understands by the term a comprehensive programme, embracing the whole range of economic activities, under which the quantity and quality of every article to be produced, from steel-plants to pins, and the occupation and payment of every individual, are prescribed in advance for a term of years by a central authority – an authority uninfluenced by the views of consumers or producers, acknowledging no responsibility, however indirect, to a representative assembly, and conducting its affairs by the issue of orders, the infringement of which is a criminal offence. Given these assumptions, it is not surprising that a Totalitarian monster should emerge as his conclusion, since he has been at pains to include Totalitarianism among his premises.[168]

Hayek's version of planning, in short, is "a possible one" but his argument is nonetheless hardly convincing; for other versions of planning simply do not have the same "horrifying consequences" or lead inevitably to the same "fatal goal". Hayek neglects the extent to which planning could be general rather than specific (involving questions of economic strategy rather than detailed budgets of production); the "serviceable drudge" (rather than "bloodthirsty Leviathan") of a democratic State; and above all fully responsible to Cabinet, Parliament and electorate ("We, in England, have repeatedly re-made the State, and are re-making it now, and shall re-make it again. Why, in heaven's name, should we be afraid of it?"[169]). Hayek would be well advised to remember that "human institutions are merely instruments. All of them – law-courts and police, armies and navies, churches and schools – can be, and have been, used for bad ends."[170] What really matters is that they need not be, for the State as such has no momentum of its own independent of the men who direct it: "Fools will use it, when they can, for foolish ends, criminals for criminal ends. Sensible and decent men will use it for ends which are sensible and decent."[171] The State, in summary, is a variable and not a constant; and while despots quite naturally behave despotically, "it is as possible to plan for freedom as for tyranny".[172]

The crucial point in Tawney's attitude to State intervention is that collective decision-making is undeniably a double-edged sword, but for that very reason a sword which can responsibly be wielded without provoking the "appalling *débâcle* foretold by Professor von Hayek".[173] The nervous student would therefore be well advised to consider carefully the following two illustrations of cases where conscious direction rather than automatic mechanism successfully allocated goods and services in accordance with the social interest.

(a) The setting of minimum wage rates under the Trade Boards Act of 1909

Tawney, concerned as he was as Director of the Ratan Tata Foundation with the relationship between pay and poverty, was greatly interested by the experiments made immediately before the First World War with the fixing of a minimum wage, and himself prepared reports on the work of the Chain Trade Board and the Tailoring Trade Board. His conclusions were entirely favourable. Higher wages did unquestionably lead to a small amount of displacement among workers whose productivity was so low as to make them not worth the minimum wage to their employers; but, Tawney notes, there are many other causes of unemployment (such as tariff policies or new inventions, compared with the impact of which the effect of the minimum wage in tailoring was "a *bagatelle*"[174]), there exist other jobs for the small numbers of those displaced to go to, and there is in any case no moral justification (not even in terms of security of employment) of low pay for the old, the slow and the weak.

On the plus-side, higher pay boosted the productivity of labour and thus to some extent itself validated *ex post* that which might have appeared undesirable *ex ante*. Better *morale* among the workers raised output per hour and in that way, as a direct result of greater cheerfulness and contentment, partially compensated firms for the rise in wages. Higher wages, moreover, improved the health, strength and general physical condition of the workers, who, being better fed and better dressed, began to be more punctual and to take more care in their work: "It is as though a weight which crushed a plant had been removed. The bent stalk gradually straightens, the crushed leaves unfold and the sap begins to circulate through the expanding veins."[175] Higher wages enabled men to work more slowly, to do justice to the work, to allow full expression to professional pride and the instinct for sound craftsmanship, and the result was a better product consequent upon a higher standard of living and the suppression of competitive sweating. As Tawney puts it, speaking of chain-making: "That bad wages produce bad work is an experience as common as it is habitually disregarded, and it is not surprising that with the advance in the prices paid the quality of the chain should have improved".[176]

The displacement of workers would have been greater had the rise in wages not had a dynamic effect on management as well as on labour. Management, rather than sitting by idly, introduced economies which would not otherwise have been made. They sought out more highly-skilled workers (often training them on the spot) and, in the enforced absence of cheap labour, complemented more efficient human inputs with a better and deeper stock of up-to-date machinery (powered, in the case of tailoring, by something more modern than the treadle, still in widespread use at the time). Again, where minimum time-rates had to be paid whether or not men on the payroll were actually producing, employers were thereby stimulated to improve their organisation, regularise the flow of output, and thus prevent workers from having to waste time waiting for work to arrive.

Looking more generally, Tawney found no evidence that the minimum wage had in practice become the maximum (although workers, theoretically speaking, could, of course, still underbid each other for jobs where the demand for labour was less than the supply of labour), and one of the reasons for this state of affairs was the fact that the institution of minimum rates actually gave an impetus to the trade union movement. Workers (especially low-paid women workers whose second income was necessary precisely because the first – that of the husband or father – was too low) were better able to pay union subscriptions out of higher wages; the very fixing of wages by the Trade Boards was an incentive to organise so as to get the most from the Act; the Trade Boards themselves fostered not the competitive rivalries of the Dutch auction but the collective solidarity of the shared problem ("The discussions and meetings which they involve tend to create the corporate consciousness of professional interests on which effective Trade Unionism depends"[177]); and, in any case, the example of minimum rates showed that pay could be raised without disaster, provoked emulation, and in that way as well led to an expansion in union membership and power. Such an expansion is a welcome development in view of the fact that unions are essential for the success of a minimum wage policy: there is, after all, the latent threat that workers will be overworked (e.g. via speeding up) so as to ensure that they earn the minimum (an easy option for a low-wage, low-profit firm which, unwilling or unable to improve its methods, nonetheless should not expect its employees to subsidise its survival).

In summary then, Tawney's observations on the minimum wage are in two stages. First, he sees no reason why the authorities should not determine a level of remuneration based on considerations of dignity and justice rather than supply and demand, the model for this form of incomes policy being the economic thought of the sixteenth century when there was popularly believed to exist "a standard of fairness in economic dealings which exists independently of the impersonal movements of the market, which honest men can discover, if they please, and which it is a matter of conscience for public authorities to enforce".[178] Second, he is optimistic about what will happen when employers are confronted with a *fait accompli* and asked to sink or to swim; for, given the choice, any reasonable man will make the effort to swim even if he does not as yet know how. The future will not be more of the same; but it is sound economics to force upon employers a change of direction which benefits all and harms none (the experience of the two industries studied demonstrating clearly that workers were able to produce as much as before in a shorter time, thereby necessitating only a small rise in prices charged to the consumer – in chain-making – or no rise at all – in tailoring – and having little or no deleterious effect on the balance of payments). Such a benefit could not have been secured by trade unionism unaided; for, while unions might be able to win a larger share in a fixed cake, minimum-wage legislation stimulates economic growth and thus generates a larger cake. There is, however, a *caveat* which has something of the character of an escape clause, and it would be wrong not to note it: "We need not raise the larger question of the social advantages of an industry which *cannot* pay the low minimum rates fixed by the Tailoring Trade Board, because the evidence suggests that the tailoring industry can".[179]

(b) Wartime economic controls

Tawney, in a memorandum prepared in 1941 for the British Government and dealing with the abolition of economic controls in the years 1918 to 1921, deeply lamented the fact that the enthusiasm and experience of wartime planning had not been utilised in the post-war period to attain socialist objectives. Instead, the controls were hastily and indiscriminately dismantled as soon as the shock of war was past, and this was a mistake: "The way to make certain that the patient's break-down would outlast the shock that had caused it was to cut off the provision which might have nursed him back to health."[180]

Tawney accepted that before 1914 some sort of self-regulating economic mechanism, although unjust, had been operative in Britain:

> Under the pre-war economic system, equilibrium, when disturbed, had been re-established by a multitude of minute, but ceaseless, readjustments, carried out, under the promptings of economic self-interest, by countless individuals. The system functioned after a fashion, though with a shocking mass of needless waste, brutality and suffering; but it could function.[181]

This was, however, no longer the case at the end of the war. The readjustments required were large rather than small (as where exports were suddenly hit by new tariffs, or where the labour force in whole industries, such as mining, contracted dramatically), the time-span for change was short rather than long (so short as to necessitate major upheavals and rapid transformation in the way of life of masses of men and women without "the healing influence of time"[182]), and collective disorganisation, "whether in a single industry, or on the larger scale of a country, required a collective effort to cope with it".[183] The British coal industry, with 1500 different companies, 3300 pits, 30,800 factors, distributing agents and dealers, simply lacked the administrative machinery collectively to co-ordinate itself, and a similar absence of internal regulation was to be remarked in the cotton industry:

> To suppose that an industry composed, on the manufacturing side, of a multitude of firms, mostly small firms, could set its house in order by uncoordinated individual efforts was as reasonable as to expect several thousand motorists to drive safely through Cheapside without a rule of the road. If the cotton industry was to adapt its pre-war organisation, with tolerable speed, to the harsh realities of the post-war world, a central authority was clearly indispensable.[184]

It is thus ironical that the Cotton Control Board, far from surviving at least long enough to smooth the "difficult passage from war to peace",[185] was actually abolished as early as 1919: speculation, crises and unemployment then resulted without any State machinery being able to check these evils.

Businessmen are not averse to controls. They knew in the post-war period (at the very time that they were clamouring for the restoration of *laissez-faire*) that "individual enterprise" was "a polite name for suicide" (analogous, in fact, to reliance on self-stabilising mechanisms in a national emergency caused by drought or flood) and consequently

> proceeded to suppress it by organising combines. It became evident, in fact, that the real object of the business world's idolatry was, not the free competition to which lip-service still continued to be paid, but a free hand either to compete or to combine as it thought most profitable, and that it had no objection to the principle of control, provided that business men, not the State, were the controllers.[186]

The war economy had accelerated the demise of perfect competition in a multitude of industries, planning had already developed in substantial segments of the private sector, and direction in short would not therefore be replacing a free economy by a regulated one. To argue otherwise is to reveal oneself intellectually out of date and the prisoner of "the last spasm of nineteenth century individualism, striving to recapture on its deathbed the crude energies of its vanished youth".[187]

Economic planning is a form of social policy, and direction is hence to be welcomed for reasons quite apart from the co-ordination of an otherwise either anarchic or else privately-regulated economic environment. Three such considerations are of particular interest.

First, concerning employment, intervention can act to redistribute jobs towards men in their prime years (among miners, between 20 and 50) and away from the young (by extending their compulsory education for anything up to two years so as to retard their entry into the labour-market) and the old (by making suitable financial provision for early retirement). The benefits from such intervention are economic but they are also social; for, in the case of "workers of the age of optimum employability", unemployment "must always be a tragedy. Not only is it such men who have the heaviest family responsibilities, but prolonged unemployment destroys the meaning of existence for them. The same is not equally true of the young and the old."[188]

Second, concerning distribution, intervention allows criteria superior to the comparison of costs and benefits to be developed and implemented. Such criteria are necessary since "in societies characterised, like Great Britain, by violent inequalities of income, effective demand is not an index of real needs":[189] "A high price does not mean that a thing is desired by many people. It may (and usually does) mean that it is intensely desired by a few."[190] Reliance upon the market mechanism thus means, for a country, the devotion of "some considerable part of its limited resources to producing the wrong things for the gratification of the wrong people".[191] It affronts morality (since the widely accepted principle of one man/ one vote is evidently suspended in the market-place, where votes are proportional to wealth and where value is in consequence no index of socially-validated need) and undermines *morale* (most dramatically where markets are dominated by profiteering and speculation in essential commodities such as food and raw materials) and must be accompanied by alternative modes of ranking desires, establishing priorities and rationing supplies. The reason is scarcity itself: "The poorer we are the *more* the need of securing equality. On a desert island or in a shipwrecked boat men must be put on rations."[192]

Third, concerning production, intervention enables an economy to match means to ends. This was the case in wartime, when scarcity of resources was accompanied by a high degree of consensus as to the nature of collective objectives:

Since victory was generally accepted as the over-ruling end to which all others must be subordinated, the commodities to be made, and the allocation of the resources required to make them, could no longer be settled by the effective demand of consumers, or cake would be produced instead of bread, high-heeled shoes in place of army boots, and motor-cars in place of shells. They must be determined by the Government in accordance with a scheme of priorities based on a decision as to the order of relative urgency in which victory required different needs to be satisfied.[193]

A policy that so effectively mobilised limited resources for victory in the national emergency of wartime can and should be continued in peacetime until other socially-validated victories as well have been won via direct control of the factors of production: "It is not equally practicable, and but little less important, to control them for the purpose of ensuring that economic resources such as land, minerals and timber, are skilfully husbanded and intelligently developed; that the population is well housed; and that the young grow up, both at home and in school, in a healthful and stimulating environment?"[194]

The two examples of State intervention which we have now considered – minimum wage rates and wartime economic controls – illustrate Tawney's view that it is as possible to plan for freedom as for tyranny and demonstrate in what way Tawney was able to reach the conclusion that "anticipations of the eclipse of political and civil liberty by any form of Socialism probable in this country seem to me to contain more emotion than reason".[195] Englishmen, he stressed, had already harnessed economic ambitions to social purposes, and the outcome had been entirely beneficial in a way that "industrialism" (i.e. that way of life which converts means into ends by making economic activity primary and the standard by which all else is to be judged) would not have been:

The increase in the freedom of ordinary men and women during the last two generations has taken place, not in spite of the action of Governments, but because of it. It has been due to the fact that, once political democracy had found its feet popularly elected chambers began, under the pressure of their electors, to prescribe minimum standards of life and work, to extend public services, to pool surplus wealth and employ it for the common good, to confer a legal status on trade unions, and generally to treat their economically weaker citizens as human beings entitled to the opportunities, advantages, and security against unmerited misfortune, which had previously been confined to the economically strong. The mother of liberty has, in fact, been law.[196]

Reflecting his general antipathy to the economizing mode, Tawney took the view that the allocative functioning of the market mechanism is not only neither *efficient* (since the market is either characterised by the mutual rivalries of multiple timorous independent price-takers–in which case it is anarchic and uncoordinated–or else dominated by monopolies, cartels and price-setting arrangements–in which case greed colludes with greed rather than holding it in check and the powerful few come to rule over their fellow citizens) nor automatically *beneficent* (since the New Leviathan of economic power gives no guidance as to the ends for which the wheels revolve and mankind labours: "Whether the chemist shall provide them with the means of life or with trinitrotoluol and poison gas, whether industry shall straighten the bent back or crush it beneath heavier burdens, depends on an act of choice between incompatible ideals, for which no increase in the apparatus of civilization at man's disposal is in itself a substitute"[197]) but is, most significantly, *unnecessary* as well. Coal, for instance, can more efficiently be distributed by local authorities than by commercial middlemen (the same sort of men, incidentally, who do not scruple to make a killing even in a period of national emergency: "On more than one occasion even during the war, when honourable men might reasonably be reluctant to take advantage of public necessities, both the Government and the private consumer have been charged prices which bore no relation to the cost of production"[198]); for then "its price will be fixed at a level sufficient to cover costs, and will not be raised, as now, whenever a 'cold snap' makes it possible to squeeze the market"[199]. Once prices come to be fixed with an eye to cost of production (including a reasonable rate of profit, but no more) rather than supply and demand, then, of course, allocation by State directives (including controls touching on such aspects of the "general welfare"[200] as output, credit policy, employment, and investment – Tawney is here far more *dirigiste* than in the model he presented twenty years earlier of the *Acquisitive Society* – becomes inevitable, as Tawney's own account of how guide-lines spiralled and multiplied in Britain in the First World War clearly demonstrates: "Once prices were fixed, the distribution of goods, whether steel, ships or food, ceased to depend on the varying abilities of would-be purchasers to pay for them. It became necessary, therefore, to allocate them on a pre-determined plan, so that recourse to some system of rationing became indispensable."[201] Tawney's account of how a few piece-meal controls led in Britain in the First World War to still more controls and ultimately to an elaborate and extensive web of State directives ("Thus a collectivism was established which was entirely doctrineless . . . without the merits or demerits of State intervention being even discussed"[202]) would seem if anything to give more comfort to his opponents than to his supporters, suggesting as it does that the design-less and independent growth of guidance from above can acquire a momentum of its own such as to perpetuate its expansion until it comes to limit the freedom of individuals to make their own personal way through life; and for that reason it is unfortunate that Tawney never directly answers Hayek's point about State absolutism, showing indeed an unusual reluctance to admit the linkages between economy and polity when he declares "Professor von Hayek has chosen as his target . . . not the economics of socialism, but the political and cultural nemesis which, he is convinced, it entails".[203] And quite apart from that, opponents of Tawney's optimism, seizing on his own undeniably over-modest assertion that he was lacking in the elaborate apparatus of formal economics ("The present writer, as his readers, doubtless, have discovered, does not, to his shame, study the works of economic theorists with the assiduity that they deserve"[204]), will no doubt wish to raise a number of questions concerning Tawney's views on production and allocation itself – questions such as why a system of flexible prices (to collect data on diverse ends and distribute scarce utilities) could not simply be complemented by selective cash hand-outs (to reallocate purchasing power in accordance with the social will and the common purpose) so as thereby to restructure rather than replace what is, after all, only a mechanism; or whether the administration of a planned economic system has costs as well as benefits (and may therefore involve waste of resources analogous to that involved in advertising which Tawney elsewhere deplores); or whether the reward to a functionless person cannot itself be functional (as where an idle landlord has no moral right to the usufruct where others sow and do not reap, and where nonetheless the rent itself has a role to play in differential pricing of an input as between alternative uses); or whether combines, mergers and other restrictive practices should be challenged by legislation such as to foster workable even if not perfect competition (he was, of course, neither the first nor the last to present a spectrum of choices as a two-pole model), a matter of particular interest in the light of Tawney's repeated examples concerning the demise of the small firm. Opponents of Tawney's optimism will no doubt wish to raise such questions; but they will be met with the answer that good results cannot come of evil motives, and that the economist should turn his attention from success to fellowship. This answer is no more an answer to their specific inquiries than God is identical to Mammon, but it is precisely the answer one would have expected from an author who believed that collective action presupposed collective mind: "The condition of effective action in a complex civilization is . . . agreement, both as to the ends to which effort should be applied, and the criteria by which its success is to be judged."[205] Agreement, moreover, implies a standard of values based on "some conception of the requirements of human nature as a whole";[206] and thus the common culture and common situation whence alone, to Tawney, all good things spring.

PART III

J. K. GALBRAITH

Biographical Note

John Kenneth Galbraith was born on 15 October 1908 in Iona Station, Ontario, and spent his childhood in a Scotch–Canadian farming community dominated by the Puritan hostility to luxury and the Calvinist work-ethic. His father was a teacher turned farmer (and in addition an active member of Canada's Liberal Party), and Galbraith originally also intended to follow some sort of agrarian career. He graduated in 1931 with a BS degree from the Ontario Agricultural College (at the time a part of the University of Toronto) and then departed for the United States (not all that foreign a country to a farm boy from Iona Station, situated as it was less than 100 miles from Detroit: heavily dependent on American markets, local farmers were well informed about economic and social conditions south of the border) to do a PhD in agricultural economics at the University of California, Berkeley. Two years later he arrived at Harvard as an instructor in economics. His starting salary was $2,400.

Berkeley in the Depression taught Galbraith about the miseries of unemployment and the tragedy of the Hoovervilles; Harvard in the New Deal convinced him of the necessity for Keynesian-type interventionist policies to combat, via reform rather than revolution, the demonstrated failures of *laissez-faire* capitalism. At Harvard he was exposed to the sophisticated arguments of Paul Samuelson, Seymour Harris, Alvin Hansen (the latter being far more of a heterodox and evolutionary economist than is usually realised, as might indeed be expected from a man who had studied with two of the giants of institutional economics, John R. Commons and Wesley Mitchell) and, of course, to the ideas of Joseph Schumpeter on technological change, the nature of the corporation and the future of economic systems. In 1937–8 he held a Social Science Research Council fellowship in Britain at Cambridge, where, although he did not meet Keynes, he deepened his knowledge of economics through wide reading and discussions with Maurice Dobb, Piero Sraffa and Joan Robinson. Meanwhile, he had gained entrée to the salons of the moneyed classes in the United States as a result of his marriage to Catherine Atwater, a modern languages student at Radcliffe.

In the Second World War Galbraith became, at the young age of 33 the Deputy Administrator in the Office of Price Administration; and was, from 1941 until the unpopularity of his policies led to his forced resignation in 1943, in charge of price control for the whole of the United States. From 1943 to 1948 he was on the board of editors of *Fortune* magazine, where he learned from Henry Luce how to write with clarity for a popular audience. In this period he was also involved in the Strategic Bombing Survey, which studied the effects of allied air attacks on the economy of Germany and Japan.

Galbraith returned to Harvard in 1949 and remained there until his retirement in 1975 (from 1959 to 1975 as the Paul M. Warburg Professor of Economics). It was in this later period that he became a celebrity in his own right. Partly this was because of his active participation in the Democratic Party, as chairman of the domestic policy committee of the Democratic Advisory Council, as president of the radical Americans for Democratic Action, as speech-writer for and advisor to Adlai Stevenson, John Kennedy (for whom he served from 1961 to 1963 as an outspoken and forceful Ambassador to India, taking time as well to warn the President against American involvement in Vietnam), Eugene McCarthy and George McGovern. Principally, it is by virtue of his position as a leading commentator on the economic, social and political problems of advanced industrial countries, however, that Galbraith has become one of the best-known intellectuals and most influential social critics of our time. A prolific if also a repetitive author, his publications range from historical accounts of the economic problem (*The Great Crash*; *The Age of Uncertainty*) through books of reminiscences (*Ambassador's Journal*; *A China Passage*) and works of fiction (*The Triumph*; *The McLandress Dimension*) to tracts on social and political reform (*How to Control the Military*; *How to Get Out of Vietnam*), and even include an often-ignored attempt to integrate price controls into the body of economic thought (*A Theory of Price Control*); but it is most of all due to four important and provocative best-sellers (books that stand alongside *The Theory of the Leisure Class*, *The Lonely Crowd*, *The Power Elite*, *The Organization Man* and *The Sane Society* as classics of modern American thought) that his ideas have come to be more widely discussed than those of virtually any other economist of his generation. Those four books are *American Capitalism* (1952), *The*

Affluent Society (1958), *The New Industrial State* (1967), and *Economics and the Public Purpose* (1973). Of those four, the second and the third are so significant that Galbraith has with some justification said of them "I have written two books in my life, and many others".

5 Convergence and Belief

Galbraith believes that "far more problems in economic behavior are common to capitalist and socialist or Communist countries than we commonly allow ourselves to suppose",[1] and that one of the choices we fortunately do not need to make in designing the ideal world of the future is whether to adopt the Eastern or the Western model: the two systems, after all, are in reality convergent.

In Section I of this chapter we will consider the evidence for convergence, and in Section II we will attempt to evaluate it.

I. THE CONVERGENCE THESIS

Galbraith notes the following eight aspects of convergence. First, in East and West alike the large firm is dominated by the need for a concentration of the powers of decision-making in the hands of highly trained specialists (the technostructure) working in committees; and it is further dominated by the imperative for large units of sector-specific capital to be committed substantially in advance of the final product being marketed. This means that in both kinds of economy prices are set by plan rather than *laissez-faire*, and the reason is advanced technology: "The enemy of the market is not ideology but the engineer."[2]

Of course, the State plays in the East a greater role in the process of planning than it does in the West, where the corporation is the source of most planning decisions: "The firm is the basic planning unit in the Western economies. In the Soviet system it is still the state."[3] The operative word here, however, is "still", for matter is in motion. In the East as in the West, the technostructure is striving for autonomy from the misguided directives of ill-informed outsiders, and in the East resents the interference of Party or Ministry no less intensely than in the West it resents the intervention of shareholders or politicians: "To gain autonomy for the enterprise is what, in

136

substantial measure, the modern communist theoretician calls reform. . . . Ideology is not the relevant force. Large and complex organizations can use diverse knowledge and talent and thus function efficiently only if under their own authority."[4] It is interesting that Galbraith was in Poland in 1958, two years after the accession of Gomulka to power and at the height of discussions on managerial independence and material incentives within a system of State ownership. Then, at the very time as Eastern managers are being upgraded from managers to planners, Western managers are being confronted with a transfer of some of their powers to the State. This is the case with wage and price controls (inevitably complementing and to a great extent superseding neo-Keynesian monetary and fiscal policies), protection of disadvantaged minorities, national economic planning and defence of the environment, particularly where these measures are backed up by extensive nationalisation of industry and by support schemes aimed at deserving sectors of economy and society. State guidance and coordination of production plans is becoming more important in the West at the same time as opportunity to plan in the East is becoming more decentralised; this suggests that a mixed system of planning is, because of the shared constraint of common circumstance, evolving on both sides of the Iron Curtain.

Second, Communist economists, like their capitalist counterparts, show a singular unawareness of the extent to which advanced technology necessitates decision making by combined expertise at the level of the production unit (subject, as Galbraith adds in his later work, to some central direction such as to ensure that microeconomic plan will mesh at the macroeconomic level). This lack of contact with the real world Galbraith attributes, in the East as in the West, at least in part to excessive concern with formal theory and irrelevant demonstrations (witness his criticism of Polish economists, that they have done so much for the theory of planning and so little for the practice[5]), together with an in-bred bias towards market-oriented explanations (witness his surprise at discovering translations of Paul Samuelson's neo-classical economics textbook in both Poland and Yugoslavia[6]). Such explanations are dangerous (since in a world of organisations convergence via models of the free market is congruence of fictions and nothing more), in the East particularly so (since they may there come to serve – a function they already fulfill in the West – as an ideological fig-leaf to the naked power of the oligarchy:

Consent for the goals of the planners must be won by all planning systems. The techniques for winning employed by the planning systems of the non-socialist states – the neo-classical ideas, the identification of the convenient social virtue, advertising and other direct propaganda, the enforcement by the Establishment of canons of reputable thought – are infinitely more diverse and subtle than those of the Communist countries. The ultimate need and purpose has much in common with theirs. Planning is planning, and acceptance of the goals of the planners by the public must be won.[7]

Rather than surrendering himself to the ideological needs of the powerful, Galbraith insists, the economist, whether in the East or in the West, should instead utilise the interdisciplinary and synthetic methodology of political economy in order best to describe the social world as it really is. Thus, introducing *American Capitalism*, he writes: "In a book like this the line between economics and politics must truly be an imaginary one – it is a parallel that must be crossed and recrossed without consultation even with the reader".[8] Galbraith clearly hopes that a similar approach will be adopted by other authors in a wide range of countries, and evidently feels confident that this will in fact be the case once economists come to perceive the error of their ways.

Third, both Communist and capitalist countries have dual economies, economies in which large-scale enterprise (the "planning system") coexists with small-scale production (the "market system"). Such duality is unavoidable, for while large organisations undeniably perform better in some fields (notably in technologically-advanced, capital-intensive industries such as those producing cars, defence equipment, petroleum products, electronic apparatus, chemicals, rubber and metals), small organisations unquestionably perform better in others (notably where individual craftsmanship is required, as in the case of the car repair shop, or where a personal service is involved, as in the case of the restaurant); and for that reason it should come as no surprise to learn that, bowing to the pressure of the inevitable, "the socialist countries . . . are making somewhat greater use of private initiative for small-scale activities".[9] Thus in Poland Galbraith was pleased to confirm that the small farmer had not been collectivised and continued to resemble his American counterpart in incentives, results and problems (and praised the Poles for having left the peasant in peace), while in China he noted that even ideology had not been enough to prevent flexibility in vegetable prices or to choke off rationing via the market with respect to perishable primary produce: "Prices vary substantially with supply and are regularly reduced – sometimes more than once a day – to clear excess supplies. Other prices are more rigid."[10] The similarity of the role played by the market mechanism in Chinese compared with Polish and American agriculture suggests a definite (and shared) awareness on the part of would-be social engineers of the true momentum inherent in economic matter.

Fourth, and turning now from supply to demand, Galbraith records that people in both Soviet-type and American-type societies are obsessed with consumer goods and a rising standard of living. Economic growth is on both sides of the Iron Curtain a central social success indicator and values are highly materialistic: "The Soviet goal is, it would appear, to live as much as possible as do middle-class Americans".[11] Production thence becomes prestigious, as the following experience in Yugoslavia illustrates: "I had hoped to wander through villages and old towns, and take pictures, and I had made my wishes tolerably clear. But the socialist inevitable happened – I was taken to an experiment station, a hybrid corn breeding station, an irrigation experimental farm, and a state farm. These are the only presentable culture."[12]

A high level of production need not mean a high level of consumption, however, and very often does not (as where a country has a deliberate policy of postponing consumption in order to favour investment). Yet Calvinist austerity is not an essential feature of Communism, and Galbraith stresses the contrast between privation in Poland and the Yugoslav view that life should be enjoyed now. Besides that, consumers, envious of high living standards in the West and not always prepared to sacrifice their own satisfaction for the sake of future generations, have tended on occasion to reject planners' time-preferences in a most spectacular fashion: "The penalty is the pain, and this cannot be avoided. The rioting in Poland in 1956 which brought Gomulka to power was occasioned in large measure by the enforcement of a rate of saving that was too stern for the people to bear. These last years on the Chinese mainland have evidently been years of serious trouble and tension."[13] Clearly there are limits beyond which even Communist planners cannot go in their attempt to postpone pleasures while not repressing pains.

Then there is another problem: even where goods are available, they are often of poor quality. While visiting the largest department store in Warsaw, Galbraith reflected that "the merchandise looks wretchedly poor" and made an interesting discovery: "I was impressed by the energy with which people dashed up the escalators until I saw that this was necessary for they were not running."[14] Elsewhere in Poland he noted that "the workmanship on the buildings is very poor – the woodwork is of poor quality, the floors are badly laid, and the masonry is poorly joined".[15] And *en route* for a tour of State farms the "tubercular car" in which he was being conveyed ("a Polish model which everyone criticizes"[16]) quietly expired: like so much else in Poland it was shoddy.

Galbraith was impressed in Poland by the "drabness of life":

One gets the impression that people put on a very brave front, but only as the result of infinite effort. I looked into a toy shop which had the worst trinkets imaginable at very high prices. There was a long queue before what I took to be a dram shop, although I am not sure. There are quite a few soldiers, mostly officers, on the streets, but they are not very noticeable, for many of the civilians wear a green-khaki coat that has the appearance of a uniform. This may be the problem of socialism. Planners can provide for everything but color . . . The people of Poland have more liberty than variety.[17]

Yet such drabness, however characteristic of Polish socialism, is not endemic to socialism in general. Witness Belgrade, where the consumer is vastly more pampered than in Warsaw: "The stores are filled with goods and, partly since there are more imports, they seem to be of far better quality. There is more traffic and the people lack the drab, uniform appearance of Poland."[18] There thus appears to be no insuperable obstacle in the Iron Curtain countries to the development of an American-type mass production/mass consumption society; and for this reason, Galbraith implies, his own strictures on the excesses of affluence are likely in Communist countries to become increasingly relevant.

Fifth, there is the complex problem of the environment, an issue with which all industrialised countries must sooner or later come to terms and which cannot be avoided by fuzzy talk of revolution that provides no blueprint for the future. Indeed, the environment "will be a problem in Heaven if that is a high-production, high-consumption society as right-thinking members of the silent majority assume it will be".[19] Galbraith was thus impressed to find the Poles aware of the problem and taking some steps to deal with it. An example: "The streets are so clean that in the moonlight they shine".[20] Unfortunately, the Poles have not always succeeded to the same extent in dealing with pressing social problems in such a way as to capture maximum environmental benefit, as the depressing example of planned provision of housing in Warsaw illustrates: "Warsaw, the planners notwithstanding, suffers from a bad case of urban sprawl – the sprawl in this case taking the form of large blocks of apartments which stand around seemingly at random. The best are ungainly and the worst are ugly."[21] If both East and West are convergent in the need to ensure social balance, they are no less convergent in the need to do so in such a way as to assign a high priority to aesthetic as well as utilitarian considerations (and this despite the inevitable opposition of the successful organisation man: he, typically conservative in his tastes and far more sympathetic to technique than to vision, prefers the functional and the realistic to those great flights of fantasy and imagination in the arts which in America he is likely to castigate as "Communist-inspired" and in Eastern Europe to brand as "bourgeois decadence"[22]).

Sixth, in both Communist and capitalist countries the military–industrial complex has won excessive influence over public spending and policy decisions, and not least because one hand washes the other across the Iron Curtain:

> It is held that if the development that renders existing weapons obsolete does not proceed in the United States, it will proceed unilaterally in the Soviet Union. This, in turn, will accord an unsupportable military advantage to that country. It seems certain that the same argument as to the danger of unilateral development by the United States is made within the planning bureaucracy of the Soviet Union. The role of innovation in creating demand for public goods is thus reinforced by what amounts to tacit co-operation between the two industrial powers.[23]

The weapons race has demonstrably not increased the relative security of either side, but has left both sides better equipped than ever before without giving either absolute superiority. It has improved the pay, prestige and promotion-prospects of bureaucrats in defence ministries and technocrats in defence industries; it has redirected resources into armaments which might otherwise have gone into more socially beneficent areas; and it has, because vested interest is reinforced by the intellectual blinkers of bureaucratic truth (by that organisational truth, in other words, which in America preaches rabid anti-Communism and ensures continuity of policies which are becoming progressively more out of touch with the world of today and yet are not brought up to date because organisation men "much in the manner of man shouting down a well . . . have heard their own voices"[24]), increased the danger of total annihilation inherent in a competitive arms build-up based upon the myth of potential belligerency. In the United States the shadow of McCarthyism has played a considerable role in causing the decisions of interested parties to be rubber-stamped to an almost unbelievable extent: "Accepted Marxian doctrine holds that a cabal of capitalists and militarists is the cutting edge of capitalist imperialism and the cause of war. Anyone who raised a question about the military–industrial complex thus sounded suspiciously like a Marxist. So it was a topic that was avoided by the circumspect."[25] The fear of being thought "soft on Communism" provided in America a source of power and immunity to material and intellectual vested interest; and it is likely that the fear of being thought "soft on capitalism" fulfills a similar function in the Soviet Union in helping to perpetuate the Cold War mentality.

Seventh, in both East and West forces are now coming into being which are working towards bilateral arms control (unilateral reduction is naturally out of the question even as far as Galbraith is concerned) and peaceful coexistence. In both East and West, moreover, the *primum mobile* is the power of public opinion: "It can safely be assumed that nuclear annihilation is as unpopular with the average Russian as it is with the ordinary American, and that their leaders are not retarded in this respect."[26] Galbraith clearly believes in the good faith of Soviet politicians, in their sensitivity to the wishes of the Soviet people and in their sincere desire to free themselves from bureaucracies bent on sabotaging arms control negotiations, and an important reason for his confidence is his conviction, as "a strong economic determinist",[27] that an increasingly complex economy is bound to lead (in the Soviet Union one day, as it did in the 1970s in Spain, Portugal and Greece) to political democratisation:

We think of parliamentary democracy as being the peculiar act of virtue of Americans and Northern Europeans. The fact is that it is something that becomes more or less inevitable when you reach a certain stage of industrial development. Then no group can have a monopoly of power. It has to be shared. The best way of sharing power is through some kind of parliamentary process.[28]

In a system of power blocs, intellectuals are likely to provide the principal impetus for reform. It is they who hound bad men from office not by "bored silence or even by a fishy stare" but by "loud and vulgar laughter",[29] "a delicately thumbed nose"[30] and "hideous noises";[31] and who, by means of their speeches, books, pamphlets, letters and lectures, help to render public opinion eminently favourable to the sensible ideas of responsible social democrats. History, moreover, is on the side of progress, for, in the East as in the West, the expansion of the education industry in order to provide skilled manpower and ensure technological advance has also meant the generation of a substantial estate of natural reformers with minds trained to question rather than to accept. This means in turn that greater political and cultural freedom must and will be introduced in Communist countries: "The requirements of deep scientific perception and deep technical specialization cannot be reconciled with intellectual regimentation. They inevitably lead to intellectual curiosity and to a measure of intellectual liberalism."[32]

Eighth, in both Communist and capitalist countries science is steadily breaking down the barriers of ideology and ensuring convergence of belief on those ideas which relate directly to the momentum increasingly revealed in matter: "In social matters, critics are an interim phenomenon. Given a little time, circumstances will prove you either right or wrong."[33] The march of events has in the West already rendered the neo-classical economics obsolete and is helping in the East to discredit the theories of Karl Marx: "In the Soviet Union and the other Communist countries, Marxists reach into the past and adjust Marx to *their* needs . . . The obvious concentration apart, I don't believe that the development of capitalism has been along the lines that Marx predicted."[34] Galbraith does share with Marx an emphasis on the concentration of industry, on the intimate links between economic and political power, on economic determinism and historical materialism, on social conflict and self-transcending contradictions; and he does, like Marx, advocate the socialisation of functionless property and the diminution of social inequalities. It would, however, be incorrect to argue, as James Tobin has done, that Galbraith is "very close to being a Marxist".[35] Galbraith has no labour theory of value, no belief in the increasing misery of the working class (nor in the profit-motive, which to Marx provides the *rationale* for economic exploitation), no conception of the reserve army of the unemployed (although since he predicts that machines will replace men in the planning system and since he makes proposals which will lead to redundancies in the market system, perhaps the welfare state which he wishes to see extended will acquire an unexpected role with respect to some future reserve army), no theory of class-conflict between capitalist and proletariat over relative shares in surplus value (even the trade unions in the Galbraithian model turn out to be firmly embedded alongside Big Business in the fabric of the Establishment), no stress on capitalist power (rather the opposite) in a world of absentee ownership and group decision-making by highly-educated technocrats with principally non-pecuniary objectives; and he anticipates neither crises and depressions (this because of his satisfaction with the efficacy of Keynesian macro-economic policies and other interventionist techniques) nor some inevitable social revolution ("I consider myself a reformer rather than a revolutionary. I have always put my faith in the idea of change from within which has continuity with the system and does not involve a radical break with the past"[36]). Galbraith is not a Marxist, and the reason is the same as that for which he rejects the outdated and unacceptable belief system of the neo-classical economics: neither ideology either describes what is or predicts what will be. That only social democracy, grounded as it is in fact rather than in myth, can do.

In summary, then, Galbraith is convinced that the juxtaposition of alternative economic systems is to a considerable extent an artificial exercise in view of the fact that American capitalism and Soviet socialism are actually converging. Man's freedom of choice, he insists, is in truth "exceedingly small":

> It is part of the vanity of modern man that he can decide the character of his economic system. . . . He could, conceivably, decide whether or not he wishes to have a high level of industrialization. Thereafter the imperatives of organization, technology and planning operate similarly, and we have seen to a broadly similar result, on all societies. Given the decision to have

modern industry, much of what happens is inevitable and the same.[37]

And from this discovery may be drawn a comforting conclusion concerning the future of the arms race, a race which neither side can hope to win: "To recognize that industrial systems are convergent in their development will, one imagines, help towards agreement on the common dangers in the weapons competition, on ending it or shifting it to more benign areas".[38]

II. CONVERGENCE RECONSIDERED

Our evaluation of Galbraith's views on convergence will be divided into two parts: first we will criticise the convergence thesis as Galbraith presents it and then, secondly, we will question the legitimacy of generalising from American capitalism to the experience of all Western societies.

(a) The case for convergence

Galbraith notes that alike capitalist and Communist countries are evolving and changing (not permanent and immutable) and, adopting the structural-functionalist view that all parts are interdependent within the framework of the whole, appears to believe that the emergence of common problems will lead to the selection of broadly similar solutions. Yet his conclusion is not entirely justifiable with respect either to the political or to the economic system.

With respect to the political system, Galbraith may justly be accused of trivializing the differences between East and West by under-estimating the perceived significance of individual liberty. He admits that the West offers more personal security and a greater guarantee of constitutional processes than obtains in the East (and notes that the Communist countries do not offer free elections, *habeas corpus*, or equality of all before the law);[39] he records that the totalitarian political systems of Communist countries treat dissident intellectuals much less gently than is the case in the United States[40] (and the Galbraithian system regards such intellectuals as the fundamental well-spring of social progress); he confesses that Communist regimes employ techniques for increasing the percentage of the national income saved such as make those utilised by the technostructure of the Western corporation for attaining precisely the opposite objective seem mere child's play ("Communist economic and political organization deals more effectively – or ruthlessly – with unproductive and excessively luxurious consumption . . . Communist organization can, within limits, squeeze blood from its turnip"[41]); and yet he nonetheless stubbornly refuses to rank very highly the problem of coercion in Communist countries (as in the following comment on Cuban socialism: "Castro brought off a social revolution, certainly at some cost to those who left. To those people who remained, he brought a sense of participation in the day-to-day affairs of their own country".[42]). Galbraith notes, for example, that in China "the Chinese are assigned to jobs, and they are required to remain where they are assigned";[43] but then he omits to ask why this is so, or to speculate on the fate of an individual who rejects his assignment and asserts his right to be different. Nor will such a non-conformist find much comfort in Galbraith's general conclusion on the system within which he feels himself imprisoned: "Let there be no doubt: For the Chinese, it works."[44] This is a dangerous doctrine: slavery worked in the South, after all, because of the success with which the powerful were able to impose their will on the weak, and under Hitler the trains were on time.

Galbraith's remarkable tolerance of present-day differences as between East and West with respect to the political system is no doubt to be explained in terms of his confident prediction that day will, on both sides of the Iron Curtain, inevitably follow night. There are reasons to think, however, that his optimism is premature. Eastern countries may increasingly experience pro-duction-fetishism and the problem-solving rationalisation of life into a utilitarian means–ends schema until they too are confronted with the excesses and inconveniences of affluence (although it must parenthetically be noted that any country which singlemin-dedly sets its sights on rapid economic growth in pursuit of baubles and trinkets is almost certain to be suffering from a serious lack of imagination); but they also retain their own cultural and historical traditions (not always democratic ones in the Westminster sense, as it happens), their ideology of Marxism (which they might not be prepared to dismiss as a spurious ideational superstructure, an outdated intellectual relic of the nineteenth century), and a political and social system dominated by the Communist Party (which can hardly be expected enthusiastically to cede its power to faceless technocrats, dissident intellectuals, or, still less likely, to the silent majority by permitting the establishment of competing parties and a genuine political market). Then, simultaneously, Western countries may increasingly temper their pursuit of individual affluence with a greater appreciation of collective consumption and noneconomic objectives (for while science can prescribe means, it cannot, obviously, impose socially valued ends); but they might in consequence introduce a wide range of *ad hoc* controls (with respect, for example, to the environment, aesthetics or the protection of disadvantaged minorities) which actually reinforce the concentrated power of the polity, threaten personal freedoms by reducing the area within which the individual can contribute to the specification of the social interest, and lead to convergence via the institution of a command society and a militarisation of social usages. It is, in short, somewhat one-sided to argue as if technology and economy were always primarily independent, society and polity always primarily dependent variables; for other determinisms are in truth no less plausible. Economic convergence need not mean political convergence; a refusal to converge in the polity might prevent convergence in the economy; and Galbraith's own model, which calls for extensive political intervention in pursuit of socially desirable objectives, does not itself convincingly demonstrate that every State will wish one day to pursue identical objectives in an identical manner, rather than to reject determinism by exercising its free will.

With respect now to the economic system, Galbraith may here be criticised for presenting as fact an eminently controversial and possibly somewhat distorted account of how modern economies actually operate. He assumes that, in the West, technocrats make decisions and shareholders are powerless; whereas other theorists would argue no less convincingly that managers exercise discipline over technocrats and that the shareholder remains the ultimate locus of power (via the Annual General Meeting and the shareholders' revolt; because ownership is often highly concentrated; and because many managers themselves own shares). He asserts that consumer sovereignty has effectively been superseded by successful manipulation on the part of corporate planners and that large organisations nowadays no longer compete for market shares; whereas other social critics would stress that individuals have genuine tastes and preferences even in a world of organisations, and furthermore that it is precisely the fact that large firms in the West do compete with one another that explains why American goods do not display the same shoddiness and drabness as Galbraith noted in Warsaw. Finally, he points to the existence of a strong link between corporate size and technological advance; whereas other thinkers would draw attention to the remarkably good track-record of the small businessman in researching and developing new goods and services, and would suggest that, in contrast to the views of Professor Galbraith, intermediate technology and the small but beautiful organisation remain valid alternatives even for a society bent on economic progress. If, of course, one accepts the interpretation of modern capitalism put forward by these other theorists, social critics and thinkers, then the Galbraithian case with respect to the convergence of economic systems loses much of its force.

Nor is Galbraith's argument with respect to economic policy any more conclusive. Galbraith presents himself as an economic determinist but he is in fact to a far greater extent than he is prepared to admit more a socialist and a social engineer than a value-free soothsayer. Thus his proposals concerning support to the welfare state suggest a definite value judgement on the optimal balance between public and private, social and market; for while universalist provision is perhaps a desirable option, it is by no means the only one (besides which, the admission that health insurance schemes *could* be fully contributory, prescriptions priced and means-tested, owner-occupied housing encouraged, the scope of voluntary organisations extended in no way implies that they *ought to be*). Similarly, his recommendations concerning prices and incomes policy as a weapon in the war on cost-push inflation are somewhat misleading, not least because the attack on positions of power is to be launched against an enemy encouraged in its resistance to a flexible and naturally selective economic system by artificialities such as State subsidies, contracts and loans which stimulate concentrated power and buttress monolithic size: rather than introducing new *ad hoc* controls (and such regulations can lead to divergence rather than convergence, as where *ad hoc* controls introduced to cope with imbalance in one market create an imbalance in others and necessitate still more controls), a case could certainly be made out for reconsidering the role of existing directives.

Once we recognise the range of choices that exists, then convergence with respect to the economic system becomes less certain a prediction than selected superficial similarities between East and West (with respect, say, to river pollution) would seem to suggest. Quite apart from that, however, a vague reference to developmental tendencies (and a tendency is not in any case a forecast) is unlikely to be a source of much satisfaction to the social democrat in Russia, Poland or Vietnam today. Confronted with the admission that "I have never known precisely what the free world was"[45] and the assertion that "the difference between a Communist jungle and a non-Communist jungle is not all that evident except to the CIA. Similarly with rice paddies",[46] he may well reply from his refugee camp, re-education centre or prison cell with "loud and insulting laughter".

(b) American Capitalism

Conjectural biography is the lowest form of art. The objective of this section is nonetheless to explore the relationship between Galbraith and his times, and specifically to consider in what way Galbraith might legitimately be seen as the sociologist of capitalism typically American. The hypothesis that Galbraith's model is in considerable measure an emanation of the material and intellectual climate of the United States will be examined under four headings: production, consumption, welfare and defence.

(1) Production

What Galbraith terms the "neo-classical economics" is to a significant extent the same as the "American Dream", with its strongly competitive, individualistic, anti-statist, naturally selective, self-interested, autoregulative bias, and the importance of this fact is not lost on him: "We have far more people who believe in the mystique as distinct from the reality of the market. We also have more economic theology than any other country. . . . So we have more people than other countries do who cling to the past."[47] It is at least in part the American obsession with competition and anti-trust laws which helps to explain Galbraith's often exaggeratedly defensive posture in his attempts to justify the giant corporation, together with the relatively modest nature of some of the proposals he makes with respect to State intervention (witness, for instance, the free enterprise orientation of the doctrine of countervailing power, which refers to self-stabilising markets where political *laissez-faire* remains in general desirable and which seeks to translate from

Constitutional law into economic theory the notion of checks and balances). More generally, the giant corporation developed at an earlier date in the United States than in, say, the United Kingdom, with the result that it has already generated substantial discussion in America on the role of big business in a democratic society. Such discussion in Britain has been more muted, partly due no doubt to a different degree of industrial concentration, but due also to the existence of a more pluralistic structure of *élites* (which tends to deflect attention from the businessman and the merchant), a collective consciousness embracing aristocratic and religious values leading to altruism in social interaction alongside the expected cult of the individual, and a lesser receptiveness than in America to economic determinisms either of the Right or of the Left.

Galbraith writes in the shadow of the demonstrated failure of the market mechanism in the 1930s; and is convinced that business prosperity and full employment were ultimately restored primarily as the result of State action, in forms ranging from Keynesian economics through the New Deal to the Second World War.[48] Such a defence of intervention may still be controversial in America, where some conservatives continue to defend macroeconomic neutrality (which they frequently take to mean a small and balanced budget). It must be remembered, however, that State action is somewhat less controversial elsewhere. Besides that, the central macroeconomic problem nowadays would appear to be inflation rather than under-employment equilibrium; and in such circumstances monetary policy might have a useful role to play (at least abroad; for not all foreign corporations are as much cushioned from deflationary price and availability effects as the American corporation – where, in the view of Professor Galbraith, new capital is normally internally generated – would appear to be). And while on the subject of inflation, it is worthwhile noting that organised labour outside the United States does not appear to have been absorbed by the technostructure to the same extent as its American counterpart: militancy on the part of shop-stewards and trades unions (which are not in all countries declining in membership), perceptions of exploitation and class-conflict (even if the resentment is directed towards powerful, wealthy and well-educated managers rather than – or as well as – towards the capitalists who own the firm), proposals for co-determination (which Galbraith would regard as eminently misguided in an era of high technology) may all suggest malintegration in Bologna, even if the *embourgeoisement* of the affluent worker truly has rendered them old hat in Detroit.

(2) Consumption

In a country characterised by substantial mobility (geographical, occupational and in terms of social station) and by weak bonds of cultural tradition, the imperative to emulate is *pro tanto* more powerful; and it is thus at least possible that American consumers are abnormally docile, conformist, and open to planned manipulation. This tendency may have been reinforced by the influx of immigrants attracted to America by a high standard of living who have traditionally sought to harness the acquisitive individualism that has stamped its mark on so much of American culture to their own desire to belong and to be accepted; for there is a clear connection between a melting pot environment and an obsession with conspicuous consumption. It is, in short, possible that the structure of American society is such as to open the door to a greater appeal to the non-rational side of human nature on the part of advertising and salesmanship than has been the case elsewhere. At the same time, of course, there is also a Puritan streak in the American personality, which Galbraith reflects and which almost certainly helps to explain his popularity: Americans like both to go the whole hog and to feel guilty for doing so.

America is a mass consumption society for sound economic reasons. As a high productivity, high wage economy (and quite apart from widespread reliance on consumer credit), its citizens have money in their pockets; and since that high productivity results in considerable measure from long production runs and economies of large scale (which reflect in turn a vast national market within which demand has been standardised, not least by reliance on television advertising), it is logical that that money should be spent on goods more homogeneous than heterogeneous. A trading country servicing a wide range of international markets might, by way of contrast, be able to offer its domestic consumers a more diversified line of commodities (although this possibly at the price of lower productivity and lower wages).

The United States as a nation probably judges its performance more in terms of goods and services produced and consumed than is the case in many other countries; and indeed, in view of the achievement-oriented nature of the American value system, it is certainly conceivable that growth worship might not be so much an imposition on American culture as an expression of it (particularly since Americans had materialistic values long before they had the technostructure). Cultures vary, however, and so by implication does the status of goods and services. In Britain, for example, benefits such as leisure enjoyed at the place of work have become so institutionalised as to constitute a not insignificant part of the British way of life; while in many less-developed societies economic growth reveals itself to be a major obstacle to the attainment of ritualistic and communitarian objectives enjoying a superior social valuation. It is, in short, possible that Galbraith, by generalising on the basis of the American experience and reducing that of other countries to casual asides and intellectual footnotes, tends to underestimate the substantial variation throughout the world in cultural attitudes to consumption.

(3) Welfare
In the case of welfare yet again, the positive and normative patterns which Galbraith describes are more typically American than, say British or Swedish: not all affluent Western industrial societies demonstrate the same hostility to the welfare state, and indeed, many (possibly due to a lower valuation of individualism and *personal* enrichment, possibly due also to a lesser hostility towards State schemes which diminish social inequalities) already possess precisely what Galbraith proposes. Then too, not only does the United States have an exceptionally intense resistance to social balance, but it may also experience an unusually high degree of imbalance: not all societies report a concentration of poor blacks in the deprived inner city and an outflow of rich whites to the suburbs (generating an erosion of the local tax base coincident with a rise in the cost of public services), nor indeed do all have the same constitutional difficulties in obtaining a tolerable mix between the equivalents of federal, state and local funding. More generally, social balance and race relations are not in all countries so closely identified as in the United States (although it must also be noted that for an American author Galbraith has surprisingly little to say either about the civil rights movement or about the problems of blacks *per se*). Nor are social balance and competition with the Soviet Union everywhere so intimately associated in the popular mind: the success of *The Affluent Society* in 1958 was due in no little measure to the climate of debate on the national purpose and on the trade-off between private enterprise and social responsibility into

which it was born and which resulted from the launching of the first Sputnik in 1957.

(4) Defence

It could be argued that nothing apart from the experience of the Great Depression affected American intellectuals of Galbraith's generation so deeply as the problem of foreign enemies, real and imaginary; and it must be recalled that some of those intellectuals accepted a Ribbentropp–Molotov pact with the aggressive foreign policy of Dulles and the witch-hunting of McCarthy whereby high defence spending served the Keynesian objective of preventing the then much feared return to the depressed conditions of the 1930s as well as acting to defend the American way of life. There was, moreover, a third party to the tacit agreement: the large military–industrial complex in the United States, comprising a number of powerful corporations and ministries dependent on defence spending for the attainment of their organisational goals.

It was against this alliance that Galbraith in the 1950s and 1960s was to a considerable extent directing his protest; and for that reason his work is in fact more radical when seen in its social context than it would appear when seen against the backdrop of, say, Britain in the same or a later period. It takes definite courage to attack rabid anti-Communism and the defence lobby in an atmosphere which is reactionary virtually to the point of national paranoia; to propose peacetime price controls in the 1950s (when Americans still vividly remembered wartime controls and still associated them with bad times and rationing); to attack private, and call for an extension of collective, consumption at a time when the consensus favoured more traditional forms of intervention (such as the tariff and price support to agriculture) and opposed any move in the direction of communalism; to defend the political as against the economic market (albeit the beautiful simplicity of the model and its evident appeal to a man who in politics as in economics is a born imperfect competitor must also be noted: the American two-party system closely corresponds to Galbraith's either/or, good/bad view of the world in a way that a multiparty system with a multiplicity of options and a need for compromises and coalitions would not). It is to Galbraith's credit that he survived the Cold War without being laughed off as a harmless crank or blacklisted for "un-American activities" (although for many years a malicious and potentially dangerous rumour that Galbraith in the 1940s was "'in favor of anything Russia was in favor of'" remained in his FBI file, together with other items including the suggestion that he was a follower of an otherwise identified subversive called Dr Ware – a mishearing of an assertion made by a Princeton professor to an FBI investigator that Galbraith was "doctrinaire", which the investigator recorded first as "doctorware", then as "Doctorware"[49]. Indeed, it is a definite achievement to write a book like *American Capitalism* during the Korean War or *The New Industrial State* at the height of American involvement in Vietnam (when, no less courageously, Galbraith not only called for American withdrawal but also went against the advice of political allies such as Senator Edward Kennedy and, like Milton Friedman, opposed conscription).

At the same time, however, other epochs and nations have other needs and problems. Defence spending may be or have been easier to get through Congress than welfare, but the reverse has often been the case in the House of Commons. Neither the arms race nor superpower status are contemporary British obsessions; and the military-industrial complex does not occupy the important role in the British power-structure that Galbraith attributes to Pentagon, State Department and associated supplier corporations in the United States. Nor does it make a great deal of sense to advise the British not to support exhausted ideas and bad rulers so as to keep Communists out; or to keep governments in that the British would not have accepted for themselves. The fact is that Britain in the post-war period has had few pretensions to acting as a bulwark against Communism. Such a role of international policeman is not widely discussed in the United Kingdom. It is much more widely discussed in the United States (and was discussed more widely still in the period of the Cold War); and for that reason Galbraith's views on questions of defence must in considerable measure seek their audience where they find their inspiration, namely at home.

This brings us to the following observation on the two-way relationship between Galbraith and American capitalism: Galbraith's ideas evolved in an American context and enjoyed their greatest triumphs against a background of black rebellion, the Vietnam War, the politicisation of young people in the 1960s ("The advent of the hippies doesn't surprise me. It seems to be a rather natural concomitant of wealth"[50]), the depoliticisation of young people in the 1970s ("One thing you can be certain of is the impermanence of student interests. . . . Anyone who expects an enduring commitment from students has no sense of history"[51]), the women's movement, the anti-pollution campaigns, the ending of the Cold War, the diminished hostility to nationalisation of industry, widespread discontent with growth and bureaucratic organisation, the personalities and administrations of John Kennedy ("a man of intelligence, judgement and inner power"[52]), Lyndon Johnson and Richard Nixon, the counter-cultural search for alternative life-styles. New values were in a process of ferment; and Galbraith, in more instances than he would care to admit, arrived *post festum* and converted dinner-party conversation into socio-economic philosophy with a dazzling turn of phrase. As Paul Samuelson put it in 1968, "Galbraith is an antenna and a synthesizer. He senses what is in the air and puts it together and packages it."[53] It might indeed be maintained that one of the principal reasons for Galbraith's success is precisely his uncanny sensitivity to what a great number of moderately anxious middle-class American liberals and progressives think they feel and are convinced they need.

Even if both the supply of and demand for Galbraith's ideas truly is, in the first instance, chiefly American in origin, however, there is still no reason to suppose that those ideas need remain chiefly American in applicability. Galbraith himself indeed tends to regard them as of general relevance in view of his conviction that America is the archetypical model of an advanced developed industrial nation. As he explained to Frances Cairncross: "The great advantage of being in the same world as the United States is that it reveals to other countries the pleasures and horrors that will afflict them only a few years hence."[54] This statement focuses on the evolutionary dimension so often neglected by orthodox economists who, anxious to model their discipline on physics, chemistry, geology and the more exact sciences, have a propensity to regard institutions as stable, fixed, exogenous and forming part of *ceteris paribus*: "It is the great desire of nearly all economists to see their subject as a science too. Accordingly, and without much thought, they hold that its matter is also fixed. . . . It is not an accident that economists who see their subject in evolutionary terms are a minority in the profession."[55] Such a propensity, Galbraith believes, is doubly unfortunate in view of the fact that economic institutions are not only situated in a historical context but play an important active part in generating the transcendence of that context and its replacement by another:

> The business corporation is the greatest of the forces for such change. In consequence of the movement it initiates, there has been a rapid alteration in the nature of the labor market and of trade union organization. Also in the class structure of modern economic society and in the resulting patterns of consumption. Also in the services and responses of the modern state.[56]

Also, indeed, in the nature of international trade, for it was the multinational corporation that vociferously demanded the multinational European Economic Community: "Intra-European trade barriers had become only a nuisance for the large corporation. . . . Farmers and other small producers would never have brought the EEC into existence."[57] From all of this comes Galbraith's conclusion concerning the importance of economic determinism ("As an experienced educator and diligent evangelist, I have learned that economic education is not that powerful, history not that easily reversed. Liberal or conservative, one must come to terms with it"[58]) and our general critique of that conclusion, that national culture, social traditions and, above all, shared values all impede convergence (between countries and within blocs) and that there is no *a priori* theoretical reason to expect purely economic and technological forces to generate common solutions to common problems. There is in all probability – although no one, of course, can say for certain what the future will bring – far more diversity and pluralism in the new industrial state than is dreamt of in Galbraith's forecasts.

If indeed they are forecasts; for Galbraith, like Adam Smith, welcomes what *will be* and *must be* with such enthusiasm that one cannot help but suspect the presence of the *ought to be* as a silent but powerful partner in the model. For such secrecy with respect to values, three possible reasons may be cited. First, the quasi-intellectual graduate now embarked upon a business career will, recognising the description of his organisation (as a group of Dupont executives on one occasion admitted to Galbraith that they had done) and anxious to be honest with himself, nonetheless have a greater willingness to accept the truth of a forecasting model predicting convergence than he would if asked to believe that democratic socialism is a state of things at which every rational community, normatively speaking, ought to aim. Then, second, Galbraith is not a Scottish Presbyterian but a Scottish Baptist by origin, and was brought up in a religious tradition which "outknoxed Knox" in the strictness of its moral code – while simultaneously stressing that values and norms are personal matters which a gentleman neither discusses nor even mentions. Finally, whereas Tawney was the product of late Victorian Oxford and its leisured humanitarian culture, Galbraith's intellectual roots are in the applied sciences and the Ontario Agricultural College, Guelph. Thus, confessing that he has a reasonable knowledge of Mill and Voltaire but a "vague knowledge of Kant", a "primitive knowledge of Rousseau", and no knowledge at all of Aquinas, Galbraith has said: "I'm weak on morality and values. I'm weak on philosophy. I have never read philophy with any comprehension or buried myself in the humane value system. It's not something with which I am at home."[59] Here he is perhaps being unduly modest: Galbraith, and despite his own protestations to the contrary, is better understood as a committed moral philosopher proposing significant reforms of mind and matter than as a detached social forecaster predicting inevitable constraints from which no collectivity, however purposive and rational, can ever escape.

6 Regulation

Galbraith's proposals in *American Capitalism* appeared so anti-statist that Joan Robinson accused him of "rebunking *laisser-faire*"[1] by seeking to limit State intervention to the creation and defence of positions of countervailing power. His argument in 1952 was in essence this: "Given the existence of private market power in the economy, the growth of countervailing power strengthens the capacity of the economy for autonomous self-regulation and thereby lessens the amount of over-all government control or planning that is required or sought".[2]

In the quarter-century following *American Capitalism*, however, Galbraith in his pursuit of a balanced society became progressively more interventionist. In this chapter we will, in six successive sections, seek to consider his attitude respectively to six forms of State regulation of the economic and social life of the nation: restrictive practices legislation, nationalisation, defence of the environment, national economic planning, protection of disadvantaged minorities and macroeconomic policy.

I. RESTRICTIVE PRACTICES LEGISLATION

It could be argued that if Jack is weak relative to Jill, their power should be equalised not simply by giving support to Jack but by taking away some of the privileges which Jill already enjoys. It could similarly be maintained that the correct way to destroy the market domination exercised by the giants of the planning system is through legislation to break up large firms into small ones.

Even the most orthodox neo-classical proponents of *laissez-faire* accept the need for State intervention to assure a competitive economy. Galbraith, however, regards such negative support to positions of concentrated power with extreme caution. The anti-trust laws in the United States are nowadays no more than "a charade",[3] and the momentum inherent in matter renders their

British counterpart likewise "more cosmetic than real":[4] "You can't drop a few stones into the river and stop the full force of the Mississippi. . . . There are some trends in social and economic affairs that are so massive and so powerful that legislation is inherently ineffective against them."[5] Restrictive practices legislation can never be more than "the fig leaf by which power is kept out of sight",[6] to argue otherwise is to "prefer hope to history",[7] and the reasons why "King Canute looks down on those who administer our antitrust laws with the utmost understanding and sympathy"[8] are the following.

First, there is the sheer magnitude of the problem. There are simply too many powerful organisations, too many potential targets, seriously to consider systematically chopping them up into a large number of small perfect competitors: "It is possible to prosecute a few evil-doers; it is evidently not so practical to indict a whole economy."[9]

Second, advanced technology and heavy capital investment make large size indispensable, both to spread the overheads of research and development and to enable the enterprise to bear the risks associated with change. Technological progress (conspicuously absent in the orthodox world of perfect markets and atomistic competition) means high productivity of labour; and the resultant high wages in the planning system suggest that the workers too, rather than resenting Big Business, will for reasons of pure pecuniary self-interest oppose any challenge to the power of the large corporation.

Third, whereas the monopolist of textbook theory restricts output in order to raise prices, the mature corporation does not; since whereas the classical capitalist sought to maximise profits, the modern technostructure seeks instead to maximise some preferred combination of job satisfaction, security and growth. Prices admittedly are not a datum to the large firm, but there is still little likelihood, because of the new imperative of sales expansion, that it is exploiting its customers by means of the old trick of restricting output in order to boost profits: clearly, "a firm that is cozening its customers in order to expand sales cannot at the same time be exploiting them in the manner of a classical monopoly".[10] Empirically speaking, the powerful planning system is overdeveloped as compared with the competitive market system, an area "not of low but of high development, not of inadequate but, more likely, of excessive resource use";[11] and this confirms that corporate prices (while they must naturally be high enough to preserve the autonomy of the technostructure from shareholder's wrath and financier's curiosity via the generation of adequate internal funds for redistribution and reinvestment) remain nonetheless low enough to attract new customers and validate expansion. It is understandable that consumers today have little sensation of price-exploitation resulting from undesirable market structures. Always more sensitive to results than to theories, they would indeed feel distinctly resentful towards any policy aimed at the dissipation of positions of power.

Fourth, much original power is already exposed to the checks and balances represented by countervailing power; and the watchdogs of the law would be ill-advised either to impede the creation of such countervailing power or to break up existing positions. In this context Galbraith refers explicitly to the "A and P Case" of 1944–9, where powerful producers were involved in a trial of strength with the A and P retailing chain. The chain was prosecuted under the Sherman Anti-Trust Act and convicted. The original power that reposed in the hands of its mighty suppliers was, however, left undisturbed. Galbraith regards this prosecution as a serious mistake, for countervailing power here did not exploit the consumer but rather prevented his exploitation by others:

> The government was in the highly equivocal position of prosecuting activities which have the effect of keeping down prices to the consumer. The positions of market power, which had given A & P its opportunity, were left untouched. . . . No explanation, however elaborate, could quite conceal the fact that the effect of antitrust enforcement, in this case, was to the disadvantage of the public.[12]

Fifth, unless a small number of giants were truly to be chopped up into a vast number of dwarfs, the effects of legislation to deal with economic overweight would almost certainly turn out to be eminently marginal. The law cannot make the large behave as if they were small or compel the powerful to act as if they were weak; and the policies pursued by a small number of large oligopolists are in consequence not likely to differ radically from those pursued by a slightly larger number of fractionally less massive oligopolists. Firms even after minor surgery remain interdependent, aware of their interdependence, and likely to form cartels or at least enter into tacit price leadership arrangements. The fact is that self-regulatory, power-free markets are a thing of the past and simply cannot be restored. Nor should they be: "There is no natural presumption in favour of the market. . . . To rely on the market where planning is in fact required, is to invite serious trouble."[13] To break up oligopoly, to deny the social benefits of size, is nowadays to attack "the very fabric of American capitalism".[14] It is a notion "which can seem sensible only to the briefless lawyer".[15]

Such is Galbraith's case against intensive reliance on restrictive practices legislation. It is a case, however, which seems to repose on a series of questionable assumptions. Chief among these is the idea that big is beautiful because it is the precondition for technological advance: "Large tasks require large organizations. That is how it is."[16] Yet small firms in truth, rather than representing essentially the vestiges of a previous stage in economic evolution, remain responsible for a large number of new products, processes and services, while many dinosaurs reveal themselves on close inspection to be clumsy, inflexible, conservative and fearful of change lest it upset the seamless web of vested interest; Galbraith himself acknowledges that research and development need not in any case be endogenous to the firm since it can be bought in from outside laboratories and institutes (some private, some State, some university); and it would in general be very wrong to treat as an iron-clad fact that which in reality is no more than a controversial assertion and a hypothesis to be tested.

Even if the large corporation were to be technologically progressive, moreover, there is still no reason to conclude that it is technologically efficient. It could be argued that the relevant unit in discussions of efficiency is the plant (even the small plant), not the entire multi-plant organisation; that many general corporate technological economies of large scale that may once have existed have long since been exhausted; that the modern corporation is often unwieldy, uneconomical and wasteful of resources due to internally-generated information costs, delays, communications failures generated by an overexpanded bureaucracy (including the specialist technostructure itself); and that such economies as do now exist are primarily pecuniary, deriving principally from the dominance exercised by the powerful. Galbraith himself is hardly reassuring, stating as he does that "the size of General Motors is in the service not of monopoly or the economies of scale but of planning. And for this planning – control of supply, control of

demand, provision of capital, minimization of risk – there is no clear
upper limit to the desirable size. It could be that the bigger the
better."[17] Yet he appears to accept the acquisition and exercise of
such naked power as the inevitable concomitant of economic
growth. He implies, naturally, that outcome matters more than
formal market structure; but his proof of the beneficent consequences of size is marred by an important confusion of a
movement along a demand curve with a shift in a demand curve.
Specifically, if it is true (as Galbraith asserts) that the giant
corporation seeks to sell a larger quantity at a lower price than the
profit-maximiser would have done (although this argument un-
justly ignores the complementarity of growth and profits to a
technostructure obsessed with its autonomy *vis-à-vis* the shareholder
and the financier), and if it is also true (as Galbraith also asserts)
that the corporation successfully deploys its powers of manipulation
in such a way as to generate a demand for its supply that would not
otherwise have existed (although it is difficult to believe that
shoppers are so lacking in personal preferences as to render
themselves the powerless automatons of advertising and
salesmanship), then it is simply not clear why the corporation in the
Galbraithian model should not consciously choose both to expand
sales and simultaneously to boost prices. Size in such a case would
mean misuse of power rather than efficiency and economy, and
hardly appears unambiguously in the public interest.

   Absolute size itself, of course, need not mean market domination,
and only does so when two further conditions are satisfied. First, the
giant must be a giant not only in absolute but also in relative terms.
Galbraith is convinced that this is typically so: "Large absolute size
and large size relative to the market do go together. Great firms –
General Motors, Standard Oil, Ford, United States Steel – are
invariably large in relation to their principal markets."[18] Yet
Galbraith neglects the implication for market structures of the
contradiction between the corporate objectives of growth and
security, namely that as a firm grows it is nowadays increasingly
likely to diversify (uni-market corporations such as those which
Galbraith cites are in that sense, as Bruce Scott has pointed out,
more characteristic of the old industrial state than of the new[19]),
invade the territory of other firms, and thus in the long-run erode
structural monopoly through cross-industry entry. In such a
situation "large absolute size" and "large size relative to the
market" do not go together. Then, second, the giant must be safe

from the aggressive competition of other giants. Galbraith once again argues that this is in truth the case: "Given the goals of the technostructure all firms will seek to expand sales. Each, accordingly, must seek to do so if it is not to lose out to others. Out of this effort, from firms that are fully able to play the game, comes a crude equilibrating process which accords to each participant a reasonably reliable share of the market."[20] Yet it is somewhat misleading to assert that the degree of competition in all oligopolistic markets is approximately the same, and that competition among the few (even where they are operating at different levels of cost) takes the form of total and complete market segmentation. Should oligopolists compete, of course, then the degree of market domination in the economy reveals itself to be somewhat less than that which Galbraith predicts on the basis of absolute size. More generally, it also reminds us that a rough sort of workable competition can still obtain in an advanced capitalist economy even where atomistic competition and the pure market mechanism can no longer be restored.

The recognition that some sort of competition remains (both positively and normatively) relevant for public policy, together with the rejection of extreme either/or formulations, then suggests that State intervention to encourage a healthy (if imperfect) price mechanism need not after all remain a "charade". Restrictive practices legislation could, for instance, be mobilised to obstruct mergers and collusive arrangements such as might reduce the stimulus of rivalry to innovation and pricing; to promote new entry; to encourage competition from abroad. It could, moreover, be utilised to ensure the abolition of practices such as resale price maintenance; for if retailing chains do in fact defend the weak consumer against the strong producer, then it is also likely that they only pass on gains to customers where there is substantial competition with one another. It could, finally, be deployed to challenge the economic power of multi-product monsters. Indeed, Galbraith himself might even accept that each division of a conglomerate could legitimately be broken up into a separate firm, for he has written as follows concerning the conglomerate mode of organisation: "The imperatives and efficiencies of large-scale production do not explain the modern conglomerate with its operations in totally unrelated fields of activity".[21]

If public policy to promote competition is today a "charade", an eminently Galbraithian explanation would be that the technostructure of the mature corporation (a special pleader at the best of times) has in the past exercised excessive influence over the State. This is not, however, Galbraith's own explanation; and he, like any good technocrat, would in the last analysis prefer the team to be nationalised rather than split up. It is curious that Galbraith does not propose induced inefficiency in the interests of economic pluralism, competition and decentralisation of decision-making, surely an odd omission from the work of a social philosopher who puts the public interest before the efficient use of scarce resources to satisfy consumer desires; who fears that the technostructure has tremendous power to impose its goals on the community; and who cannot be unaware that the dissolution of the strong is bound to increase the relative power of the weak.

II. NATIONALISATION

Private enterprise is an essential part of the American Dream, and it is by no means popular in the United States to argue that the solution to the twin problems of size and power is to take giant corporations into the public sector. Nationalisation has, however, since 1952 become of increasing importance to Galbraith, who has in this respect moved further and further to the Left. His evolution is marked by four main stages.

First, in *American Capitalism*, he recommended nationalisation of those industries where the presence of natural monopoly is matched by the absence of opportunity to develop countervailing power. This is the case, for example, with the railways, the highways, and the electricity-supply industry: here, "where market power is inherent in the structure of the industry and where the development of countervailing power cannot be counted on by the great mass of consumers",[22] there is no alternative to public ownership.

Second, in the late 1960s, he became concerned about the problem of defence-related industries, and specifically about specialised weapons firms such as Thiokol, Lockheed, General Dynamics, North American Rockwell, Aerospace, Grumman and others. These he came to regard as private in name but public in reality, being in actual fact extensions of the government in finance and administration:

For the large, specialized weapons firms the cloak of private enterprise is already perilously, and even indecently, thin. General Dynamics and Lockheed, the two largest specialized defence contractors, do virtually all of their business with the government. Their working capital is supplied, by means of progress payments on their contracts, by the government. A not inconsiderable portion of their plant and equipment is owned by the government. Losses are absorbed by the government, and the firms are subject to financial rescue in the event of misfortune. Their technostructures are the upward extension of the hierarchy of the public bureaucracy; generals, admirals, subordinate officers and civil servants, on completing their careers in the public bureaucracy, proceed automatically and at higher pay to the corporate bureaucracy. The corporate bureaucracy, in return, lends its personnel to the upper civilian levels of the Department of Defense.[23]

Galbraith in the late 1960s was fully aware of the case for making *de jure* that which was already *de facto*. Yet he made no plea for State ownership of defence firms, recognising (as he explained in 1969) that nationalisation was bound to be unpopular:

That we should pretend that the big specialized military contractors, those that do all or the bulk of their business with the Pentagon, much of it as the only source of supply, are really private firms – a stalwart manifestation of private enterprise – seems to me a unique bit of nonsense. There would be many advantages in recognizing the reality which is that they are public extensions of the Pentagon. Some day we must do so. But this would not solve the problem of military power. In my view the Services, not their industrial suppliers, are the prime wielders of this power. Only a ubiquitous and often unconscious Marxism causes us to assume that, if there is a capitalist in the background, he must be powerful. So nationalization of the big arms firms would not solve the problem of military power. And it would cost something in public support. So one thing at a time.[24]

Third, in 1969, Galbraith, unable any longer to stomach an asymmetrical system whereby the large weapons firms were allowed to keep their profits but the government agreed to cover their losses, ultimately came down in favour of State ownership in an article entitled "The Big Defense Firms are Really Public Firms and

Should be Nationalized" and published in *The New York Times Magazine*. In 1973 he returned to the attack in his book *Economics and the Public Purpose*, where he advised that the "new socialism" ought to embrace not only the weakest sectors of the economy (sectors such as the social services) but also some of the strongest: "The large weapons firms are already socialized except in name; what is proposed here only affirms the reality."[25] Specifically, the proposal was this: "As a rough rule a corporation (or conglomerate subsidiary) doing more than half of its business with the government should be converted into a full public corporation."[26]

Fourth, and perhaps most surprisingly of all, Galbraith, in 1974, astonished readers of *The New Republic* by unexpectedly calling for nationalisation of all corporations where the shareholder had become a powerless and "purely passive recipient of income" and where management was in consequence a "self-governing, self-perpetuating bureaucracy".[27] Within a period of only a year or two, in other words, Galbraith had moved from advocating the conversion of the weapons industry into a series of public corporations to prescribing the same medicine, in theory at least, for the remaining sectors of corporate capitalism: "Were the criterion for this action that the firm be a full, self-governing bureaucracy – that the power of the management be plenary and that of the stockholder nil – some hundred or more of the largest industrial firms in the United States would be eligible, together with a fair number of the larger utility, transportation, financial and merchandising corporations".[28] This implies a comprehensive shopping-list featuring such celebrated names as General Motors, Exxon, General Electric and Shell[29] to name but a few. In the short-run, however, and because he is "a man of recognized caution",[30] Galbraith is prepared to compromise on the question of ownership and to confine himself to three categories of corporation.

First, the big weapons firms.

Second, the failures, the natural losers, the lame ducks of corporate capitalism who are dependent on public assistance to avoid bankruptcy. The fact is that "in all modern countries socialism has become the ash heap of capitalism"[31] as failed private enterprise collapses into the public sector. This is inevitable, and "has nothing to do with either accident or ideological preference":[32] "It is now taken for granted that the state will inherit the turkeys. And this is necessary; we can't get along without railroads, banks or perhaps even the Chrysler Corporation".[33]

Third, the oil majors: "These have a strong environmental impact, a large influence on foreign policy and a stranglehold on the public pocketbook. Public ownership in this field has worked well elsewhere, notably in Britain, Austria and numerous other countries. It would, no one should doubt and least of all the oil men, be widely popular."[34] The oil majors, moreover, are profitable corporations; and the gains from these "predators" can thus be mobilised to help offset the operating losses of less-fortunate undertakings such as British Leyland or the Penn Central.

By limiting himself in practice to the public takeover of so few technostructure-run enterprises while simultaneously arguing in theory that all are ripe for socialisation, Galbraith is demonstrating his not uncommon predilection for approaching the hurdle at a gallop and then refusing to jump. It must be emphasized, however, that his fundamental strategy is long-term, and depends on the creation of a favourable climate of public opinion through the demonstration effect of repeated success within an existing State sector: "Extension of the area of public ownership is only possible politically or economically as the reputation for efficient public management is affirmed. That is now the absolute essential."[35]

Socialisation means a new source of public finance (corporate profits flowing into public coffers) and the end of an old abuse (corporate profits flowing into private pockets). Furthermore, "as equity passes to the public, so would capital gains. Thus would be eliminated a wholly adventitious source of public enrichment derived extensively from the accident of parentage or grandparentage."[36] Once again, however, Galbraith recommends compromise: the shareholder who has "no power and hence no role in the running of the firm" is to lose his "private participating interest",[37] but he is to be compensated with bonds guaranteeing him a fixed return. Socialisation, in other words, would not mean sequestration: "The common stock would be valued, perhaps by reference to past stock market prices or perhaps by more specific appraisal of assets, and the stockholder paid off with fixed, interest-bearing securities. . . . It should be noted that no public expenditure would be involved in this transaction, only an exchange of assets."[38]

Socialisation is a necessary but not by itself a sufficient condition for the subordination of the planning system to the national interest: few, after all, would "think the Department of Defense more subject to public pressure and concern than the American Telephone and

Telegraph Company".[39] The modern corporation is "a creature in the service of its own bureaucracy",[40] and will consequently continue to serve "the purposes of its own management"[41] should socialisation merely dispose of powerless capitalists while leaving powerful technocrats in full control. To ensure that the public interest is defended and not neglected, to prevent the technostructure from twisting social goals to match its own, something more substantial is needed than simply the conversion of a private into a public bureaucracy. What is called for is the establishment of a "board of public auditors" (replacing the existing board of directors) in each enterprise socialised:

> This board should be of moderate size – perhaps eight members. A minority of the members, perhaps three, should be selected, as now, by the management. This minority would include the senior executives of the firm. The remaining five would be designated as public members by the state. Like judges, they should be men and women of quality and strong public instinct. They should not be of excessive age; they should be of persistent, informed and disciplined curiosity. They would be expected to take their jobs seriously, meet at least monthly, and they would be paid. Since the board of public auditors would have no operational duties, I do not see it as a useful place for the exercise of trade union or other specific participant interest. . . . The defense of the worker interest is more effectively served by traditional trade union means. That the board of public auditors would reflect the consumer interest is inherent in its public character. The consumer *is* the public and vice versa.[42]

The role of the board is to monitor the financial affairs of the corporation and also to exercise "a continuing social audit" on its sensitivity to the public interest. To this end it must have "full access to the information available in the firm – to prices, costs, investment planning, product design, advertising and merchandising methods and plans, and much more".[43] It should appoint top management (usually from the ranks of existing middle management) and set executive remuneration (keeping in mind that, "while to reduce executive compensation in the new public corporations to civil service levels might be too radical a step, there is no excuse for the present munificence"[44]). It should, moreover, exercise surveillance over corporate contacts with political authorities.[45] And it should (in some ways not unlike the present-day Annual General Meeting of the shareholders) serve as a valuable talking-shop and sounding-board for public opinion: since "both the findings and deliberations of the board of public auditors should be known", the board "would also generally be the place for informed discussion of the public impact of the major policies of the firm".[46]

Public inspection and reaction would in turn provide guidance to legislators on economic and social questions: "From this information and discussion would also come the raw material for legislation setting and refining the rules on what can be done to air, water, the tranquillity of life, the safety of consumers and by way of public bamboozlement – in short, for establishing the parameters within which corporate growth and profit-making should proceed".[47] It is vital to remember, however, that these limits are in the last analysis to be set by politicians, and not by technostructure, management, or even board of public auditors: "It is a sound rule that matters of public urgency – those pertaining to the environment, product design, advertising – should be controlled by general law, not by individual company decision".[48]

The conversion of private into public corporations does not mean that the technostructure completely loses its autonomous powers of decision-making. Policy directives issued by the board of public auditors are, of course, to be binding; but Galbraith also believes that such directives should be issued "sparingly". Even in the public corporation, "management must retain the major powers of decision and therewith the capacity to perform. And it must be held responsible for effective performance."[49] The technostructure must, in other words, because of its monopoly of information and expertise, remain firmly in control:

> One reason the private stockholder was excluded from management was that his intrusion, since it was uninformed, was damaging. So it is with any outsider; a public owner cannot and should not participate in the routine of management. This has come to be well understood in many countries, with the consequence that public ownership has been reconciled with extensive managerial autonomy and marked commercial success. The example of automobile manufactures – Renault, Alfa Romeo, Volkswagen – is especially impressive.[50]

The crucial problem in the industrial state appears to be the trade-off between accountability and autonomy: whether in private or in public enterprise the danger is that, by subjecting the specialists to outside command and direction, efficiency will be sacrificed on the altar of democracy. Looking round the world, it is hard to be totally optimistic about social control of the technostructure, as Galbraith indicated in the following eminently depressing passage from *The New Industrial State*:

> The misfortune of democratic socialism has been the misfortune of the capitalist. When the latter could no longer control, democratic socialism was no longer an alternative. The technical complexity, planning and associated scale of operations that took power from the capitalist entrepreneur and lodged it with the technostructure, removed it also from the reach of social control. . . . The choice being between success without social control and social control without success, democratic socialism no longer seems worth the struggle.[51]

This bleak picture antedates by some seven years Galbraith's proposals for a "board of public auditors", however, and reflects most of all his disillusionment with the two principal non-Communist incarnations of nationalised enterprise: the British model and the Indian model.

The British model is one of autonomous public corporations. In Britain the technostructure of these corporations, wishing to be free from interference in the decision-making process on the part of non-specialised outsiders with inadequate access to the collective pool of essential information, has successfully attained autonomy (save for the occasional and rather ineffectual Parliamentary debate) as the precondition for efficiency. Unfortunately, denial to the uninitiated of the right to participate also means a State within the State. In Britain, because of nationalisation, "puzzlement over capitalism without control by the capitalist" is replaced by "puzzlement over socialism without control by the society".[52]

The Indian model, on the other hand, is one of continuous political interference in the affairs of the public corporation. Such "control by the society" is intended to subject the corporation to socially-determined goals and to give it a sense of public purpose. Denial of autonomy, however, is not without its disadvantages.

First, external interference in the public corporation distorts its "synthetic personality", that combination of integrated and complementary skills which enables the technostructure to do "what no individual can do": "The intrusion of politics and patronage into the public corporation is deeply subversive of the subtle relationships on which an effective development of this synthetic personality depends."[53]

Second, there is the problem of divided loyalty:

> If individuals within the corporate organization are servants of a force outside the organization, they will no longer think automatically of the goals of the organization. They have, at best, a dual obligation; one part of the obligation runs to the firm and the other to the external authority. One eye is on the organization; the other is on the parliament or other public authority. Decisions will not automatically be attuned to the needs of the corporation. Some will be related to the external political requirements. The dual obligation is inconsistent with the requirements of the corporate personality, which calls for the implicit commitment of many people to the common goal.[54]

The dual obligation means that some public policies may be imposed, but at the cost of some professional resentment and some loss in professional competence.

Third, external interference generates both conservatism and delay on the part of corporate servants:

> The man who must answer to a parliamentary committee or brief a minister will always reserve to himself the right to review the decisions that he must later defend. Moreover, executive departments and parliaments are ordinarily aroused over the wrong decision. It is on these that a man can score points and, hence, on which others can lose points. The result is centralized decision to avoid error but with the greater wastes of delay.[55]

Where resources lie idle while decisions are triple-checked to avoid eventual embarassment, the loss of time is also a loss of money.

Fourth, and as a direct result of all the above, State control of the Indian type means costs and wages that are higher, prices that are lower, than they would have been had they been set by the technostructure acting with complete autonomy. This tends in turn to eliminate net savings, to cause the corporation to run at a loss, to necessitate a substantial subsidy out of public funds and to put the technostructure even more at the mercy of the ill-informed politician.

Galbraith's own proposals for public corporations supervised by a "board of public auditors" seek to reconcile the two seemingly contradictory goals of democratic control and independence of decision-makers in a way that neither the British nor the Indians have succeeded in doing. The former goal is unquestionably desirable: "The public enterprise in the parliamentary democracy is publicly owned for a purpose. The most obvious purpose is to exercise a measure of democratic control over the enterprise. This control ensures that the firm's procedures and decisions will be in the public interest, that its decisions are sound and sensible and serve the general good."[56] In Galbraith's model, this control is to be exercised by a board of eight wise men, in consultation with the public and the politicians. Such control overcomes Galbraith's principal criticism of the public corporation as it exists in Britain, namely the absence of adequate accountability in the here-and-now.

At the same time, however, since independence of decision-makers (the latter goal) is also unquestionably desirable, such control is to be discrete, not continuous. Business leaders, like military leaders, are to be given general targets to reach, but they are also to be given relative autonomy in the techniques they employ to attain those ends: "Autonomy does not mean less public accountability. On the contrary, it means more. But it is account-ability not for method, procedure, or individual action, but for result."[57] The nature of these results, moreover, is clearly economic, the public corporation being assigned the duty to finance expansion out of its own earnings and the obligation to apply orthodox standards of cost and return: "This is not a capitalist test of efficiency; it is the universal and only test."[58] That being the case, and while the odd miscalculation ought to be tolerated in the public sector just as it would have been tolerated in private business, continued failure to attain solvency should not be regarded with complacency. Thus, for instance, "where the return to an enterprise is intrinsically negative, this should be provided for by a subsidy determined *ex ante*, not by an automatic covering of the deficit."[59] Furthermore, the public corporation is not to be treated as if it were an extension of the social welfare complex. Hence, for example, "the problem of unemployment must never be solved by the provision of unnecessary jobs in socialist enterprises. The word never means *never*."[60] In these ways the technostructure is to be insulated from the State, thereby meeting Galbraith's main criticism of the public corporation as it exists in India, namely excessive political interference on a day-to-day basis.

Galbraith's proposals ensure that even in the world of the public corporation decision-making can nonetheless remain decentralised, a welcome result in view of his own repeated assertion that, precisely because there are in each firm a multitude of complicated decisions to be taken on matters ranging from output and pricing to technology, no State administrative machine could be equal to the multiplied challenge: were there to be referral and appeal all the way up a hierarchy of bureaucrats, "the process of reaching final decisions in a modern economy with a wide variety of products would be almost incredibly difficult".[61] Centralised decision-making is in practice only administratively feasible where production is confined to a relatively small number of relatively standardised products: "There is a popular cliché, deeply beloved by conservatives, that socialism and communism are the cause of a low standard of living. It is much more nearly accurate to say that a low and simple standard of living makes socialism and communism feasible."[62] Since the consumer goods industries are evidently considerably more vulnerable to the insensitive and deadening hand of the civil service than are, say, the railways, there would then appear to be a presumption that capitalism is an institution with a high income elasticity which survives "because there isn't anything administratively workable to take its place".[63]

Ease of administration is clearly a point in favour of capitalism: "Capitalism, as a practical matter rather than as a system of theology, is an arrangement for getting a considerable decentralization in economic decision. An examination of the prospects for capitalism . . . becomes, in the last analysis, an examination of the prospects for decentralized decision."[64] Concentration of power in the modern economy is, however, clearly a point against capitalism:

> In its pricing, procurement of materials, persuasion of consumers and distribution of the resulting income, the modern large corporation, numerous scholars now concede, functions increasingly as an independent force – as an instrument for the exercise of power in which there is responsibility primarily to itself. And this power is independent of, perhaps even above, the modern state.[65]

Galbraith believes that the benefits of decentralisation can be wedded to a sense of public responsibility in no other way than by

socialising the giant corporation while at the same time safeguard-
ing its operational autonomy. Loose governmental controls
(controls involving, say, taxation, licensing, public contracts and
the generation of countervailing power) are simply not adequate to
defend the public interest. That only public ownership can do.

Galbraith came round to the idea of expropriation wedded to
autonomy very late in his career; and it is surely at least in part an
autocritique when he expresses his sincere regret that "we are
concerned here with a subject on which almost nothing has been
said".[66] In fact, much has been said. Simply, it has not been said by
Galbraith.

Galbraith believes that the technostructure of the mature
corporation controls us and that we ought to control it. Whether his
proposals concerning nationalisation would in fact succeed in
converting today's master into tomorrow's servant depends,
however, on the resolution of three crucial difficulties in the model
with respect to the locus of power.

First, it is by no means clear why a technostructure in the State
sector should be more sensitive to social goals and public opinion
than a technostructure in the private sector; or should, once
socialised, eschew self-interested goals (such as the pursuit of rapid
corporate growth so as to improve the personal position of the
decision-makers) and anti-social techniques (such as the reliance on
manipulative advertising and political lobbying) despite the fact
that Galbraith himself regards these goals as common to all
bureaucratised organisational structures and these techniques as
essential to the very process of planning in an era of corporate
enterprise. Galbraith, of course, would argue that the goals and
techniques of organisation men would be humanised through
exposure to the countervailing power of the board of public
auditors. Yet for such power to be exercised, the board must first
comprehend the issues at stake (and the Galbraithian model, which
stresses how easily the present-day technostructure can dazzle its
non-specialist directors and ignorant shareholders through its
command of complicated technical data expressed in unintelligible
jargon, does not augur well for the end of interested bamboozlement) and be prepared to challenge the advice of the
full-time expert (which few outside generalists would wish to do,
partly because they appreciate that the Galbraithian-type public
corporation is to be run on commercial lines and not as a social
service, partly because one-third of the board is in any case to be

made up of well-informed insiders able to argue a technocrat's case). Then there is the problem of the relationship between competition and co-ordination: it is not clear, for example, what would happen in the economy if technostructure A were to be set a ceiling growth-rate of 5 per cent by its environmentally conscious board, while technostructure B in the same industry were simultaneously to be given the go-ahead to aim at 25 per cent by its highly materialistic auditors. The problem could be partially overcome were the State to have a comprehensive national plan that prescribed growth-targets and market-shares for each producer; but this Galbraith does not propose and would probably not welcome, believing as he does in the general efficacy of decentralised decision-making processes with the technostructure at the helm.

Second, it is a matter of debate whether the workers, expressly denied participation on the "board of public auditors" (although three executives are to be included, presumably because their recommendations would reflect greater knowledge, expertise and disciplined intelligence than would those even of trade union leaders, and certainly of the men on the production line) and evidently not to benefit from profit-sharing schemes (since in the Galbraithian model, corporate profits flow to the central government and are clearly earmarked as a reward for ownership rather than labour, at least until they are later used to finance collective consumption), will be entirely satisfied with a system which glorifies productive efficiency (even where the goods actually produced are, in an affluent society, as trivial and frivolous as "a lawn mower that can be guided by transcendental meditation"[67]) and fears social experimentation (even where the result might be a more convivial if also a less productive society). Extreme Leftists will complain that the Galbraithian model means a treble alienation for the worker (alienation from power, alienation from surplus-value and alienation from a product in which no self-respecting creator can see his face reflected), while trade unionists will draw attention to surviving causes of class conflict. Thus the workers might, for example, seek by direct action to twist differentials towards the lower paid and away from the executive and technocratic estate; or they might demand complete expropriation of the *rentier* class (since even fixed-interest bonds are a concealed multiplier of inequality and a reward to a group that Galbraith, like Tawney, calls "functionless"). Whatever they seek or demand, however, they do so as outsiders in a world unquestionably closer to American capitalism than to the Yugoslav socialism which the model superficially recalls.

Third, there is some question surrounding the future role of bureaucrats and politicians. Regarding bureaucrats, there is the threat that nationalisation would put the ultimate seal of approval on organisational symbiosis, since public ownership brings bureaucrats in the private sector closer than ever to bureaucrats in the civil service: not only are their objectives the same (job-satisfaction, security and growth) but so as a consequence of nationalisation is their employer. Regarding politicians, there is the threat that nationalisation would prove incompatible with organisational autonomy – partially because of the inevitable discovery that the auditors are unable to control the technostructure, arrest the process of production for its own sake, or control manipulative advertising; partially because the State itself benefits directly from high profits (and not simply via tax-revenues, as at present) and suffers from losses (which it may willy nilly have to cover). Historical evidence in countries following the British as well as the Indian model demonstrates how often political rather than simply commercial considerations have governed prices and incomes in public corporations; implies that "never" might *not* mean "never" when it comes to using nationalised industries for social purposes; and suggests that the marriage of two monoliths has its costs as well as its benefits. As Galbraith himself confirms, "the instinct which warns of dangers in [the] association of economic and public power is sound".[68] Since he asserts that this instinct "comes close to being the subject" of *The New Industrial State*, since the same is clearly true of his later writings as well, it is perhaps somewhat remarkable that he has made himself the advocate of policies which might actually lead to an even closer alliance between Big Business and Big Government than exists at the present-day. Galbraith, however, would reply simply that, while concentration of ownership-rights undeniably *can* lead to concentration of decision-making powers, there is still no reason to think that it *will* or *must* do so, and that the success of socialist policies quite reasonably presupposes sensible leadership and a modicum of common sense. This is not too much to expect, particularly when we reflect that power in itself by no means corrupts a good man: "My impression is that most people react rather responsibly to power; it often brings out a side to their character, a depth of concern, that they hadn't previously displayed."[69]

III. DEFENCE OF THE ENVIRONMENT

Galbraith believes that private enterprise regrettably does not take into account the damage to the physical and social environment that arises as a by-product of the twin processes of producing and consuming. At present production rises, but "the price of increasing production is unpleasant and even lethal surroundings. The air is less breathable, the water less potable, the countryside is invisible and the air waves unbelievable."[70] Private enterprise may be able to deliver the goods, but it also is responsible for air and river pollution (including car exhaust and smoking in public places), health hazards (consider the examples of road accidents, alcohol and cigarettes, which lead to loss of working days and pressure on hospital beds), uglification of the landscape (as in the case of roadside advertising, rural land development, urban blight, sub-urban sprawl, or functional architecture) and other social dis-amenities (such as the effects of a commercial culture on psychological discontent, of television entertainments depicting violence on crime rates, of the rat race on mental illness). Private enterprise is responsible for causing such damage to the environment. It is society as a whole, however, that pays the bill: "Economic growth is increasing in response to wants, which those that benefit from the growth themselves stimulate, and the costs, increasingly, are borne by the community."[71]

Galbraith was among the first to call attention to the dark side of affluence, to point out the extent to which technocrats, managers and owners are indifferent to environmental considerations, and to argue that State intervention in this area is inescapable. The real question is what form such action should take, and here Galbraith examines four possible strategies.

First, the government could by law impose maximum rates of economic growth. Galbraith, however, while far from believing growth in the GNP to be the supreme social goal, nonetheless feels that a ceiling rate ought not to be imposed by statute, but should rather emerge naturally and spontaneously from a long-term reform of consciousness. There is also the point that a ceiling on growth is only acceptable where incomes are more equal than they are at present: otherwise "people or groups are frozen in the consumption they now have",[72] a proposition substantially more appealing to the affluent than to the poor. Besides that, a society which seeks to combine an expansion in State intervention with protection of the environment through a slow or a zero growth rate will experience the massive social bitterness associated with "a quarrel over the division of a fixed product": "I have never quite agreed with the advocates of zero growth. Growth and increasing income ease a good many social problems."[73]

Second, the government could extend its use of corrective measures in the defence of the environment. This means increased expenditure of public money on, say, the depollution of rivers or to clean up the streets. Unfortunately, corrective measures, although unquestionably useful, are by themselves inadequate, for they are not merely costly but in any case only necessary be definition when the damage (the destruction of a beauty-spot, for example) has already been done.

Third, the government could introduce preventive measures backed up by penal sanctions. Preventive measures would require the producer himself to ensure that abuse of the environment does not occur in the first place; while penal sanctions would internalise externalities by imposing on the offending enterprise the cost of cleaning and depolluting or of providing compensation to the community for irreversible damage done. Yet preventive measures presuppose that the locus of responsibility can be found (and in the case of litter, traffic-congestion or cigarette smoke, to name but a few, this is not always easy); and penal sanctions are subject to difficulties of quantitative assessment (as in attempting to calculate the disamenity value of ravished countryside, aircraft noise or smoky rooms). Clearly, if the public interest is to be defended, then more intensive solutions are called for; and this brings us to the only one of the four courses of action examined that Galbraith himself feels able with any enthusiasm to recommend.

Fourth, the government could allow growth to continue as now but insist that its direction be influenced by legislative guidelines formulated in such a way as to take into account environmental considerations and the public interest. For example:

> Automobile use in the central city, aircraft travel adjacent to populated areas, supersonic travel, random residential use of land are all cases where the advantage to the particular consumer is outweighed by the adverse effect on the community as a whole. In the past the presumption has favoured individual convenience even in face of larger social cost, and this has reflected the purposes of the planning system. The rational legislative decision

requires the exclusion from consumption of products, services and technology where the social cost and discomfort are deemed to outweigh the individual advantages.[74]

Social planning of town and country is thus evidently to be the principal solution to the problem of the environment. The State should have strict zoning policies and arrange for parks and open spaces to be protected from industry and advertising; while factory location should be decided with an eye to clean air and a pleasing landscape rather than exclusively to efficiency in the production of goods (even if the result is "higher cost, smaller output or both"[75]). The State should legislate where possible against noise-nuisance and the use of disposable containers or non-degradable detergents; it should finance research into problems of pollution and environmental disamenity to ensure that such research is in fact performed; and it should prevent property-developers from ravishing beauty-spots or razing historical buildings. The State should not hesitate to make compulsory land-purchase and clearance orders;[76] to employ good architects and artists in its own building programmes (thereby gaining the benefit of their aesthetic experience and at the same time providing them with a valuable outlet for creative but non-commercial projects); and should take pride in the appearance of the social infrastructure. Urban blight naturally necessitates urban renewal; but urban renewal must be accompanied by urban planning in order to ensure a cohesive and aesthetically satisfying environment. Good architecture, after all, is "mostly meaningless unless it is within a consistent framework": the Taj Mahal "would lose much of its queenly elegance if surrounded by modern service stations",[77] and St. Mark's "might well lose some of its charm were the Piazza San Marco surrounded by Gulf, Esso and Texaco stations, a Do-nut shop, with Howard Johnson's at the end".[78] Since "such grotesque arrangements are strongly defended by the competitive ideology",[79] it is clear that State rather than market must act as arbiter of public taste if the wider needs of the community are to be taken into account: "Where there is a conflict between industrial and aesthetic priorities, it is the state which must assert aesthetic priority against the industrial need".[80] The alternative is no less hideous than private enterprise, insensitive to questions of amenity and environment and orientated purely towards "the best commercial opportunity, in the manner of the vertical greenhouses on modern Manhattan".[81]

Few will disagree with Galbraith that economic growth must proceed within the constraints of some framework of legal parameters; and some of the specific guidelines which he proposes with respect to the environment do appear to make a good deal of sense. It is obvious that aircraft noise disturbs my sleep, that cigarette smoke pollutes my trip on the Underground, and that advertising hoardings spoil the view from my car window. Less obvious, however, are certain other points which figure in his argument.

First, it is not obvious that planners will dependably maximise beauty and amenity (always assuming that these can be defined in a way which is electorally as well as aesthetically satisfying) while simultaneously minimising unnecessary interference with individual liberties and avoiding substantial administrative costs associated with the policing of an ever-larger number of rules.

Second, it is not obvious that the State, and the State alone, can and must intervene to deal with the environmental disamenities of change. When it comes to litter, for example, there is some reason to think that citizens should take pride in, and responsibility for, their environment; and, regarding businesses, there is much to be said for internalising diseconomies (including the cost to the public sector of unsnarling traffic jams and widening roads) imposed by some producers and consumers on all members of the community.

Third, it is not obvious that public amenity is more important at the margin than private consumption. It is superficially clear, for instance, that a road is somewhat more than just "an efficient instrument of commerce",[82] and that motorway construction should not simply be concerned "with moving the maximum number of vehicles in the minimum of time with the greatest commercial advantage to all in a position to seize it"[83] but should reflect aesthetic and environmental considerations as well: "It is not imperative that the road which winds pleasantly along the lake or which accepts the contours of the valley should be widened and straightened today or even tomorrow. Those who use it can take a little more time in getting to their destination."[84] Such sentiments will, however, have far greater appeal to the investment banker *en route* for the week-end to his country cottage than they will to the small farmer attempting to convey his crops at a reasonable cost to a market-place where they will be bought by old-age pensioners as well as by company executives. The farmer and the pensioner, in contrast to the banker and the executive, may still argue for efficiency and consumption as opposed to elegance and amenity; and only in a world of general rather than partial affluence can one presume to say categorically that they are wrong.

IV. NATIONAL ECONOMIC PLANNING

The term "planning" to Galbraith means the systematic exercise of foresight, coupled with the ability to shape and mould the economic environment: "The more responsive the producer must be to consumer choice, the more it is a market economy. The greater his power to establish prices and to persuade, command or otherwise arrange the consumer response at these prices, the more it is a planned economy."[85]

Such planning rather than the free market is, as we have already seen, now the order of the day in the world of corporate enterprise, and helps to explain much of its success: "There would be no flights to the moon and not many to Los Angeles were market incentives relied upon to bring into existence the required vehicles."[86] Yet in the absence of the market mechanism, and despite the matrix of interlocking contracts, there remains a real danger that microeconomic planning might mean macroeconomic anarchy and a lack of overall co-ordination in the economy. There is no reason to expect gears to mesh, and inspection demonstrates that they very often do not:

> The expansion that rewards the industrial bureaucracy proceeds at different rates in different industries – in automobiles more rapidly on occasion than in refining capacity, in air conditioning more rapidly than in power supply, in advertising more rapidly than in newsprint. Nothing reliably relates growth in one industry to growth in related and dependent industries; thus we have fuel crises, power crises, newsprint crises.[87]

These crises have already forced governments to reject the "impersonal magic of the market"[88] and to plunge, pushed by circumstances, into the world of democratic planning. These crises, joined to the criticisms of Meade and others levelled against *The New Industrial State* (notably that Galbraith was there concerned exclusively with how a single firm plans, but not at all with how those plans become aggregated into a macroeconomic whole)[89] also brought about in the 1970s Galbraith's own belated adoption of the idea of national economic planning.

Planning authorities are assigned by Galbraith two distinct functions to perform. First, they are to make independent forecasts, isolate probable future bottlenecks, and co-ordinate plans throughout the economy. They are also to work in collaboration with similar authorities in other countries so as to ensure that the smooth adjustment of production and consumption operates on a global scale: the private planning system, after all, already plans via the multinational corporation for the world as a whole.

What is lacking here in the Galbraithian model is, however, any detailed discussion of the mechanism by which micro-plans in a mixed economy are to be made consistent with each other in such a way that aggregate planned output is equal to total demand for each particular product. The problem is this: even if the State were to provide forecasts of future demand for a commodity, the reader is still not told how individual corporations would share out aggregate future supply as between themselves. Galbraith does not recommend that each firm be given a quota to fulfill, which implies that he expects each firm to continue to formulate its micro-plans in total ignorance of the micro-plans of its competitor corporations. He appears still to be convinced that market shares are fixed by convention, and that guesstimation at present refers principally to aggregates; so that if your micro-plan in a world of specified totals is inconsistent with my micro-plan, the explanation is to be sought along lines such as inadequate or over-adequate sales effort on either your part or mine. Here his habitual assumption of sleepy inflexibility rather than wide-awake voracity renders unnecessary the use of complex input–output tables and precisely-specified micro-targets on which many planning authorities in the real world have had to fall back.

Second, planning authorities ought not simply to co-ordinate the plans of others; they ought also to impose targets of their own (concerning, say, the optimal rate of growth or the maximum tolerable level of unemployment) and to have a clear order of priorities. Naturally, once the planners begin to make independent decisions involving the public interest, they will have to be "under the closest legislative supervision. For here will be encountered the most difficult of all the problems of the public cognizance. That will be to have planning that reflects not the planning but the public purpose."[90] This is a form of imperative planning; but indicative planning based on the autonomous verdict of the market mechanism is likely, in Galbraith's view, to be something of an anachronism in a world of post-competitive conditions.

Galbraith thus believes that the planning authorities should not simply provide forecasts and market information but should also set goals and macro-objectives that reflect the public interest. Yet what is not made clear is whence these social goals are to be derived. The collective consciousness, after all, is notoriously difficult to consult when it comes to trade-offs between quality and quantity, aesthetics and convenience, welfare and profits, amenity and expansion; and Galbraith's theory of producer sovereignty and manipulated markets implies definite limitations on the scope for citizen-consultation and consumer-participation. Galbraith's theory of national economic planning is in essence one of polity divorced from society; and its attraction to the reader thus varies depending on the extent to which one has confidence in intellectuals, specialists and moral *élites*.

V. PROTECTION OF DISADVANTAGED MINORITIES

It appears that white males in 1969 (although representing only 52 per cent of all wage and salary earners in the American economy) held 96 per cent of jobs paying over $15,000 per annum. This suggests that measures are necessary to integrate women and members of racial minorities into the mainstream of economic life. The ending of educational segregation and the extension of voting rights will help in this respect, as will improved social balance in the form of better housing and schooling; but there is also a need for direct State intervention to secure equal opportunity for all.

To this end Galbraith (together with Edwin Kuh and Lester C. Thurow) in 1971 outlined MAP (the Minorities Advancement Plan) and proposed that it have the force of law: "We propose that the Congress now enact legislation declaring it to be national policy that employment of women, blacks, American Indians, Spanish-speaking minorities be in accord, throughout the various salary brackets in industry and government, with the numbers in the working force."[91]

The adoption of MAP is to be made compulsory by the end of a transitional period of ten years for all firms with over 2000 employees (smaller firms are to be exempt and firms with only

2000–5000 employees are to be allowed an extra three-years grace). Its enforcement is to be policed by a Minorities Advancement Commission, fully representative of all minority groups to be assisted.

MAP is to apply only to salaried personnel (to top jobs, in other words, and not to the shop floor) and, indeed, only where salaries are equal to at least 150 per cent of national average earnings of fully employed males. Its aim is thus to ensure that the executive hierarchy in the corporate sector is roughly similar to the structure of the working population. The three top executives of the firm, however, are to be exempted from MAP, and may be appointed purely on grounds of merit regardless of race or sex.

MAP is to be enforced on the basis of the local labour catchment area, not the national labour force; for whereas women are distributed throughout the whole country, racial minorities are not. Within a given catchment area, where inadequate numbers of the disadvanged are forthcoming due to poor education, the Federal Government should promote the formation of specialist and executive talent through special grants to the States for the intensive training of minority groups. In any case, firms should be allowed to compensate for undercompliance in the employment of one category of labour (say, blacks) through overcompliance in the employment of another (say, women).

MAP is only to extend to unintegrated minority groups. Thus, for instance, it imposes no quotas for Jews, since the average Jew already enjoys above-average earnings.

MAP will help to improve the power position of women in society. If there is to be genuine equality between the sexes and the true liberation of women, however, then it must be accompanied by further measures (this time of a voluntary rather than a compulsory nature) intended to improve the power position of women in the home as well. Specifically, Galbraith in *Economics and the Public Purpose* puts forward three proposals for consideration.

First, household tasks should be shared among all members. One sex should not be subordinate to another, and hence men and women both should share domestic chores such as shopping, cleaning and cooking.

Second, income-earning should be shared. At the moment one partner tends to earn the income while the other tends to administer its expenditure. Were women to contribute more fully to household finances, however, then they would be in a stronger position to influence household decisions. Women should not, of course, be compelled to work; but they should at least be given a meaningful chance to do so, through equal opportunity laws, greater provision of professional care for small children, more flexible working hours, expanded educational facilities (including positive discrimination in favour of women in the short-run in order to redress past neglect).

Third, there should be increased buying-in of services. If both men and women are increasingly to take jobs outside the home, then there is a clear case for more restaurants (providing professionally cooked food) and more laundries (replacing wife-operated domestic washing machines). The non-availability of housewife labour will thus stimulate the small-scale service firm in the market system and increase its countervailing power in the economy, in the same way that the conversion of that housewife into a top executive will increase her countervailing power in the home.

Looking at Galbraith's proposals with respect to the protection of disadvantaged minorities, it is clear that the compulsory measures are more controversial than the voluntary ones; since while the latter imply no more than the creation of an infrastructure which the individual remains free to reject as well as to utilise, the former represent legally enforceable prescriptions, and prescriptions at that whose content seems at variance with consensual notions concerning the superiority of achieved over ascribed status and the evils of market distortion. One cannot help but note, furthermore, that compulsory measures are bound to be socially divisive to the extent that they generate new resentments. An Ulster Catholic who is denied a particular job because only a Protestant need apply is likely to experience some bitterness, as is a white man turned down for promotion because a statutory black woman is required (bitterness magnified by the fact that, in view of the unwillingness of many working women to accept top jobs, it may prove easier for the particular woman to be promoted than it would have been for the particular man). Quotas are likely, in other words, to generate a certain amount of frustration and unhappiness based on the perception that one belongs to the wrong race or sex. It must be added, however, that such frustration and unhappiness is far from being new, and that it in fact constitutes the very problem which quotas are intended to resolve.

At the same time, nonetheless, there is something to be said for attempting to escape from the straitjacket of the zero–sum game (where Jack's gain is by definition Jill's loss) and to seek in a more general way to discover those social conditions which spontaneously foster tolerance of diversity. One alternative – a liberal alternative and one, incidentally, which Milton Friedman praises with particular warmth in Chapter Seven of his *Capitalism and Freedom* – is the institution of unadministered and anonymous markets orientated towards what men and women can perform, not who they are. Galbraith himself has eloquently described how contract rather than status adequately ensured minority rights in seventeenth-century Amsterdam:

> It was, like all successful merchant cities, a tolerant place; men who wanted to make money could do business here regardless of race, creed or national origin. Much of Amsterdam's prosperity was the achievement of its large settlement of Huguenots and Portuguese and Spanish Jews. The city had a reputation for doing business with anyone who wished to do business, including, on occasion, those who might be fighting the Dutch.[92]

A second alternative – a more socialist alternative, one both anti-capitalist and anti-mercantile – is the encouragement of a common culture via the establishment of a non-antagonistic mode of production, distribution and exchange. Both of these alternatives focus on society rather than polity, on what we can do for ourselves rather than on what should be done for us, and remind us that, even if "the state remains the essential instrument of reform",[93] political action will only in the long-run be successful where its principal effect is to alter social attitudes.

VI. MACROECONOMIC POLICY

Galbraith was an early convert to Keynesian ideas, but he is a Keynesian with a difference: he is convinced that policies intended to combat recession and inflation via the manipulation of total demand will only succeed in the small firm sector, and that the general market regulation favoured by Keynes will unfortunately fail to stabilise the world of large organisations, which must for that reason become subject to specific and direct controls on wages and prices instead.[94]

In the planning system, firms have power in their respective markets, and so in consequence do unions. The latter push for and obtain pay above that level that would have been set by supply and demand and risk no unemployment, since the modern corporation is able to pass on a wage rise in excess of productivity gains via a rise in the price of final output (at the expense of the powerless consumer and the small business) or through a reduction in distributed profits (at the expense of the powerless shareholder). Because the technostructure has the power to export cost-push inflation to other sectors of the economy, traditional class antagonisms have been replaced by excellent and amicable relations between labour and management.

Demand-pull inflation in the market system is a problem which could be dealt with by use of monetary and fiscal policy, although for humanitarian reasons these tools should in practice be handled with care: a rise in interest rates or reduction in the supply of bank loans, quite apart from the fact that their consequences are unpredictable and often perverse, tend to victimise the small and the weak (since the rich and the powerful grow fat on internally generated funds and, should they need to borrow, not only enjoy an excellent credit rating but are able as price-setters to cost-push the burden of interest on to the final consumer), while a reduction in government expenditure (even where accompanied by an increase in direct taxation: being progressive, this is a valuable means for securing redistribution of incomes as well as a useful source of public finance) diminishes the scope for essential public regulation and support and must therefore be avoided. Cost-push inflation in the planning system, however, is a problem which is insensitive to solution via demand-management policies and which necessitates the institution of permanent pay and price controls applicable to all large organisations (in the USA, those with at least a thousand members or employees: hence the administrative burden would not be excessive, since only a few hundred strong unions and one or two thousand powerful corporations would be affected). These controls should not only attempt to prevent the planning system from holding the community for ransom, but should also seek to adjust differentials in favour of the lower-paid. The policy should be enforced by a tripartite commission representing the three sides of industry (labour, management, the public) and its recommendations should be legally binding.

Galbraith's views with respect to macroeconomic policy are controversial ones. He assumes that unions and corporations do in fact have the power to cost-push (whereas what may simply be happening is that a weak government creates demand after the wage round and the price rise so as to validate the higher level of wages and prices and thereby forestall redundancies); he leaves himself with virtually no policy-instrument to deal with the problem of excessive total demand (since interest rates are to be pegged at a permanently low level, the money supply not to be controlled, government expenditure never to be reduced in a boom although always increased in a slump; and since there must inevitably come a point when taxation simply cannot be boosted still further, especially since it will never again be cut); and he is being somewhat optimistic with respect to the acceptability and workability of ambitious incomes policies which seek to combine macroeconomic stability with perceived social justice. The success of such incomes policies, after all, presupposes not merely co-ordination in administration but also consensus with respect to pay norms that are to be regarded as socially just in a way that traditional differentials are not to be, coupled with a willingness on the part of strong unions to contribute to the success of policies which virtually by definition give them less money than the free-for-all of collective bargaining would have done. This is not to say that incomes policies will never succeed, only to imply once again that a mechanistic rather than a motivational form of democratic socialism is unlikely in the long run to be able to do the trick.

7 Support

Galbraith believes that the State should do more than merely regulate the conditions within which economic and social activity takes place. It should also provide direct governmental support of various kinds to deserving but weak sections of the community. Particularly important are support to the creative arts, to the planning system, to the market system and to the welfare state; and it is with these forms of support to positions of weakness that we shall be concerned in this chapter.

I. SUPPORT TO THE CREATIVE ARTS

Consider

the traditional relationship between art and economics. There is none. Art has nothing to do with the sterner preoccupations of the economist. The artist's values – his splendid and often splenetic insistence on the supremacy of aesthetic goals – are subversive of the straightforward materialist concerns of the economist. He makes the economist feel dull, routine, philistine, and uncomfortable and also sadly unappreciated for his earthly concern for bread and butter, including that which nourishes the artist. Not only do the two worlds not meet, but the regret in each is evidently negligible.[1]

Galbraith, author of two works of fiction and co-author (with M. S. Randhawa) of a book on Indian painting,[2] understandably deplores the mutual alienation of the artist from the practical man of affairs. He also believes that a close relationship between aesthetics and economics is simply not to be expected automatically to develop either in poor or in rich countries.

In poor countries the problem is basically lack of material well-being and absence of adequate leisure; for while the artist may be a

Hungerkünstler, "not so his audience. It turns to art after it has had dinner."[3] Then too, living standards must not only be high but secure, as only a secure man can divert his thoughts from the risk and hardship of a fall in his accustomed level of consumption to less pressing matters such as an appreciation of the arts. Uncertainty may be (as the Social Darwinists maintained it was) an indispensable antidote to sloth and an essential stimulant to industry; but it also equates a competitive environment with an aesthetically barren desert, since it fosters a "full-time concern with making money" through the medium of the "omnipresent possibility of failure".[4] As Galbraith puts it, his views reflecting no doubt the personal experience of a childhood spent in a farming community where the functional was preferred to the beautiful and architecture "was intrinsically an eyesore":[5]

> That the successful lawyer should have a concern for painting does not surprise us. But not the successful cattleman. He is the man for whom the calendars and the *Saturday Evening Post* covers are drawn. As his income increases, he may develop an interest in a better automobile, possibly in an aeroplane, and certainly in an array of consumers' goods. That he should develop a serious concern for painting or sculpture or even for domestic architecture is not expected. A farmer has too many other worries. He cannot be frivolous or eccentric. Unlike the more secure lawyer, it is in fact taken for granted that his pecuniary concerns are pre-emptive.[6]

In rich countries, the most charitable thing that can be said is that the economic climate is radically different while the alienation of art from economics remains substantially the same. In America material affluence combined with the progressive supersession of insecurity (at least for the large corporation and the organisation man) has done little to foster an environment in which creative activity can flourish. For this unfortunate state of affairs, the following reasons may be adduced.

First, there is the mystification of reality that results from reliance on a vestigial economic ideology couched in terms of small producers. In truth, as it happens, "the myth of the insecure, tough, competitive enterprise has outlasted the reality. Business is assumed still to require a total concentration of energies; anything less is still deemed to be out of character."[7] Several generations ago successful tycoons and self-made millionaires built up great art collections to prove that "they were not mere money-grubbers. . . . Now the organization man may seek to prove the opposite."[8]

Second, the technostructure of the modern corporation finds it difficult to absorb the creative artist since the latter, prizing his independence, does not fit easily into a team or submit willingly to the discipline and goals of organisation (save possibly within the context of an artistic organisation such as a symphony orchestra or ballet company). In some cases the firm gets round this problem by buying in design from outside eccentrics; but in most cases it prefers to employ its own tame if second-rate talents. Such second-rate talents, because their primary loyalty is to the economic rather than the artistic life, will not hesitate to perform those tasks which the true creative artist is himself unable to perform without ceasing altogether to be creative.

Third, the organisation man tends to formulate decisions on the basis of commercial and utilitarian rather than aesthetic criteria. Ideally, design should "reflect the artist's sense of what is good, not the technician's knowledge of what can be efficiently produced or the marketing man's sense of what can be sold".[9] In the modern industrial system, however, the artist's view is subordinated to that of the technocrat; and the technocrat is bound to vote for "long runs, technical efficiency, low costs and a considered marketing strategy at the expense of good design".[10]

Fourth, commercial advertising contributes to the estrangement of aesthetics and economics by propagandising on behalf of privately-produced commodities but not in favour of cultural and artistic achievement. The consumer nowadays undeniably prefers the quantitative to the qualitative: "The inhabitants of a three-bedroom house are thought 'better off' than those of a two-bedroom house; they gain further distinction from having a fully equipped kitchen and being a two- as opposed to a one-car family."[11] Such preference-patterns, however, are induced and not autonomous; for clearly "the technical character and novelty of goods, not their beauty, is stressed in advertising".[12] Advertising, indeed, may be positively deleterious to the artistic response, as where it not only aims at the inculcation via an appeal to psychological and cultural insecurities of a consumption mentality but also comes intentionally to be based on "a jarring of the aesthetic sensibilities. An advertising billboard that blends gracefully into the landscape is of little value; it must be in sharp contrast with surroundings."[13] Such dissonance provokes competitive dissonance from other firms, and the result is that the individual in the long-run loses much of the sensitivity to beauty he might otherwise have developed: "Good theatre and good music require the protection of a mood; they cannot be successfully juxtaposed to rhymed jingles on behalf of a laxative."[14]

In a nutshell then, the crisis in the creative arts may be summarised as follows: whereas once the arts were an index and source of social prestige (say, in the Florence of the Renaissance), nowadays science and engineering are generally regarded to be the foundation of a nation's standing, education is increasingly orientated towards the practical rather than the imaginative, and the public on balance prefers technological innovation to artistic perfection (indeed, while it loves new products, it laughs at new art-forms). The consumer-citizen is not to blame for this social outlook, for it has been imposed on the community not by the majority but by a minority, and specifically by the technostructure of the mature corporation:

> No one will be in doubt as to the source of these attitudes. It lies with the technostructure and the planning system and with their ability to impose their values on the society and the state. The technostructure embraces and uses the engineer and the scientist; it cannot embrace the artist. Engineering and science serve its purpose; art, at best, is something which it needs but finds troublesome and puzzling. From these attitudes come those of the community and the government. Engineering and science are socially necessary; art is a luxury.[15]

Fortunately, there is reason to hope that the alienation of art from economics will one day be transcended. Rising living standards, increasing economic security and the decline of the myth of the aggressive entrepreneur are all welcome developments, as is the spread of education (which by its very nature, and independent of the subjects actually studied, tends to expand horizons and inculcate new tastes somewhat different from those preferred by the large corporation); and projects such as the Rockefeller Center in New York demonstrate that the American businessman is not congenitally incapable of an aesthetic as well as a commercial response. Furthermore, craftsmanship-intensive firms do even now exist (which, while admittedly producing at higher cost than do their corporate rivals, nonetheless provide an outlet for artistic freedom and expand the range of choice of the connoisseur) and are likely in future to increase in numbers (since products such as handmade jewellery enjoy a high income elasticity of demand: "At some point, as consumption expands, a transcending interest in beauty may be expected"[16]). Finally, the deplorable nature of the alienation of art from economics is bound to be brought home to hard-headed businessmen by the balance of payments argument: preference for quality rather than quantity now causes many American lovers of good things to purchase Danish furniture or Italian ceramics instead of the mass-produced domestic article, proving conclusively that the American failure in the field of design has financial as well as purely aesthetic consequences.

Despite these encouraging tendencies, however, Galbraith is nonetheless convinced that there is no substitute for an expansion in State support to the creative arts. Witness the miracles such patronage has wrought in the Soviet Union: "The cultural life of the great Soviet cities is intense, professional, and interesting. Music, classical ballet, and the traditional stage are all excellent and enthusiastically supported. If some great novels get suppressed, some rather good ones now get published. The universities are large, well attended, and well equipped. The intellectual is a person of prestige."[17] These miracles, Galbraith maintains, are long overdue in the United States.

Advocates of consumer sovereignty will object that Galbraith is being arrogantly élitist in so far as he is proposing to spend public money on goods and services for which the public undeniably does not now vote in the market-place; for traditional economics teaches that "to intervene is to substitute an élitist and snobbish preference for the honest democratic philistinism of the masses".[18] Galbraith, however, because he believes that popular taste can in substantial measure be traced back to producer sovereignty, would reply to the neo-classical economist and the utilitarian that he sees no reason to treat as sacred those desires (say, for toothpaste rather than museums) with which the technostructure has inseminated the consumer; and would in addition draw attention with regret to the absence of countervailing power to be exercised by the artist (who is likely in any case to anticipate an inverse relationship between merit and pecuniary success, and may fear to lobby for support lest compensation prove a threat to talent and performance[19]) on behalf of those desires which for the technostructure serve no function. Hence the case for State action, and specifically for the following.

First, the State should give direct grants and subsidies to the arts. At present State support is heavily biased in favour of applied science and engineering, while the creative arts (being adequately subsidised neither by State nor by technostructure) are left in considerable measure dependent on private benefactors. Such patronage is welcome but it is inadequate.

Second, the state should work via education to counteract the sterility of the technostructure (which *de facto* conditions public opinion against that which it cannot absorb). All education in itself instils a deep and general appreciation for culture and the intellect; but the State should go beyond the mere provision of schools and universities and ensure that adequate scholarships and facilities are available for students wishing to specialise in not only chemical engineering and business mathematics but poetry and music as well.

Third, the State should commission artist and architects to design and decorate buildings in the public sector. This it does not do with any real frequency at the moment: the nature of public works tends to be functional, and the aim to get the project completed cheaply and rapidly (or, as in the 1930s, to create employment). It is, of course, comprehensible that, as long as taxation is a synonym for coercion and State support to the arts a synonym for waste, public building will have to remain inconspicuous rather than ostentatious, efficient rather than aesthetically pleasing. Brazil and Pakistan have built attractive new capitals; and much of the best American architecture in the State sector is represented by her embassies abroad. At home, however, false austerity rules out imaginative projects and dictates that the objective of construction in the public sector should be simply "to enclose the greatest number of bureaucrats at the lowest cost".[20]

Such an obsession with function and cost Galbraith naturally regrets. After all, "the return on a public structure is not merely the task that it facilitates. It is the whole pleasure that it provides the community. Accordingly, a building can be very expensive but a rare bargain for the pleasure it provides."[21] There is more to the Taj Mahal than can be expressed in terms of cost curves and double-entry bookkeeping.

Pleasure, unfortunately, is a highly subjective sensation; and support to the arts is certain to arouse controversy, if only because there is unlikely to be a consensus on standards of beauty. Clearly, "there need be no debate over what building will do its job at the lowest price. This can be calculated. But there is bound to be a debate over what building gives the most pleasure to the public."[22] Controversy is inevitable; but so is State support to the creative arts. Inevitable it may be, but Galbraith's views on support to the arts nonetheless leave three important questions unanswered.

To begin with, there is the question of how much support is to be provided to spheres of activity which at least some members of the general public will regard with cold indifference or even overt hostility. The pensioner or the urban black might not regard a guaranteed salary to painters or a subsidy to build a new opera house with the same enthusiasm as he might higher pensions or better housing; and a stronger case must be made for politicians to disobey the instructions of their constituents in the interests of a high and noble ideal than a straightforward appeal to Galbraith's own preference-patterns (even if one in fact happens to agree with them), implicitly supported by the specialist advice of experts in the field (whose guidance is likely understandably to be value-laden and biased).

Then there is the question of who benefits from support to the arts, an important issue in view of the fact that the audience at a symphony concert is no more representative a cross-section of the national population as a whole than is the audience for a Christian rock group and the choice of what to support is also one of whom. Hence it could be argued that the subsidy paid to a ballet company is unacceptably regressive in its nature (even if one by-product of ballet being subsidised for many rich men is that it will in consequence be available for some poor ones as well) and that the affluent can afford to pay the economic cost of their High Culture in a way which the audience at an experimental pop concert, an open-air folk festival or a socialist fringe theatre might not be able to do. It must also be stressed that the mode of provision itself is important: cultural diversity might be better fostered, for example, by support being directed to subsidised galleries open to all artists and concert halls open to all musicians than predominantly to the artists and the musicians themselves, particularly since where individuals are subsidised directly there is always the danger that the new and the unusual will not be subsidised at all. This possibility Galbraith tends to play down because of his general belief in the non-problematic nature of that which is truly good.

Finally, there is the question of censorship. Galbraith notes that the United States has an advantage over the Soviet Union in

modern literature, theatre, painting, architecture, precisely because there is not in the United States that constraint of dogma and
directive which reduces so much of Soviet art to banality,[23] but he
does not mention that the same constraint could well come into
operation in Western countries were a governing *élite* to arrogate to
itself the right to exercise countervailing power on behalf of beauty.
The liberal ideology that pushpin is as good as poetry (and that the
market researcher rather than the cloistered aesthete or the
Professor is the proper arbiter of taste) at least has the advantage
of generating decentralised decision-making mechanisms.
Galbraith's approach, on the other hand, because it assumes that
the artist who must aim at the popular market will frequently
pander to the lowest common denominator and thereby debase his
art if not protected from his customers by State action, raises the
spectre of centralised monopolistic power. It must be stressed,
however, that the threat of censorship does not necessarily imply the
fact of censorship; and that if an Arts Council did refuse, in the
interests and name of a viable social consensus, to subsidise
revolutionary and anarchist plays advocating the overthrow of the
existing social order, so almost certainly would commercial man-
agements and private businessmen. It is not only the government, in
other words, which is able to exercise effective censorship on the
creative arts.

II. SUPPORT TO THE PLANNING SYSTEM

Galbraith believes that the State has a positive duty to provide
support to the large corporations (there are in the United States
something like 1000–2000 of these) of the planning system, and the
reasons are as follows.

First, the State must finance research and development such as to
encourage a great leap forward in risky areas where there is no
alternative source of funds:

> For the development of atomic energy in the advanced countries,
> there was no alternative to government action. Similarly with
> space exploration. The initial passages to the moon will cost some
> tens of billions of dollars. This will almost certainly discourage the
> average tourist and prevent the business from soon being placed
> on a paying basis. Accordingly, apart from the hideous possibility

of remaining at home, there is no alternative to government-sponsored moon travel. The old-fashioned subsonic jet passenger transport would not have existed except as a by-product of government-sponsored military development. The development of supersonic transport has had to wait on government initiative. One rewarding result of these necessities has been the discovery of how much government initiative is welcomed in a capitalist economy once it is discovered that capitalism cannot do the job.[24]

Many new products and new processes, socially desirable but commercially unattractive, would have been ignored had it not been for the State: "Though no one doubts the vigour with which it addresses itself to travel within the United States, General Motors has little interest in travel through space."[25]

The techniques employed by the State for underwriting technological advance are well-known, and include straightforward research grants (to private industry, research institutes in public or private sector, and the universities), guaranteed markets (say, to the weapons industry, thereby ensuring the security of supply price and quantity demanded so essential for forward planning), and provision of capital, both working (as where the State gives progress payments in advance of completion of a long-term contract) and fixed (as where the State supplies all or part of the plant employed by munitions and other firms). The State, furthermore, is known to be a sympathetic lender of last resort to large firms facing temporary insolvency. The conclusion then follows that "the planning system has a powerful commitment to independence from the state except where public action is required. There is much to the increasingly common observation that the modern economy features socialism for the large corporation, free enterprise for the small."[26]

Second, the State must provide a social infrastructure complementary to the goods and services generated in the private sector, including the planning system. Thus it must supply sufficient educational services to provide adequate skilled manpower (a policy which *de facto* treats the large corporation as a preferred claimant on resources, since it is there that training is most at a premium), and it should not forget that an increasing supply of roads must be forthcoming to accommodate an increasing supply of motor-cars. Besides that, the State must continue to demonstrate its sensitivity to the needs of (if not only of) the powerful through its macroeconomic stabilisation policies: clearly, the security of the technostructure would be threatened by unpredicted fluctuations in sales and earnings (resulting, say, from a sudden and uncompensated rise in household savings), while the growth objective would be frustrated by unexpected spending cuts and other restrictive measures (since only in an expanding economy can all firms taken together be certain of finding markets for their increased output, and only where the trend in expansion is stable can output successfully be planned years in advance).

Third, the State, by the very fact of its intimate relationship with the large corporations, gives the organisation man something he desperately needs and greatly values, namely the sensation of a social mission. Indeed, because over half of American public expenditure is directed towards defence and defence-related projects (including the space programme),[27] the State unambiguously allows the technostructure to rationalise manifest interference with free enterprise in terms of the need for national preparedness and the defence of free enterprise. Such expenditure is adequate and stable, moreover, since it is unchallenged, precisely because of the national security connection, by conservative politicians who would virulently have opposed equivalent public expenditure on schools and hospitals. This means that national security and the security of the mature corporation are closely associated, both on a microeconomic ("for no other products can the technostructure plan with such certainty and assurance"[28]) and on a macroeconomic level ("Military expenditures are what now make the public sector large. Without them the federal government would be roughly half its present size. It is most unlikely that this would exercise the requisite leverage on the private economy."[29]) Such an imbalance in public expenditure can, however, paradoxically, also prove a threat to security, in so far as it ties managerial and technocratic capitalism (and the trade unions) to the arms race and causes it to oppose peaceful coexistence on the grounds of the case for Cold War confrontation; for an ideology of competitive militarism can all too easily lead to a holocaust. Defence-linked projects are a dangerous way of underwriting corporate capitalism (despite the welcome spin-off in the form of, say, peaceful uses of nuclear power, computers and communications satellites) since, "given a sufficient rate of technical progress . . . all the beneficiaries will be dead".[30] This has the effect of "associating great and exciting scientific advances with an atmosphere of fear and even terror",[31] a curious means indeed of enlisting the enthusiasm of organisation men in the service of the community as a whole.

Galbraith believes that State support to the planning system is indispensable, and is critical not of its existence but of its direction. It must continue to provide attractive financial incentives in order to stimulate maximum interest in technological advance (even if more concerned with exploration of space or of the sea-bed, or the study of how to alter the world's weather, and substantially less concerned with the development of advanced weaponry[32]); and it must in future continue to supply inputs complementary to those produced by private enterprise (which means, for example, that while State schooling is to become marginally more humanistic in its orientation, it must nonetheless remain the principal source of trained manpower in the economy). Strikingly merciful to his enemies, Galbraith appears to be calling for a direct transfer of resources *within* the planning system (and specifically, from swords to ploughshares) but not for an overall reduction in the total financial burden on the State which support to the planning system represents. Galbraith, in other words, although he does in some passages perhaps somewhat confusingly appear to juxtapose market poverty to planning affluence (as in the following: "Numerous industries – textiles, shoes, railroads, shipping, machine tools – make or render old-fashioned products or services with obsolete equipment. The developmental energy and capital that might have altered this situation is invested in supersonic fighters, an anti-ballistic missile system and expeditions to the moon, Mars and beyond."[33]), in no way seeks to rob Peter to pay Paul; and clearly intends that additional support to the market system (as indeed to the creative arts and the welfare state) should be new money, not old money newly shared out.

One hopes at least that the money will be well spent, but here again there is some confusion concerning criteria. Should the goal be the optimal allocation of the community's resources, then there is perhaps a case for the natural death of the lame ducks in question, followed by their rebirth in some more viable incarnation; while should the goal be non-economic (say, the preservation of jobs in an organically linked traditional community with a cultural identity rooted deeply in the past), then it should be made clear that the corporation is here to be supported not because it is efficient or technologically progressive but because it is part of a way of life. Whatever the reasons for support, however, they should be clearly

specified if society truly is to benefit from the application of the
social welfare principle of unilateral transfers to the uncharitable
world of industry and trade.

It is not in any case self-evident that the large corporations
already in receipt of State support have benefited quite as much as
Galbraith asserts. Professor Demsetz has tested Galbraith's claim
that the defence industries are optimally suited to planning their
future with certainty because the State is their principal client, and
reports as follows on the prevalence of risk he discovered in the
stock-market behaviour of the relevant shares:

> I analyzed a sample of defense stocks to see what evidence could
> be brought to bear on this claim. The sample contained 13 of the
> top prime defense contractors for whom defense contracts
> accounted for over 30 percent of sales. These stocks over the
> period of 1949–64 offered to investors about 21 percent more risk,
> measured by fluctuations in year-to-year rates of return to
> shareholders, than did randomly selected portfolios of 13 stocks
> per portfolio.[34]

Were such experience to be general, then many a technostructure
could, with justice, demand protection from its friends and call for a
movement towards *laissez-faire* in the interests of job-satisfaction,
security and growth.

III. SUPPORT TO THE MARKET SYSTEM

The modern economy, Galbraith believes, is a dual or bimodal one
in which the members of the market system are price-takers while
the members of the planning system are price-setters, and where the
latter (being large and powerful) are consequently able to dictate
prices (both for inputs and for outputs) to the former (who are small
and weak, and in addition starved of State support). Galbraith
believes that orthodox economic theory, because it does not
recognise the problems inherent in the contemporary imbalance of
power (and, by extension, income and development), is demonstrably irrelevant to the needs of the exploited. He also believes
that State must acknowledge the existence of domestic imperialism
in a wide range of markets; comprehend that there is no automatic
tendency towards equalisation of factor-rewards as between the two

systems; and intervene in the cause of social justice by assisting the disadvantaged to acquire power of their own.

Thus, he argues, the State should itself either perform or finance research and development on behalf of small business. This represents a valuable external economy (particularly since each small farmer or entrepreneur cannot afford his own laboratory, or even to make a modest contribution towards a co-operative effort), and may also lead to the improvement of many vital products (such as low-cost housing, a field in which technological advance is neglected by the technostructure and as a result by the community as a whole). The results of government-sponsored research and development projects should, of course, be made generally available (should not, in other words, be protected by secrecy or patents); and their implementation should be facilitated, in case of need, by State provision of capital and even by State advertising campaigns (say, of milk on behalf of dairy farmers).

Then too, Galbraith argues, the State should lend its support to schemes which seek to improve the bargaining power of the small and the weak (say, by aiding them to form coalitions and cartels, to consolidate and merge, to limit new entry into a trade). Help of this nature is vital, and much has in fact already been forthcoming: witness Federal support to farmers in the form of guaranteed minimum prices, production quotas and State purchases (all of which tend to minimise the impact on the producer of fluctuations in supply and demand and hence his insecurity and uncertainty), or the encouragement accorded to American trade unions by the provisions of the Wagner Act. Further measures along these lines are clearly in the national interest since they help to strengthen the position of the market system as a whole (and of each individual beneficiary within it) and since they thus help to improve the domestic (inter-systemic) terms of trade (by raising the prices charged by small firms relative to those charged by large corporations with pre-existent original power).

The State should not only lend support to the development of countervailing power, but it should also extend general exemption from prosecution under restrictive practices legislation to such positions. It would, for instance, "be broadly in harmony with the distinction between original and countervailing power to exclude labour and farm organizations from prosecution under the antitrust laws".[35] Indeed, this once again has in the United States already been done: the Sherman Act (1890) makes no mention of trade unions, and the Clayton Act (1914) expressly excludes unions and farming co-operatives from sanctions concerning collusive and other restrictive practices. Offsets to original power should naturally be kept under review lest they themselves come to represent anti-social positions with respect to prices and production; but they should not automatically be broken up in the name of competitive markets which today might well prove illusory. It would clearly be nonsensical for the State to encourage banding together on the one hand, while on the other prosecuting organisations which do actually attempt to equalize economic and social power through the collective action of the weak *vis-à-vis* the strong.

Power equalisation is not, of course, simply a domestic problem; and in an open economy it is therefore incumbent on the government to ensure that adequate countervailing power operates internationally as well as at home. On the international scene, the large firm can protect itself through its sheer size and through the possibility of becoming multinational; while the small firm, by contrast, may need State support to its power, in the form of quotas, tariffs and international commodity agreements. These measures are, admittedly, interferences with free trade; but it must be recognised that free trade itself has unwelcome redistributive consequences insofar as the weak tend to suffer more than the strong from the bracing cold shower of international competition. The strong have already escaped from the shackles of the market; it is only just that the weak should now be assisted to do so as well.

The State should help to redress the inter-systemic imbalance of power, but it should not forget to correct the intra-systemic imbalance as well; and should in particular help to buttress positions of weakness *within* the market system, where many of the greatest abuses of power are today to be found. Here Galbraith has four specific proposals to make.

(1) Unionisation
Employees in the market system often have minimal bargaining power because they negotiate as individuals rather than as groups; and the State should therefore give support to unionisation drives (such as that of Cesar Chavez among hired workers in Californian agriculture[36]) in order to generate strong unions capable of carrying out effective negotiations on behalf of their members.

(2) Directive

Workers in the market system are notoriously difficult to unionise (as in the case of agricultural labourers, who are geographically dispersed and often migrant); and hence unionisation programmes should be accompanied by laws specifying minimum notice of dismissal and guaranteeing a reasonable floor income ("The minimum wage is the poor man's union; it serves the same function as a union for the poorest members of the working force"[37]). Furthermore, since many small firms are only able to survive because of the deplorable self-exploitation of the entrepreneur and his own family, Galbraith also recommends a legal ceiling on the hours worked by the self-employed in an attempt to protect the petty capitalist from his own propensity to substitute overwork for efficiency.

(3) Redeployment

Many low-paid jobs are at present performed simply because there is no tolerable alternative. Hence retraining schemes and measures to terminate racial discrimination should be introduced in order to free the prisoners of the market system and permit them, should they wish to do so, to take jobs in the more attractive planning system, and there is a strong case as well for unemployment benefits such as would terminate the practice whereby the market system acts as employer of last resort:

> There is a conflict between the goal of full employment and the unsatisfactory terms on which employment takes place in the weak or self-exploitative parts of the market. I would have some unemployment as the price of maintaining the standards of those who are employed. Unemployment with an adequate guaranteed income may be more civilized than employment with an inadequate one.[38]

For example:

> I remember a year or two ago, at the meeting of the American Economic Association in New Orleans, I was having my shoes shined by an elderly arthritic man at the shoeshine stand across from the hotel. Had he any alternative income, this poor old man would be unemployed. Is this such a bad thing? Instead of having to accept a derogatory form of employment, he would have an

alternative. Such unemployment seems to me desirable. It
confines the employment of people as shoeshine operators to the
number who can be paid a decent wage.[39]

(4) A negative income tax
Many workers will despite unionisation, minimum wage laws,
assisted passages to greener systems and the alternative of gainful
unemployment still be "low paid" (say, by comparison with those in
the planning system); and in order to reduce the effective differential their earnings should be supplemented by means of a negative
income tax. Thus an unemployed man would in consequence of the
subsidy be prepared to accept employment at a low wage and would
know with certainty that idleness will not be better rewarded than
activity: "It is right, as all present proposals provide, that the
individual who works should get more income than the one who
does not. When he takes a job, he should lose some but not all of his
alternative income so that he will always be better off working than
idle."[40]

Looking at Galbraith's proposals concerning support to the
market system, it is clear that not all are advantageous in every
respect. The tariff is an implicit subsidy to non-competitive
domestic producers which leads to higher prices in the shops; while
minimum grain prices ultimately become minimum bread prices (a
state of affairs which would hardly minimise social tensions should
the consumer in practice resent the marriage of high prices and high
taxes or look with horror on the resultant stockpiles that develop as
the result of a policy orientated towards an unknown peasant with
twenty-five acres and a goat). Besides that, it is simply not clear why
Galbraith wishes to help small producers in the market-system, or
why in the absence of public support they would be unable to
compete in the modern economy.

Most controversial of all are Galbraith's proposals to assist the
less-privileged worker. He intends that more extensive unionisation
and/or a statutory minimum wage should narrow the inter-systemic
pay-differential, and this the measures proposed will almost
certainly accomplish. What is likely to happen in addition,
however, is, at least within the confines of a theory of minimum
wages substantially different from the more sophisticated model
presented by Professor Tawney, somewhat less cheering.

First, the burden of higher wages will where possible be passed on to the consumer in the form of higher prices. It is, after all, unlikely that the small, perfect competitor in the market system (in contrast to the large corporation in the planning system) can afford to absorb the entire increase; and it is, moreover, certain that the new union will fight to prevent the small businessman from reducing wages to their minimum levels with the same tenacity that the government displays when it strives to prevent him from putting in excessive overtime and thus exploiting himself through overwork. Yet, as the firm was presumably initially maximising profits, higher prices *ceteris paribus* will then mean "smaller purchases, smaller output and less employment in the market system than would otherwise be the case. This must be accepted."[41] What must be accepted must, of course, be accepted. Few friends of the market system will, however, be entirely happy with measures which threaten to replace the small trader by the large corporation in yet more spheres of economic life; and which challenge the widely-held view that the right to overwork in the interests of job-satisfaction, independence or social approbation (even if the latter only reflects some technostructure-induced "Convenient Social Virtue") are integral parts of the amorphous complex known as individual freedom.

Second, higher nominal wage rates do not mean higher pay where the low-paid in consequence merely experience a change of crisis and become the unemployed. Galbraith does not regard this problem as intractable since, as we have seen, he anticipates that those who lose their jobs in the market system will be offered guaranteed unemployment compensation and retrained for the well-paid planning system (which, moreover, and despite its propensity to prefer machines to men, is apparently eager to receive them); so that the average wage in the economy will gradually rise, while simultaneously workers will no longer be expected to subsidise inefficient employers by accepting low incomes. Yet Galbraith implicitly assumes that all or most workers are capable of acquiring the skills needed for high-productivity, high-income employment; and also that higher pay and lower job satisfaction seldom go together. Casual empiricism suggests that he is wrong.

IV. SUPPORT TO THE WELFARE STATE

Social action costs money, as Galbraith is quick to stress: "There are few problems in New York City which would not be solved by doubling the city budget".[42] When it comes to welfare, he insists, we must stop using "sociology as a substitute for higher taxes".[43] At the same time, he admits, there is considerable reluctance to do this: social services are today underprovided relative to the baubles and trinkets supplied by private enterprise and there consequently exists public poverty amidst private affluence.[44]

The reasons for this imbalance are numerous and include the traditional (if outdated) view that only the private sector can create wealth (a stance which makes roads, parks and schools unproductive, cars, alcohol and school desks productive, since the supply of the latter alone is in response to effective individual demand and thus an indication of genuine expected utility), the truce on inequality (much of taxation being progressive, an expansion in public services has levelling properties on the side of costs which not all advocates of the associated welfare-state benefits would also support), and the absence in the State sector both of consumer-credit and of want-creation. Because of these and other factors, the public lags behind the private sector, and this is unfortunate inasmuch as the case for public spending reposes more on circumstance and necessity than on preference and ideology: many goods and services (for example, refuse collection, law and order, roads, mass education) must be provided for all if they are to be provided for any, and cannot by their very nature adequately be supplied by private enterprise.

Social balance is capable of doing many things which economic growth by itself cannot do at all or else does badly: social insurance can ensure security of income (whereas only a ruinously rapid rate of economic growth could ensure continued full employment embracing even the most marginal members of the labour force), education, retraining, slum clearance and health schemes can combat poverty and inequality of opportunity (whereas economic growth benefits most those who already have most, and least those who are now ill, alcoholic, illiterate or geographically isolated), and it is from greater generosity rather than greater output that aid to developing countries must come (since greater output by itself does not mean greater compassion and might mean greater selfishness). One thing is certain, and that is that economic growth in isolation cannot, in affluent societies, be taken as an indication of social progress: the goods produced are increasingly frivolous and trivial and the wants which they are presumed to satisfy increasingly inculcated by the wiles and deceptions of advertising and salesmanship. This is not an argument for zero growth (rather the opposite: "It will be easier and safer if movement toward greater equality can come gradually as reform rather than abruptly as the result of a quarrel over the division of a fixed product"[45]), simply an assertion that growth by itself is not the solution to all major contemporary social problems: "I'm not saying that increasing prosperity isn't important, but it's clear that this is not a remedy for the distress in our cities."[46]

Galbraith has over time marginally softened his *critique* of increasing prosperity, and this would appear to be a step in the right direction. People do not, after all, as they grow richer, principally purchase the electric toothbrush or the gold-plated mousetrap, but other goods and services towards which it is more difficult to be intolerant (the package holiday abroad, for example, or the pocket calculator); and the socially undesirable side effects of advertising and salesmanship should not be exaggerated in view of the fact that the impact of persuasion is greatest when it is appealing to some fundamental if unexpressed desire which the consumer already experiences (as ascertained via market research) rather than seeking to vend some fantastical new product by means of an extensive and expensive campaign of bamboozlement and mendacity. There must in any case, in a modern democracy, be a presumption that a man who can vote responsibly for political leaders to govern him can also select a tube of toothpaste or a packet of cigarettes without being deceived by the picture of a pretty girl or the recommendation of a famous film-star.

Galbraith assumes that the poor benefit more than the rich from social welfare policies, but it is by no means certain that this will be so. On the side of costs, and while he personally would like to see greater reliance on the progressive income tax, he is prepared to countenance an expansion of the welfare state out of higher indirect taxation, a compromise solution which separates the issue of equality of opportunity from that of equality of income and is in that sense liberal rather than socialist. On the side of benefits, while it is clear that the poor gain disproportionately from some services (notably where selective discrimination is involved, as in Galbraith's proposals for low-cost housing and municipal swimming-pools in the slums), it is less clear that they gain from others (witness the overwhelmingly middle-class clientele of the universities).

More generally, Galbraith couches his recommendations for the welfare state in the somewhat misleading terms of lame-duck socialism (misleading since if the State *ought* to supply medical care, it is still not clear that the private sector *cannot* in any institutional environment in fact satisfactorily do so) and technological determinism (misleading since, although social welfare is taken to be unquestionably good, nonetheless no moral choices involving cohesion and altruism are to be made; and since, while there is understandably little scope for consumer-consultation and self-help schemes in a model which assumes that the experts know best, the absence of success indicators is another matter).

Because of his reliance on the residual supplier argument and his faith in benevolent paternalism, Galbraith never states at what precise point social balance may be said to have been attained. Yet the very concept of balance implies that a community can have too much as well as too little of a good thing. To those selfish tax payers and malintegrated ratepayers who insist that the problem today is public affluence and private poverty, not the opposite, Galbraith has in the last analysis no answer at all beyond the rejoinder that they are wrong.

PART IV

CONCLUSION

8 Adam Smith and Market Capitalism

In an era when doctrinaire acceptance or dogmatic rejection so often replace sincere discussion and reasoned argument, the haunted intellectuality of Adam Smith appears as out of place as Gulliver amongst the Lilliputians; and yet the real importance of Adam Smith is in truth to be found rather in the questions he asked than in the answers he provided. Smith was not unique in associating market capitalism with individual freedom. He was unique, however, in developing a guarded and careful institutionalist approach to market equilibration, anthropocentric rather than reiocentric and dynamic rather than static in nature; and in stressing that price sensitivity is not the only kind of sensitivity that obtains even in the free market place.

It will be the task of this chapter to demonstrate that Adam Smith's greatest relevance to thinkers two centuries after the publication of *The Wealth of Nations* lies rather in his method than in his model. We shall proceed as follows: in Section I we will examine Smith's theory of free markets; in Sections II and III we will look more closely at the supply and demand curves respectively; and in Section IV we will summarise what we regard as Adam Smith's chief contribution to the discussion of market capitalism.

I. THE CASE FOR THE MARKET

Adam Smith believed in the beneficial effects of competition, the profit motive and the free market mechanism, and recommended that matters of business be delegated to businessmen, whose self-interest has the unintended outcome of benefiting the community. In the marketplace, he noted,

> every individual is continually exerting himself to find out the most advantageous employment for whatever capital he can

command. It is his own advantage, indeed, and not that of the society which he has in view. But the study of his own advantage naturally, or rather necessarily leads him to prefer that employment which is most advantageous to the society.[1]

It is as if the businessman were led by an invisible hand to promote group interests while only seeking to further his own, a distinction between manifest and latent functions which optimistically suggests that private vices might turn out to be public virtues. After all, while "the brewer and the baker serve us not from benevolence, but from self love",[2] at least they do serve us and advance our material welfare, and this points to the following general rule:

> The natural effort of every individual to better his own condition, when suffered to exert itself with freedom and security, is so powerful a principle, that it is alone, and without any assistance, not only capable of carrying on the society to wealth and prosperity, but of surmounting a hundred impertinent obstructions with which the folly of human laws too often incumbers its operations.[3]

The fact is that matter has a momentum of its own "altogether different from that which the legislature might choose to impress upon it";[4] and for this reason idealistic "men of system",[5] who like all other confused and misguided fanatics are exposed to "innumerable delusions"[6] in their attempt to lead nature rather than follow her, are doomed to failure. Smith recorded that he had "never known much good done by those who affected to trade for the public good"[7] and recommended the dissolution of interventionist and restrictive institutions, thereby allowing matter to find its own level and nature's laws to be observed in both senses of the word. Smith's example of the "natural price" (defined as "the central price, to which the prices of all commodities are continually gravitating"[8]) illustrates his admiration for "the superior genius and sagacity of Sir Isaac Newton"[9] and reminds us that he regarded trade secrets, collusive arrangements, settlement laws, primogeniture, entails, monopolies granted by charter and statutes of apprenticeship as undesirable impediments to the law of gravity applied to social phenomena.

Once human frustration of natural momentum has been terminated, "the obvious and simple system of natural liberty establishes itself of its own accord",[10] and this development is to be welcomed. For one thing, natural liberty is so pleasing from an aesthetic point of view that utility may indeed be an unintended outcome of the pursuit of beauty: after all, "fitness" and "happy contrivance" are beautiful in themselves, and it is only human nature that "the exact adjustment of the means for attaining any conveniency or pleasure should frequently be more regarded than that very conveniency or pleasure".[11] Moreover, natural liberty is optimally suited to the attainment of the end for which the beautiful and well-oiled machine of human society was designed, as surely the promotion of human happiness as the end for which the watch is intended is "the pointing of the hour".[12]

Just as the perfection of the watch makes us praise the watchmaker, so the smooth functioning of natural liberty increases our respect for Divine benevolence and design. The hand of the Creator is visible at the level of means (witness the key role of instinct, as crucial for economic as for population growth[13]) and also at the level of ends. Smith believed that God's will is to be derived empirically from God's works, often manifested in man's practice, and drew the conclusion that God was opposed to asceticism and the mortification of the flesh: "The happiness of mankind, as well as of all other rational creatures, seems to have been the original purpose intended by the Author of Nature when he brought them into existence",[14] a fact to which all "the works of Nature"[15] testify. Clearly, Smith's plea for the "obvious and simple system of natural liberty" (in place of "preference" and "restraint"[16]) was also a defence of the "Superintendent of the Universe" against the challenge of the "man of system"; and his stress on induction from experience (in place of dependence on "the abstruse syllogisms of a quibbling dialectic"[17]) was also an invitation to trust in God.

If God's goal is human happiness, then there is much to be said for the sensitivity of the market mechanism, as a simple example will demonstrate. Suppose, starting from a position of market equilibrium, that there is a shift outward in the demand curve for a commodity, caused either by a sudden emergency (as where "a public mourning raises the price of black cloth"[18]) or simply a rise in income (in "wealth and wanton luxury"[19]). Competition among would-be consumers of the good drives up prices and profits and stimulates capitalists to transfer their capital from lower-return employments (allowing for non-pecuniary considerations and assuming perfect knowledge of alternative opportunities).[20] New entry and increased competition among would-be sellers lead in turn to a fall in the price of the good and thus increased consumption, since purchasers act as if they face a downward-sloping demand curve.[21] Indeed, the percentage rise in quantity demanded may actually exceed the percentage fall in price (the reason that coal proprietors "find it more for their interest to sell a great quantity at a price somewhat above the lowest, than a small quantity at the highest"[22]). Yet high profits will only induce still more new entrants and encourage still more competition, until ultimately "perfect liberty" leads to the establishment of an "ordinary rate of profit", the lowest with which a mobile and profit-oriented investor "can content himself without being a loser".[23] At that point a new market equilibrium will be established, market signals having brought about a new "natural balance of industry, or a disposition in the people to apply to each species of work precisely in proportion to the demand for that work".[24]

In summary, the "higgling and bargaining of the market" ensures a "rough equality"[25] of value in exchange and an allocation of resources so efficient and so sensitive that it must serve as a shining example to schemers who design wasteful interventionist measures such as the Navigation Laws.[26] There is, all in all, a strong case for nature and market compared with politician and plan.

II. SUPPLY

Adam Smith believed that "the uniform, constant, and uninter-rupted effort of every man to better his condition [is] the principle from which public and national, as well as private opulence is originally derived".[27] What he did not make entirely clear, however, is whence springs that self-love which so powerfully promotes the welfare of the community.

The source might be human nature. Smith argued that men are made of "coarse clay"[28] and have a "base and selfish disposition",[29] and stated categorically that the desire to better our condition "comes with us from the womb, and never leaves us till we go into the grave".[30] A psychological explanation of pecuniary self-love as intrinsic to human nature, however, much understates Smith's conviction that social survival is as important to a sensitive man as physical survival. Man has, Smith believed, "an original desire to please, and an original aversion to offend his brethren",[31] and it is this drive which makes him both a scientist (since observation of habitual associations and the multiplied reactions of our fellow men is the key to social standards of propriety) and a conformist (since our peers love the norm, and "the chief part of human happiness arises from the consciousness of being beloved"[32]). Evidently pecuniary self-love is not to be seen in isolation but is instead to be derived from love of fellowship and "sympathy" (the coincidence of sentiments).

This does not, of course, imply that an individual ought to neglect his material interests. On the contrary, since virtue consists in balance, some "prudence" appears eminently proper when combined with some "benevolence" and some "justice": "Regard to our own private happiness and interest . . . appear upon many occasions very laudable principles of action".[33] The point is simply that self-interest must be constrained by self-control to a degree prescribed by society if we are to escape the proper "hatred or contempt"[34] of our fellows. Thus a money-grubbing wheeler-dealer might become rich, but he would also be condemned for putting excess before moderation and made to feel rejected, an outsider, a hideous specimen (since aesthetic pleasure is related to "whatever we have been used to"[35] in a particular breed as seen through a particular social looking-glass). And even if others were unaware of his failing, the Don Juan of the business world would still himself suffer from a guilty conscience and spoiled identity (becoming as he would "the object of his own hatred and abhorrence"[36]). The fact is that men desire "not only praise, but praise-worthiness, or to be that thing which, though it should be praised by nobody, is, however, the natural and proper object of praise",[37] at least at a particular time and in a particular place.

Basically, the self-interested businessman, should he want sympathy for his passion, has no choice but to "flatten . . . the sharpness of its natural tone, in order to reduce it to harmony and concord with the emotions of those who are about him".[38] His primary objective is neither riches (although utility may be an unintended outcome of propriety) nor applause (since the real spectator is often biased or misinformed), but to win the entire approbation of the impartial spectator (who knows the whole truth about the individual's motivations and society's standards of right and wrong) by prospering with propriety. The businessman tries to see himself as others see him and to act the part others expect of him, for he knows that mankind tends to respect those who approach the mean type of conduct associated with each calling and to censure deviation: "We expect in each rank and profession a degree of those manners which, experience has taught us, belonged to it. . . . A man, we say, should look like his trade and profession."[39] *What is* acquires the force of *what ought to be* as norms are internalised: "Our continual observations upon the conduct of others insensibly lead us to form to ourselves certain general rules concerning what is fit and proper either to be done or to be avoided".[40]

A businessman acts as a businessman habitually does in a given society lest he render himself "the proper object of the contempt and indignation"[41] of the collectivity. Curiously, however, the behaviour patterns to which he conforms are also uniquely appropriate to one in his station; for "the objects with which men in the different professions and states of life are conversant being very different, and habituating them to very different passions, naturally form in them very different characters and manners".[42] We have here a case of existence, not essence; of man in situation rather than the cult of the individual; of economic determinism rather than the unfolding of innate gifts. We have here a case where society takes a malleable lump of wax and moulds it into the shape that the group not only by tradition is used to seeing but also needs; a case of co-ordination not through the price-mechanism but through the work-function, since a man's character is more the result than the cause of the way in which he earns a living. None of us is likely to have a useless or improper essence precisely because what we are seems to arrive *post festum*.

Consider some examples. Indolence and extravagance are both natural and proper in a nobleman (whose mind seldom faces any challenge save possibly "to figure at a ball' or "to succeed in an intrigue of gallantry"[43] and whose revenue renews itself year after year without any effort on his part[44]); abstract contemplation and severe gravity in a clergyman (whose mind is continually focused on the "awful futurity"[45] facing man); dissolution in a soldier (whose pay is unrelated to effort[46] and who is in any case never far from death[47]); "hardness of character"[48] in a customs inspector. The work-function also renders the factory-operative "stupid and ignorant"[49] due to overconcentration on a single repetitive operation and the absence of intellectual challenge.[50]

The general rule is this: "The understandings of the greater part of men are necessarily formed by their ordinary employments".[51] Applied to the businessman, this rule helps to explain that industry and trade naturally form in him habits of "order, œconomy and attention"[52] and "probity and prudence"[53] (but unfortunately also vices such as "mean rapacity"[54] and "avarice and ambition",[55] perhaps to be expected in an insecure social climber whose income and position depend on nothing but "the labour of his body and the activity of his mind"[56]). Such a man has no time for political responsibilities; is cold but correct in personal relationships; avoids excessive risks. He is able to evaluate new investments carefully; and "if he enters into any new projects or enterprises, they are likely to be well concerted and well prepared".[57] Businessmen are honest and "faithful to their word",[58] since at all times "a dealer is afraid of losing his character".[59] They seek out "new divisions of labour and new improvements of art"[60] in order to squeeze "as great a quantity of work as possible"[61] from a given quantity of input, for they know that they can "justle" existing competitors out of a trade "by no other means but by dealing upon more reasonable terms".[62]

In short, the conditions of the business life "breed and form"[63] habits of frugality, industry and self-sacrifice, as these are the preconditions for adaptation to a particular environment. A man does not become a businessman because he is frugal and honest but is made frugal and honest by his job, since a merchant indulging excessively in "liberality, frankness, and good fellowship"[64] would soon be ruined and thus no longer a merchant at all. Clearly, if citizens of a mercantile commonwealth typically are to be recognised by their "narrowness, meanness, and selfish disposition",[65] they are not to blame: such conduct, as we have seen, has "a propriety independent of custom".[66]

Since work makes men, it is understandable that Smith viewed the classes associated with the State with great reservation. Competition among politicians is likely to mould an "insidious and crafty animal",[67] forced to intrigue and scheme by a frantic and factious environment where ambition is likely to get out of hand.[68] And the bureaucrat is apathetic and inefficient because of lack of challenge and incentive. On the Crown lands revenue is low in large measure because of bad management, the "abusive management" of "idle and profligate bailiffs",[69] the "negligent, expensive, and oppressive management" of "factors and agents".[70] There is little incentive to maximise revenues in which one has no share,[71] and Smith made clear that bureaucrats are not at fault for acting as their situation naturally directs: his censure was directed toward "the situation in which they are placed", not "the character of those who have acted in it".[72] At the same time, a healthier situation should be created, not least by selling off the Crown lands to industrious farmers whose private interest in productivity corresponds to that of the nation.

As it happens, however, bureaucracy is not purely a problem of the public sector. In the private sector the South Sea Company, for example, like the East India Company, had suffered from "the loss occasioned by the negligence, profusion, and malversation of the servants of the company".[73] The problem arose because it had an "immense capital divided among an immense number of proprietors",[74] few of them able to understand the Company's business, all of them willing simply to "receive contentedly such half yearly or yearly dividend, as the directors think proper to make to them".[75] The owners did not exercise the necessary "vigilance and attention" to prevent "wasting", "embezzling", "disorderly conduct",[76] "folly" and "depredations"[77] on the part of their managers, and it was only natural that those managers chose to turn a sick situation to their own advantage: "The directors of such companies . . . being the managers rather of other people's money than of their own, it cannot well be expected, that they should watch over it with the same anxious vigilance with which the partners in a private copartnery frequently watch over their own."[78]

Business requires "such an unremitting exertion of vigilance and attention, as cannot long be expected from the directors of a joint stock company".[79] Here free trade is the answer, for Smith believed such companies (having no genuine economies of scale and considerable diseconomies due to the indifference of managers) only survived because of monopolies artificially created by charter. Free trade means the reversal of the managerial revolution and the replacement of salaried bureaucrats by wide-awake entrepreneurs, a process from which the nation as a whole cannot but gain.

With hindsight, it is clear that Smith underestimated the future of the corporation. He did note that some industries (iron-works,[80] coal-mines,[81] the silk industry,[82] the capital goods industry[83]) were fixed-capital intensive and expensive to enter; but apparently regarded industrial economies of scale (together with the cost of large-scale enterprise, probably beyond the purse of the owner–operator) as the exception rather than the rule and tended to apply the model of the small-scale corn merchant to industry as well as trade. Then, too, he also believed that, while the business of invention and innovation was clearly passing from the worker to a new class of specialists (a "very few people"[84] whose trade it is "not to do any thing, but to observe every thing"[85]), the brains of this technostructure could nonetheless be bought in without making research and development a fixed cost to the firm.

Naturally, Smith would have wanted to re-think the role of the State in a world of economies of scale (if only because a smaller number of firms can more easily indulge in "a conspiracy against the public"[86] to raise prices in the absence of social regulation of restrictive practices) and corporate bureaucracies similar in goals and structure to the civil service. After all, he was not hostile to the State on principle, and noted that in some foreign republics State enterprise had proved a success: witness the fact that the government of Berne did a flourishing trade in loans to other states[87] and the government of Hamburg ran a public pawn-shop, wine-cellar, apothecary and bank.[88] The problem was not simply government in general, but the British government in particular; for whereas the administrators of Venice and Amsterdam had proven themselves "orderly, vigilant, and parsimonious",[89] the British government had typically demonstrated "slothful and negligent profusion".[90] Historically speaking, England had "never been blessed with a very parsimonious government",[91] but had been saddled with leaders showing more of the idleness and indolence,[92] the dissolution of manners,[93] the wastefulness[94] of the landed classes than the parsimony and industry of the merchant. Moreover, the British government had come under the influence of vested interests offering biased advice: clearly it was not a nation of shopkeepers but "a nation whose government is influenced by shopkeepers"[95] that had instituted the Mercantile system at the expense of their countrymen (thereby proving yet again that greedy peddlars "neither are, nor ought to be, the rulers of mankind"[96]). In Britain, weak leaders misinformed about trade had in the past been all too often swayed by "the passionate confidence of interested falsehood"[97] to "warp the positive laws of the country from what natural justice would prescribe"[98]; and even the political balance of powers (represented by the fact that the House of Commons had been absolute in money bills since 1688[99]), while desirable in itself, would not make State regulation an adequate substitute for the market and the law of gravity.

Even for a country such as Britain, however, Smith did envisage a role for State intervention, not just in ensuring defence and justice but in providing public works where social exceed private benefits (say; in aiding the education industry to teach the masses "the elementary parts of geometry and mechanics", so useful to productivity in any "common trade"[100] if still not an antidote to the occupational hazard of "mental mutilation"[101]). He also recommended that the State use its powers of discriminatory taxation for gentle social engineering, albeit *via* the market: hence he advised *ad valorem* taxation rather than taxes on bulk (since precious commodities are often light[102]) and a highway toll levied most heavily on luxury carriages (to penalise "the indolence and vanity of the rich"[103]). And he advocated nationalisation of the postal system.[104]

Perhaps in a more parsimonious and balanced commonwealth Smith would have proposed a greater role for the State in economic affairs. It is only fair to note, however, that the foreign republics he singled out for praise were not only characterised by a good balance of power between hereditary and mercantile classes, but also by a total lack of popular participation. Smith feared the "thoughtless extravagance"[105] of democracies; believed that a man with a mutilated mind is likely to be deceived by "quacks and imposters"[106] (although the mob had of course been able to play an intelligent part in the primitive democracies of hunting societies anterior to the division of labour[107]); and was convinced that the *canaille* prefer paternalistic to representative government in any case.[108] Such élitism was common currency in the eighteenth century. It is unlikely to be common currency today.

III. DEMAND

Adam Smith was in no doubt that economics is about scarcity and stressed the need to provide "a plentiful revenue or subsistence for the people".[109] He announced that "the riches of a country consist in the plenty and cheapness of provisions"[110] and made a growing supply of goods and services (along with provision of revenue for the State) one of the twin goals he proposed for political economy.[111]

Smith also believed that the problem of scarcity was on the way to being solved. He noted that nowadays economic activity is often oriented towards satisfying "many insignificant demands, which we by no means stand in need of",[112] and implied that even the lower classes now participate in the affluent society (since wages are clearly above subsistence).[113] This does not, of course, mean that such luxuries ought not to be consumed. While Smith noted that the "great wants of mankind" (for food, clothing and housing)[114] are so modest that they can be satisfied "by the unassisted labour of the individual"[115] even without the division of labour, he hardly adopted a puritanical attitude towards cultural needs over and above "the gratification of the bodily appetites".[116] On the contrary, he stressed that consumer preferences are not random but laid down by society, and that men thus have a positive duty to observe the customary proprieties: "When we say that a man is worth fifty or a hundred pounds a-year . . . we mean commonly to ascertain what is or *ought to be* his way of living, or the quantity and quality of the necessaries and conveniencies of life in which he can *with propriety* indulge himself".[117]

Obedience to social norms concerning the habitual association of subject and symbol substantially restricts the freedom of choice. In the case of dress, for example, custom has in England rendered leather shoes a necessity for both sexes and all classes (although not in Scotland or France),[118] and an Englishman afraid of mockery and anxious to win "the entire approbation of the impartial spectator"[119] would also be well advised to wear a linen shirt;[120] for truly "a man would be ridiculous who should appear in public with a suit of clothes quite different from those which are commonly worn, though the new dress should in itself be ever so graceful or convenient".[121] Clearly "grace" and "convenience" are inadequate to explain choice without reference to "the peculiar manners and customs of the people".[122] In such a world, social facts are to be explained by other social facts and individuals are seen to behave in a manner both predictable and aesthetically pleasing out of a love of social survival: obviously no sensitive man wants to be as ridiculous, as out of place, as a sow in a drawing-room or Gulliver amongst the Lilliputians.[123]

Smith was thus concerned with relative rather than absolute deprivation, for he identified commodities largely as socially-prescribed status symbols. He recorded that "with the greater part of rich people, the chief enjoyment of riches consists in the parade of riches";[124] and implied that it is the desire for increased conspicuous consumption that causes a man to sacrifice still more of "his ease, his liberty, and his happiness"[125] in order to obtain still more command over commodities (for a poor man simply cannot afford to buy the expensive status symbols of a higher social station).

Smith recognised that people want goods. He was not, however, convinced that people need them. Students schooled in the textbook theory of consumer sovereignty will be shocked by his arrogant dismissal of many effectively-demanded commodities as "trifling",[126] "frivolous",[127] "contemptible",[128] "childish",[129] by his intolerance towards "trinkets and baubles",[130] by his cavalier rejection of the verdict of the market whenever it offended his philosophical sensibilities. Students trained in the inductivist approach to total demand will be astonished by his stoic apathy and his refusal to identify increased commodity consumption with increased human happiness: "Happiness and misery . . . reside altogether in the mind",[131] he argued, and observed that "the beggar, who suns himself by the side of the highway, possesses that security which kings are fighting for".[132] This suggests that, since there is little difference between one permanent situation and another, the obvious solution to the problem of scarcity is not to increase supply but to reduce demand. After all, for most men work is unpleasant (even Oxford dons face an upward-sloping supply curve for labour,[133] and this would not be the case if their duties were as enjoyable as, say, hunting and fishing[134]); and it hardly seems worthwhile to sacrifice one's energy, one's tranquillity, one's peace of mind, if at the end of the day one can but fall back exhausted on the blissful banks of a mirage.

Clearly, since he believed that for most men "consumption is the sole end and purpose of all production"[135] and since he also believed that consumption is without any doubt a "deception",[136] it follows that Smith could have recommended repose rather than change. He chose not to do so, however, for two reasons: first, because he recognised, as a scientist, that the philosopher cannot turn the acquisitive society on its head simply by propounding his own opinions while ignoring the momentum inherent in matter, and, second, because he in fact welcomed the social dynamism that industry put in motion. After all, by producing commodities men produce institutions as well; and Smith, a believer in social progress, was convinced that the latent function of the "deception" of commodity-utility was likely to be major social change which the philosopher could contemplate with the utmost pleasure. He hoped, in other words, via the free market mechanism, to harness the stallion of economic determinism to the plough of social reform. Seldom has so massive an attempt at social engineering been more skilfully presented or more carefully concealed, as will be evident from an example of the way in which Smith believed demand-led growth could act as the motor of social progress: the resounding defeat of the Roman Catholic Church.

In the Middle Ages the Church, like any other great landowner, maintained private armies out of its agricultural surplus, and it deployed them according to "one uniform plan"[137] as ordered by "one man".[138] The concentrated monolithic, monopolistic, multi-national power of the Church made it "the most formidable combination that ever was formed against the authority and security of civil government, as well as against the liberty, reason, and happiness of mankind".[139] Fortunately, the market is the enemy of the Pope. To begin with, the introduction of an exchange economy (emanating in the first instance from the mercantile ports[140]) meant that clerics, like secular landowners, began to use the surplus for their own "vanity, luxury, and expence"[141] rather than waste it on retainers and charity. This weakened their military might and also alienated the masses who, "provoked and disgusted",[142] were ready to be plucked by even "the most ignorant enthusiast".[143] Then too, not only did the market pave the way for Reformation by undermining the power and prestige of the clergy, but it provided a model for the future. Smith proposed that there should not in a country be one Church but "two or three hundred, or perhaps . . . as many thousand small sects",[144] all competing for customers. In a situation of perfect competition such sects are bound to gravitate towards a natural price, "that pure and rational religion" which wise men have always and everywhere "wished to see established";[145] whereas oligopolists are likely to employ "all the terrors of religion"[146] and the "grossest delusions"[147] in order to consolidate and expand business (as the examples of France[148] and Ireland[149] indicate). Finally, market capitalism is responsible for "order and good government"[150] and economic growth; and both security and freedom from want are essential if men are to be set free from "pusillanimous superstition"[151] and directed towards experiment, observation and induction of God's will from the study of God's works.

Such institutional change, however desirable, is not obtained without a cost, since demand-led growth implies a double veil of tears. Men sacrifice themselves first at the stage of production and then at the stage of consumption, and never grasp that the economic weapon is only the motor of progress so long as they do not see that it is powered by a "deception". Manipulation via demand-led growth is more powerful than manipulation by advertising and more successful than manipulation by politicians, precisely because it is the most hidden of the hidden persuaders.

IV. CONCLUSION

Adam Smith's relevance to the modern reader is to be found more in his method than in his model, and specifically in the following features of his approach.

First, a stress on the momentum inherent in matter (which in the economic sphere could be respected by a system of free enterprise, perfect competition, political *laissez-faire* and market pricing based on conditions of supply and demand) and a warning that it is virtually impossible save by induction from unfettered experience for man to derive knowledge about mechanistic forces, natural laws and positions of equilibrium.

Second, a belief that economy, society and polity ought to be studied together as mutually determinant within the framework of a large-scale interdisciplinary systemic whole; a conviction that even Economic Man must be seen as a social animal; a sociologist's awareness of conventions, status-groups, classes (as in his more corporatist than individualist attitudes to consumer behaviour and character patterns).

Third, a theory of social causality based on a marriage between the assumption of sensitivity (that men record group standards of propriety and then conform to these norms so as to deserve approbation in the process of human interaction) and the postulate of malleability (that human nature is basically wax or clay, to be moulded by the invisible hand of economic determinism).

Fourth, a normative as well as a positive dimension imposed by the simple fact that a vote for the market is also a vote for massive social change in a world where reality is not static but dynamic and the observer is compelled to regard the present as but a moment in history; and thus a philosophical orientation imposed by the need to choose between two social matrices.

Fifth, a recognition of overdevelopment as well as of under-development and a hint that the price of progress can be measured in units such as the mental mutilation of the factory operative, the spread of commodity hedonism, the triumph of utility over sensitivity and propriety, the universality of a base and selfish disposition, excessive ambition, the decay of martial virtues. To this list we might wish to add the problems of seller-manipulation, corporate government and oligopolistic distortion (for a theory of markets need not be a *Loblied* to private enterprise, and in the case of Adam Smith most assuredly was not).

Adam Smith did not adequately explore the question of overdevelopment, partly because the problems with which he was more immediately concerned lay far to the other side of the Golden Mean, partly because he, like the rest of us, did not and could not have all the answers. Perhaps today, however, that which was to Smith *obiter dictum* has become to us *sine qua non*. If so, then in any future discussion of the relationship between men and things, between society and economy, between State and Welfare, there is no better example to follow than that of the haunted intellectuality of Adam Smith.

Reference Notes

2. CULTURE AND CONDITION

1. R. H. Tawney, *Equality* (1931) (London: George Allen & Unwin Ltd., 1964), p. 82.
2. *Equality*, p. 81.
3. *Equality*, p. 40.
4. *Equality*, p. 40.
5. *Equality*, p. 85.
6. *Equality*, p. 108.
7. *Equality*, p. 108.
8. *Equality*, p. 43.
9. "Christanity and the Social Revolution" (1935), in R. H. Tawney, *The Attack and Other Papers* (London: George Allen & Unwin Ltd., 1953), pp. 160, 161.
10. *Equality*, p. 43.
11. *Equality*, p. 43.
12. *Equality*, p. 113.
13. *Equality*, p. 113.
14. "An Experiment in Democratic Education" (1914), in R. H. Tawney, *The Radical Tradition*, ed. by Rita Hinden (abbreviated to *RT*) (Harmondsworth: Penguin Books, 1966), p. 76.
15. "Social Democracy in Britain" (1949), in *RT*, pp. 145–6.
16. "A Note on Christianity and the Social Order" (1937), in *The Attack*, p. 170.
17. "A Note on Christianity and the Social Order", in *The Attack*, p. 182.
18. "A Note on Christianity and the Social Order", in *The Attack*, p. 190.
19. "A Note on Christianity and the Social Order", in *The Attack*, p. 188.
20. "A Note on Christianity and the Social Order", in *The Attack*, p. 184.
21. "A Note on Christianity and the Social Order", in *The Attack*, pp. 176–7.
22. "A Note on Christianity and the Social Order", in *The Attack*, p. 173.
23. "A Note on Christianity and the Social Order", in *The Attack*, pp. 182, 181.
24. "A Note on Christianity and the Social Order", in *The Attack*, p. 183.
25. "A Note on Christianity and the Social Order", in *The Attack*, pp. 183–4.
26. "Christianity and the Social Revolution", in *The Attack*, p. 163n.
27. "Christianity and the Social Revolution", in *The Attack*, p. 164.
28. "Christianity and the Social Revolution", in *The Attack*, p. 164.
29. "Christianity and the Social Revolution", in *The Attack*, p. 165.
30. "Christianity and the Social Revolution", in *The Attack*, p. 165.
31. "Christianity and the Social Revolution", in *The Attack*, pp. 165–6.
32. "British Socialism Today" (1952), in *RT*, p. 176.
33. "Christianity and the Social Revolution", in *The Attack*, p. 166.
34. "The Choice before the Labour Party" (1934), in *The Attack*, p. 66.

35. "The Choice before the Labour Party", in *The Attack*, p. 57.
36. "The Choice before the Labour Party", in *The Attack*, p. 64.
37. "The Choice before the Labour Party", in *The Attack*, pp. 57–8.
38. "The Choice before the Labour Party", in *The Attack*, p. 63.
39. "The Choice before the Labour Party", in *The Attack*, p. 58.
40. R. Terrill, *R. H. Tawney and His Times* (Cambridge, Massachusetts: Harvard University Press, 1973), p. 247.
41. J. M. Winter and D.M. Joslin (eds.), *R. H. Tawney's Commonplace Book* (abbreviated to *CB*) (Cambridge: Cambridge University Press, 1972), p. 53. Italics mine.
42. *CB*, p. 54.
43. *CB*, p. 67. Italics mine.
44. *CB*, p. 9.
45. *CB*, pp. 53–4.
46. R. H. Tawney, *The Western Political Tradition* (London: SCM Press, 1949), p. 18.
47. *The Western Political Tradition*, p. 19.
48. *The Western Political Tradition*, p. 15.
49. *The Western Political Tradition*, p. 16.
50. *The Western Political Tradition*, p. 17.
51. *The Western Political Tradition*, pp. 16–17.
52. *CB*, pp. 78, 79. Italics mine.
53. *The Western Political Tradition*, p. 18.
54. R. H. Tawney, *Religion and the Rise of Capitalism* (1926) (abbreviated to *RRC*) (Harmondsworth: Penguin Books, 1977), p. 229.
55. R. H. Tawney, "Introduction" to M. Beer, *A History of British Socialism*, 1, (London: G. Bell & Sons, Ltd., 1919), p. xvii.
56. R. H. Tawney, "Max Weber and the Spirit of Capitalism" (1930), in J. M. Winter (ed.), *History and Society: Essays by R. H. Tawney* (London: Routledge & Kegan Paul Ltd., 1978), p. 195.
57. "The Study of Economic History" (1933), in *History and Society*, pp. 59–60.
58. "Max Weber and the Spirit of Capitalism", in *History and Society*, p. 196.
59. "Max Weber and the Spirit of Capitalism", in *History and Society*, p. 192.
60. "Max Weber and the Spirit of Capitalism", in *History and Society*, p. 195.
61. *RRC*, p. 125.
62. *RRC*, p. 123.
63. *RRC*, p. 101.
64. *RRC*, p. 225.
65. R. H. Tawney, "Introduction" to J. P. Mayer, *Political Thought: The European Tradition* (London: J. M. Dent & Sons Ltd., 1939), pp. vi–vii.
66. "Introduction" to Beer, *A History*, p. xvii.
67. "Introduction" to Mayer, *Political Thought*, p. vii.
68. *The Western Political Tradition*, p. 17.
69. *RRC*, p. 245.
70. *RRC*, p. 245.
71. *RRC*, p. 26.
72. *RRC*, p. 26.
73. *RRC*, pp. 271–2.
74. "Introduction" to Mayer, *Political Thought*, p. xviii.

75. "Introduction" to Mayer, *Political Thought*, p. xix.
76. *CB*, p. 66.
77. *CB*, p. 76.
78. *CB*, p. 50.
79. *CB*, p. 12.
80. *CB*, p. 12.
81. *CB*, p. 12.
82. *CB*, p. 13.
83. *CB*, p. 13.
84. *CB*, p. 17.
85. "Social History and Literature" (1950), in *RT*, p. 206.
86. "Devon and Dr. Hoskins" (1954), in *History and Society*, p. 219.
87. *CB*, p. 11.
88. *CB*, p. 14.
89. *CB*, p. 14.
90. *RRC*, p. 32.
91. *CB*, p. 67.
92. *Equality*, p. 224.
93. "Introduction" to Mayer, *Political Thought*, p. vi
94. *The Western Political Tradition*, p. 7.
95. "Introduction" to Mayer, *Political Thought*, p. xvi.
96. "Introduction" to Mayer, *Political Thought*, p. vi.
97. "Introduction" to Mayer, *Political Thought*, p. xiii.
98. *CB*, p. 53.
99. *CB*, p. 53.
100. *CB*, p. 25.
101. *CB*, p. 25.
102. *CB*, p. 25.
103. *The Western Political Tradition*, p. 9.
104. "Introduction" to Mayer, *Political Thought*, p. ix.
105. *The Western Political Tradition*, p. 9.
106. *The Western Political Tradition*, pp. 9–10.
107. "Introduction" to Mayer, *Political Thought*, p. viii.
108. *The Western Political Tradition*, p. 15.
109. *RRC*, p. 18.
110. *Equality*, p. 47.
111. *Equality*, p. 50.
112. "A Note on Christianity and the Social Order", in *The Attack*, p. 183.
113. *Equality*, p. 86.
114. *Equality*, pp. 49–50.
115. *Equality*, p. 235.
116. *Equality*, p. 59.
117. *Equality*, p. 60.
118. *Equality*, p. 60.
119. *Equality*, p. 62.
120. *Equality*, p. 63.
121. *Equality*, p. 63.
122. *Equality*, p. 64.
123. *Equality*, p. 61.

124. *Equality*, p. 58.
125. *Equality*, p. 196.
126. *Equality*, p. 69.
127. *Equality*, p. 69.
128. "British Socialism Today", in *RT*, p. 181.
129. *Equality*, p. 72.
130. "British Socialism Today", in *RT*, p. 185.
131. *Equality*, p. 86.
132. *Equality*, p. 38.
133. *Equality*, p. 77.
134. "The Problem of the Public Schools" (1943), in *RT*, p. 65.
135. *Equality*, p. 96.
136. *Equality*, p. 103.
137. *Equality*, p. 104.
138. *Equality*, p. 103.
139. *Equality*, p. 110.
140. *Equality*, p. 159.
141. *Equality*, p. 75.
142. *Equality*, pp. 69–70.
143. "The Conditions of Economic Liberty" (1918), in *RT*, p. 107.
144. *Equality*, p. 166.
145. *Equality*, p. 172.
146. *Equality*, p. 172.
147. *Equality*, p. 191.
148. *Equality*, p. 70.
149. *Equality*, p. 167.
150. *Equality*, p. 37.
151. *Equality*, p. 42.
152. *Equality*, p. 37.
153. *Equality*, p. 37.
154. *Equality*, p. 74.
155. *Equality*, p. 80.
156. "The Choice before the Labour Party", in *The Attack*, p. 67.
157. *CB*, p. 55.
158. "Introduction" to Mayer, *Political Thought*, p. xxi.
159. *CB*, p. 70.
160. *CB*, p. 13.
161. *CB*, p. 70.
162. *CB*, p. 40.
163. *CB*, p. 40.
164. *CB*, p. 37.
165. R. H. Tawney, "Poverty as an Industrial Problem" (1913), in R. H. Tawney, *The American Labour Movement and Other Essays*, ed. by J. M. Winter (Brighton: The Harvester Press, 1979), p. 112.
166. "Poverty as an Industrial Problem", in *The American Labour Movement*, p. 113.
167. "Poverty as an Industrial Problem", in *The American Labour Movement*, pp. 112–3.
168. "Poverty as an Industrial Problem", in *The American Labour Movement*, p. 114.
169. "Poverty as an Industrial Problem", in *The American Labour Movement*, p. 119.

170. "Poverty as an Industrial Problem", in *The American Labour Movement*, p. 115.
171. "Poverty as an Industrial Problem", in *The American Labour Movement*, p. 116.
172. *CB*, p. 61.
173. *CB*, p. 65.

3. THE WELFARE SOCIETY

1. "The Rise of the Gentry, 1558–1640" (1941), in *History and Society*, p. 99.
2. "Harrington's Interpretation of His Age" (1941), in *History and Society*, p. 71.
3. *Equality*, p. 196.
4. "Introduction" to Mayer, *Political Thought*, p. xiv.
5. *Equality*, p. 87.
6. *Equality*, p. 81.
7. *Equality*, p. 40.
8. *Equality*, p. 113.
9. *Equality*, p. 113.
10. *Equality*, p. 150.
11. R. H. Tawney, *The Acquisitive Society* (1921) (abbreviated to *AS*) (London: Collins, 1961), p. 38.
12. *AS*, p. 39.
13. *Equality*, p. 27.
14. AS, p. 177.
15. *Equality*, p. 134.
16. *Equality*, p. 135.
17. *Equality*, p. 136.
18. *Equality*, p. 133.
19. *Equality*, p. 122.
20. *Equality*, p. 123.
21. *Equality*, p. 124.
22. *Equality*, p. 125.
23. *Equality*, p. 125.
24. *Equality*, p. 126.
25. *Equality*, p. 127.
26. *Equality*, p. 126.
27. *Equality*, p. 154.
28. *Equality*, p. 154.
29. *Equality*, p. 139.
30. *Equality*, p. 155.
31. *Equality*, p. 139.
32. *Equality*, p. 140.
33. *Equality*, p. 155.
34. "Social Democracy in Britain", in *RT*, p. 157.
35. *AS*, p. 146.
36. "The Conditions of Economic Liberty", in *RT*, p. 110.
37. "The Problem of the Public Schools", in *RT*, p. 64.
38. *Equality*, p. 43.
39. *Equality*, p. 27.
40. *Equality*, p. 52.

41. *Equality*, p. 106.
42. *Equality*, p. 116.
43. "A Note on Christianity and the Social Order", in *The Attack*, p. 184.
44. *Equality*, p. 106.
45. "A National College of All Souls" (1917), in *The Attack*, p. 32.
46. "A National College of All Souls", in *The Attack*, p. 30.
47. "A National College of All Souls", in *The Attack*, p. 30.
48. "A National College of All Souls", in *The Attack*, p. 32.
49. "Some Reflections of a Soldier" (1916), in *The Attack*, p. 25.
50. "A National College of All Souls", in *The Attack*, pp. 29–30.
51. "The Conditions of Economic Liberty", in *RT*, p. 102.
52. "The Conditions of Economic Liberty", in *RT*, p. 104. Italics mine.
53. "The WEA and Adult Education" (1953), in *RT*, pp. 87–8.
54. *Equality*, p. 145.
55. "The Problem of the Public Schools", in *RT*, pp. 58–9.
56. "The Problem of the Public Schools", in *RT*, p. 65.
57. "The Problem of the Public Schools", in *RT*, p. 63–4.
58. "The Problem of the Public Schools", in *RT*, p. 62.
59. *Equality*, p. 144.
60. "The Problem of the Public Schools", in *RT*, p. 72.
61. *Equality*, p. 145.
62. "The Problem of the Public Schools", in *RT*, p. 63.
63. "The Problem of the Public Schools", in *RT*, p. 63.
64. *Equality*, p. 146.
65. *Equality*, p. 146.
66. *Equality*, p. 148.
67. *Equality*, p. 148.
68. *Equality*, p. 148.
69. *Equality*, p. 148.
70. "A Note on Christianity and the Social Order", in *The Attack*, p. 169.
71. "The Nationalization of the Coal Industry" (1919), in *RT*, pp. 128–9.
72. "The Nationalization of the Coal Industry", in *RT*, p. 127.
73. *Equality*, p. 120.
74. *Equality*, p. 186.
75. *Equality*, p. 187.
76. *Equality*, p. 188.
77. *Equality*, p. 205.
78. "British Socialism Today", in *RT*, p. 186.
79. *Equality*, p. 157.
80. *AS*, p. 69.
81. R. M. Titmuss, *Essays on 'The Welfare State'*, 2nd edition (London: George Allen & Unwin Ltd., 1963), p. 39.
82. R. M. Titmuss, *Commitment to Welfare* (London: George Allen & Unwin Ltd., 1968), p. 150.
83. R. M. Titmuss, *The Gift Relationship* (Harmondsworth: Penguin Books, 1973), p. 17.
84. Titmuss, *Essays*, p. 109.
85. Terrill, *op. cit.*, p. 67.
86. *Ibid*, p. v.

87. "The Study of Economic History", in *History and Society*, p. 48.
88. "The Study of Economic History", in *History and Society*, p. 49.
89. "Beatrice Webb, 1858–1943" (1943), in *The Attack*, p. 105.
90. R. H. Tawney, *The Establishment of Minimum Rates in the Chain-Making Industry under the Trade Boards Act of 1909* (London: G. Bell & Sons Ltd., 1914), p. xi.
91. Letter from Tawney to Professor J. U. Nef, 26 September 1938 (Nef Papers, in Joseph Regenstein Library, University of Chicago)
92. R. M. Titmuss, "Richard Henry Tawney, 1881–1962", *L.S.E. Magazine*, November 1971, p. 6.
93. "A History of Capitalism" (1950), in *History and Society*, p. 205.
94. "The Study of Economic History", in *History and Society*, p. 63.
95. "The War and Social Policy" (1950), in *The Attack*, p. 147.
96. "The War and Social Policy", in *The Attack*, pp. 147–8.
97. "An Occupational Census of the Seventeenth Century" (1934), in *The American Labour Movement*, p. 238.
98. "Introduction" to Mayer, *Political Thought*, p. xxii.
99. "The Study of Economic History", in *History and Society*, p. 54.
100. R. M. Titmuss, F. J. Fisher and J. R. Williams, *R. H. Tawney: A Portrait by Several Hands* (London: privately published and printed by the Shenval Press, 1960), pp. 30, 31. Cf. the view of Talcott Parsons:

> "R. H. Tawney was one of the seminal minds who contributed to a number of the most important intellectual and cultural movements that have been central to the social sciences of our time, and particularly to sociology. . . . The link between the historical interests of Tawney and his role as an active labor intellectual was provided by the economic component, since the critical problems of his own time were defined by him and others as 'economic'. Hence it seemed almost obvious that their antecedents should also be looked for in the economic situations of earlier periods . . . Tawney may be considered, for the sociologist, to have been among the most important figures in his generation in forming the climate of opinion in which an important part of contemporary sociology is working. The broad field of his primary relevance may be said to be 'economic sociology'." (T. Parsons, "In Memoriam: Richard Henry Tawney (1880–1962)", *American Sociological Review*, vol. 27, 1962, pp. 888, 890.)

101. "The Condition of China" (1933), in *The American Labour Movement*, p. 187.
102. "The Study of Economic History", in *History and Society*, p. 54.
103. "The Study of Economic History", in *History and Society*, p. 56.
104. "The Study of Economic History", in *History and Society*, pp. 54–5.
105. "The Study of Economic History", in *History and Society*, p. 55.
106. "The Webbs and Their Work" (1945), in *The Attack*, p. 131.
107. Titmuss *et al.*, *op. cit.*, p. 21.
108. "Poverty as an Industrial Problem", in *The American Labour Movement*, p. 111.
109. Titmuss, *Essays*, p. 15.
110. *CB*, pp. 30–1.
111. *CB*, p 31.
112. *CB*, p. 31.

113. *CB*, p. 32.
114. *CB*, p. 30.
115. *CB*, p. 31.
116. Dr Ann Oakley, letter to author, 25 June 1980.
117. R. H. Tawney, *Land and Labour in China* (London: George Allen & Unwin Ltd., 1932), p. 69.
118. "The WEA and Adult Education", in *RT*, p. 93.
119. "Social Democracy in Britain", in *RT*, p. 165.
120. "The War and Social Policy", in *The Attack*, p. 149.
121. Titmuss *et al.*, *op. cit.*, pp. 29–30.
122. *Equality*, p. 197.
123. "The American Labour Movement" (1942), in *The American Labour Movement*, pp. 72–3.
124. Titmuss *et al.*, *op. cit.*, p. 28.
125. "British Socialism Today", in *RT*, p. 176.
126. *CB*, p. 34.
127. Speech at Manchester University to the WEA. See Tawney papers, Box 19 (Section 18/9), pp. 19–20, kept at the British Library of Political and Economic Science.
128. "Introduction" to Mayer, *Political Thought*, pp. xxi–xxii.
129. R. H. Tawney, *The British Labor Movement* (New Haven: Yale University Press, 1925), p. 72.
130. R. M. Titmuss, *Social Policy* (London: George Allen & Unwin Ltd., 1974), pp. 149–50.
131. *CB*, p. 13.
132. *Equality*, p. 223.
133. "British Socialism Today", in *RT*, p. 181.
134. *CB*, p. 14.
135. "The War and Social Policy", in *The Attack*, p. 151.
136. "The War and Social Policy", in *The Attack*, p. 156.
137. *CB*, p. 46.
138. Margaret Gowing, conversation with author, London, 6 June 1980.
139. Pearl Buck, conversation with Ross Terrill, Danby, Vermont, 26–27 December 1971. I am grateful to Professor Terrill for permission to quote from unpublished notes concerning that meeting.
140. Portrait speech at LSE. See Tawney papers, Box 19 (Section 18/10), p. 11.
141. *Ibid.*, p. 9.
142. "The American Labour Movement", in *The American Labour Movement*, p. 9.
143. "The American Labour Movement", in *The American Labour Movement*, p. 45.
144. Titmuss *et al.*, *op. cit.*, pp. 28, 33.
145. Titmuss, "R. H. Tawney, 1881–1962", *loc. cit.*
146. H. Gaitskell, Address at a Memorial Service for R. H. Tawney at St. Martin-in-the-Fields, on Thursday, 8 February 1962 and reprinted in *RT*. The quotation appears on p. 223.

4. PRODUCTION AND ALLOCATION

1. "The Study of Economic History", in *History and Society*, p. 61.
2. "The Study of Economic History", in *History and Society*, p. 62.

3. *CB*, p. 72.
4. *AS*, p. 179.
5. *AS*, p. 23.
6. *AS*, p. 24.
7. *AS*, p. 23.
8. *AS*, p. 23.
9. *AS*, p. 48.
10. *AS*, p. 70.
11. *AS*, p. 35.
12. *AS*, p. 43.
13. *AS*, p. 43.
14. *AS*, p. 44.
15. *AS*, p. 80.
16. *AS*, p. 13.
17. *AS*, p. 10.
18. *AS*, p. 11.
19. *AS*, p. 48.
20. *AS*, p. 180.
21. *AS*, p. 16.
22. *AS*, p. 16.
23. *AS*, p. 15.
24. *AS*, p. 18.
25. *AS*, p. 190.
26. *AS*, p. 183.
27. *AS*, p. 185.
28. *AS*, p. 185.
29. *AS*, p. 185.
30. *AS*, p. 186.
31. *AS*, p. 184.
32. *AS*, p. 185.
33. *AS*, p. 187.
34. *AS*, p. 189.
35. *AS*, p. 27.
36. *AS*, p. 57.
37. *AS*, p. 28.
38. *AS*, p. 78.
39. *AS*, p. 57.
40. *AS*, p. 57.
41. *AS*, p. 57.
42. *AS*, p. 126.
43. *AS*, pp. 40–1.
44. *AS*, p. 41.
45. *AS*, p. 68.
46. *AS*, p. 40.
47. *AS*, p. 42.
48. *AS*, p. 142.
49. *AS*, p. 171.
50. *AS*, p. 27.
51. *AS*, p. 30.

52. *AS*, p. 106.
53. *AS*, p. 178.
54. *AS*, p. 178.
55. *AS*, p. 122.
56. *AS*, p. 122.
57. *AS*, p. 144.
58. *AS*, p. 145.
59. *AS*, p. 36.
60. *AS*, p. 38.
61. *AS*, p. 151.
62. *AS*, p. 78.
63. *AS*, p. 161.
64. *AS*, p. 100.
65. *AS*, p. 32.
66. *AS*, p. 177.
67. *AS*, p. 32.
68. *AS*, p. 35.
69. *AS*, p. 173.
70. *AS*, p. 37.
71. *AS*, p. 79.
72. *AS*, p. 94.
73. *AS*, p. 46.
74. *AS*, pp. 97–8.
75. *AS*, p. 121.
76. *AS*, p. 97.
77. *AS*, p. 115.
78. *AS*, p. 114.
79. *AS*, p. 116.
80. *AS*, p. 97.
81. *AS*, p. 173.
82. *AS*, p. 80.
83. *AS*, p. 112.
84. *AS*, p. 81.
85. *AS*, p. 121.
86. *AS*, p. 113.
87. *AS*, p. 129.
88. *AS*, p. 89.
89. *AS*, p. 90.
90. *AS*, p. 90.
91. *AS*, p. 91.
92. *AS*, p. 148.
93. *AS*, pp. 153–4.
94. *AS*, p. 176.
95. *AS*, p. 65.
96. *AS*, p. 66.
97. *AS*, p. 149.
98. *AS*, p. 92.
99. *AS*, pp. 129–30.
100. *AS*, p. 121.

101. *AS*, p. 123.
102. *AS*, p. 92.
103. *AS*, p. 90.
104. *AS*, p. 90.
105. *AS*, p. 105.
106. *AS*, p. 82.
107. *AS*, p. 118.
108. *AS*, p. 126.
109. *AS*, p. 70.
110. *AS*, p. 70.
111. *AS*, p. 70.
112. *AS*, p. 72.
113. *AS*, p. 85.
114. *AS*, p. 77.
115. *AS*, pp. 179–80.
116. *AS*, p. 175.
117. *AS*, p. 168.
118. *AS*, p. 168.
119. *AS*, pp. 168–9.
120. *AS*, p. 40.
121. *Equality*, pp. 209–10.
122. *AS*, p. 149.
123. *AS*, p. 149.
124. *AS*, p. 155.
125. *AS*, p. 90.
126. *AS*, p. 89.
127. *CB*, p. 79.
128. *AS*, p. 155.
129. *AS*, p. 156.
130. *AS*, p. 156.
131. *AS*, p. 157.
132. *AS*, p. 157.
133. *AS*, p. 183.
134. *AS*, p. 152.
135. *AS*, p. 56.
136. *AS*, p. 103.
137. *AS*, p. 160.
138. *AS*, p. 149.
139. *AS*, p. 149.
140. "John Ruskin" (1919), in *RT*, pp. 44–5.
141. "British Socialism Today", in *RT*, p. 182.
142. *AS*, p. 83.
143. *AS*, p. 14.
144. *AS*, p. 31.
145. *AS*, p. 133.
146. *AS*, p. 174.
147. *AS*, p. 174.
148. *AS*, p. 179.
149. *AS*, p. 155.

150. *AS*, p. 165.
151. *AS*, p. 156.
152. *AS*, p. 156.
153. *AS*, p. 135.
154. *AS*, p. 94.
155. *AS*, p. 109.
156. *AS*, p. 111.
157. *AS*, p. 85.
158. *AS*, p. 12.
159. *AS*, p. 10.
160. *AS*, p. 146.
161. *AS*, pp. 136–7.
162. *AS*, p. 147.
163. *AS*, p. 149.
164. "We Mean Freedom" (1944), in *The Attack*, p. 93.
165. "Social Democracy in Britain", in *RT*, p. 172.
166. "British Socialism Today", in *RT*, p. 178.
167. "British Socialism Today", in *RT*, p. 179.
168. "Social Democracy in Britain", in *RT*, p. 170.
169. "Social Democracy in Britain", in *RT*, p. 172.
170. "We Mean Freedom", in *The Attack*, p. 94.
171. "Social Democracy in Britain", in *RT*, p. 172.
172. "We Mean Freedom", in *The Attack*, p. 97.
173. "We Mean Freedom", in *The Attack*, p. 94.
174. R. H. Tawney, *The Establishment of Minimum Rates in the Tailoring Industry under the Trade Boards Act of 1909* (London: G. Bell & Sons Ltd., 1915), p. 165.
175. *The Establishment of Minimum Rates in the Chain-Making Industry*, p. 101.
176. *The Establishment of Minimum Rates in the Chain-Making Industry*, p. 113.
177. *The Establishment of Minimum Rates in the Tailoring Industry*, p. 91.
178. R. H. Tawney, *The Agrarian Problem in the Sixteenth Century* (London: Longmans, Green & Co., 1912), p. 307.
179. *The Establishment of Minimum Rates in the Tailoring Industry*, p. 105.
180. "The Abolition of Economic Controls, 1918–21" (1941), in *History and Society*, p. 154.
181. "The Abolition of Economic Controls", in *History and Society*, p. 164.
182. "The Abolition of Economic Controls", in *History and Society*, p. 165.
183. "The Abolition of Economic Controls", in *History and Society*, p. 165.
184. "The Abolition of Economic Controls", in *History and Society*, p. 168.
185. "The Abolition of Economic Controls", in *History and Society*, p. 165.
186. "The Abolition of Economic Controls", in *History and Society*, p. 170.
187. "The Abolition of Economic Controls", in *History and Society*, p. 155.
188. "The Abolition of Economic Controls", in *History and Society*, p. 169.
189. "The Abolition of Economic Controls", in *History and Society*, p. 180.
190. *CB*, p. 36.
191. "The Abolition of Economic Controls", in *History and Society*, p. 180.
192. *CB*, p. 70.
193. "The Abolition of Economic Controls", in *History and Society*, p. 161.
194. "The Abolition of Economic Controls", in *History and Society*, p. 180.

195. "We Mean Freedom", in *The Attack*, p. 99.
196. "Social Democracy in Britain", in *RT*, p. 169.
197. *RRC*, p. 277.
198. "The Conditions of Economic Liberty", in *RT*, p. 118.
199. "The Nationalization of the Coal Industry", in *RT*, p. 130.
200. "We Mean Freedom", in *The Attack*, p. 95.
201. "The Abolition of Economic Controls", in *History and Society*, pp. 161–2.
202. "The Abolition of Economic Controls", in *History and Society*, p. 139.
203. "Social Democracy in Britain", in *RT*, p. 170.
204. "Social Democracy in Britain", in *RT*, p. 169.
205. *RRC*, p. 277.
206. *RRC*, p. 277.

5. CONVERGENCE AND BELIEF

1. J. K. Galbraith, *Journey to Poland and Yugoslavia* (Cambridge, Mass.: Harvard University Press, 1958), p. v.
2. J. K. Galbraith, *The New Industrial State* (abbreviated to *NIS*), revised edition (Harmondsworth: Penguin Books, 1974), p. 51.
3. *NIS*, p. 117.
4. *NIS*, p. 383.
5. *Journey to Poland and Yugoslavia*, p. 12.
6. *Journey to Poland and Yugoslavia*, pp. 58, 91.
7. J. K. Galbraith, *Economics and the Public Purpose* (abbreviated to *EPP*), (Harmondsworth: Penguin Books, 1975), p. 239.
8. J. K. Galbraith, *American Capitalism* (abbreviated to *AC*), revised edition (Harmondsworth: Penguin Books, 1967), p. 10.
9. J. K. Galbraith and Nicole Salinger, *Almost Everyone's Guide to Economics* (Boston: Houghton Mifflin Co., 1978), p. 29.
10. J. K. Galbraith, *A China Passage* (London: André Deutsch, 1973), p. 48.
11. J. K. Galbraith, *Economic Development* (abbreviated to *ED*) (Cambridge, Mass.: Harvard University Press, 1965), p. 3.
12. *Journey to Poland and Yugoslavia*, p. 83.
13. *ED*, p. 29.
14. *Journey to Poland and Yugoslavia*, p. 44.
15. *Journey to Poland and Yugoslavia*, p. 34.
16. *Journey to Poland and Yugoslavia*, pp. 44–5.
17. *Journey to Poland and Yugoslavia*, p. 28.
18. *Journey to Poland and Yugoslavia*, p. 76.
19. "Richard Nixon", in J. K. Galbraith, *Economics, Peace and Laughter* (abbreviated to *EPL*) (Harmondsworth: Penguin Books, 1975), p. 228.
20. *Journey to Poland and Yugoslavia*, p. 34.
21. *Journey to Poland and Yugoslavia*, p. 3.
22. "Economics and Art", in J. K. Galbraith, *The Liberal Hour* (abbreviated to *LH*) (Harmondsworth: Penguin Books, 1960), p. 58.
23. *EPP*, p. 169.
24. J. K. Galbraith, "An Agenda for American Liberals", *Commentary*, June 1966, p. 33.

25. J. K. Galbraith, *How to Control the Military* (abbreviated to *HCM*) (Garden City: Doubleday & Company, 1969), p. 36.
26. *HCM*, p. 55.
27. Quoted in F. J. Pratson, *Perspectives on Galbraith* (Boston: CBI Publishing Company, Inc., 1978), p. 232.
28. *Ibid*, p. 158.
29. J. K. Galbraith, "The Age of the Wordfact", *The Atlantic*, September 1960, p. 90.
30. "Richard Nixon", in *EPL*, p. 227.
31. J. K. Galbraith, "Reflection on the Asian Scene", *The Journal of Asian Studies*, August 1964, p. 504.
32. "The World Through Galbraith's Eyes", *The New York Times Magazine*, 18 December 1966, p. 92.
33. J. K. Galbraith, *The Affluent Society* (abbreviated to *AS*), revised edition (Harmondsworth: Penguin Books, 1973), p. 21.
34. *Almost Everyone's Guide to Economics*, pp. 21, 22.
35. Quoted in B. Collier, "A Most Galbraithian Economist", *The New York Times Magazine*, 18 February 1973, p. 60.
36. Quoted in Pratson, *op. cit.*, p. 232.
37. *NIS*, p. 388.
38. *NIS*, p. 384.
39. *ED*, pp. 33–4.
40. *NIS*, p. 329.
41. *ED*, p. 29.
42. Quoted in Pratson, *op. cit.*, p. 212.
43. *A China Passage*, p. 132.
44. *A China Passage*, p. 137.
45. "Critic of Affluence", *The Listener*, 6 May 1965, p. 658.
46. J. K. Galbraith, "The Case for George McGovern", *Saturday Review*, 1 July 1972, p. 26.
47. *Almost Everyone's Guide to Economics*, p. 116.
48. See, for example, *AC*, p. 78 and J. K. Galbraith, *The Age of Uncertainty*, (London: British Broadcasting Corporation and André Deutsch, 1977), pp. 221, 255.
49. See "My Forty Years with the F.B.I.", in J. K. Galbraith, *Annals of an Abiding Liberal* (Boston: Houghton Mifflin Co., 1979).
50. Quoted in *Playboy*, June 1968, p. 168.
51. Quoted in Pratson, *op. cit.*, p. 219.
52. The passage is quoted from an unpublished speech prepared for delivery in the 1960 Presidential campaign. The entire text may be found in the Papers of John Kenneth Galbraith (Box 75) which are kept by the John F. Kennedy Library, Boston, Massachusetts.
53. Quoted in "The Great Mogul", *Time*, 16 February 1968, p. 18.
54. "Galbraith", interview with Frances Cairncross, *The Observer*, 22 November 1970, p. 25.
55. "The Valid Image of the Modern Economy", in *Annals of an Abiding Liberal*, p. 4.
56. "The Valid Image of the Modern Economy", in *Annals of an Abiding Liberal*, p. 4.

57. "The Valid Image of the Modern Economy", in *Annals of an Abiding Liberal*, p. 18.
58. "Defenders of the Faith, I: William Simon", in *Annals of an Abiding Liberal*, p. 108.
59. J. K. Galbraith, conversation with author, Cambridge, Massachusetts, 15 August 1980.

6. REGULATION

1. J. Robinson, "*American Capitalism*", *Economic Journal*, 1952, p. 928.
2. *AC*, p. 165.
3. *NIS*, p. 202.
4. *Almost Everyone's Guide to Economics*, p. 39.
5. *Almost Everyone's Guide to Economics*, p. 40.
6. *NIS*, p. 194.
7. *Almost Everyone's Guide to Economics*, p. 39.
8. *Almost Everyone's Guide to Economics*, p. 39.
9. *AC*, p. 65.
10. *EPP*, p. 294.
11. "Power and the Useful Economist", in *Annals of an Abiding Liberal*, p. 356.
12. *AC*, p. 156.
13. *NIS*, p. 356.
14. *AC*, p. 68.
15. *AC*, p. 68.
16. *The Age of Uncertainty*, p. 277.
17. *NIS*, p. 91.
18. *NIS*, p. 47n.
19. See Bruce R. Scott, "The Industrial State: Old Myths and New Realities", *Harvard Business Review*, 1973.
20. *NIS*, p. 211.
21. *Almost Everyone's Guide to Economics*, p. 49.
22. *AC*, p. 189.
23. *EPP*, pp. 302–3.
24. *HCM*, p. 7.
25. *EPP*, p. 303.
26. *EPP*, p. 303.
27. "What Comes After General Motors", in *Annals of an Abiding Liberal*, p. 81.
28. "What Comes After General Motors", in *Annals of an Abiding Liberal*, p. 81.
29. J. K. Galbraith, "Tasks for the Democratic Left", *The New Republic*, 16 August 1975, p. 20.
30. "What Comes After General Motors", in *Annals of an Abiding Liberal*, p. 81.
31. "Tasks for the Democratic Left", p. 19.
32. "Tasks for the Democratic Left", p. 20.
33. "What Comes After General Motors", in *Annals of an Abiding Liberal*, p. 82.
34. "What Comes After General Motors", in *Annals of an Abiding Liberal*, p. 82.
35. "Tasks for the Democratic Left", p. 20.
36. "What Comes After General Motors", in *Annals of an Abiding Liberal*, p. 82.
37. "What Comes After General Motors", in *Annals of an Abiding Liberal*, p. 79.

38. "What Comes After General Motors", in *Annals of an Abiding Liberal*, p. 81.
39. *EPP*, p. 238.
40. "What Comes After General Motors", in *Annals of an Abiding Liberal*, p. 77.
41. "What Comes After General Motors", in *Annals of an Abiding Liberal*, p. 77.
42. "What Comes After General Motors", in *Annals of an Abiding Liberal*, p. 83.
43. "What Comes After General Motors", in *Annals of an Abiding Liberal*, p. 83.
44. "What Comes After General Motors", in *Annals of an Abiding Liberal*, p. 84.
45. "What Comes After General Motors", in *Annals of an Abiding Liberal*, p. 83.
46. "What Comes After General Motors", in *Annals of an Abiding Liberal*, p. 83.
47. "What Comes After General Motors", in *Annals of an Abiding Liberal*, p. 84.
48. "What Comes After General Motors", in *Annals of an Abiding Liberal*, p. 84.
49. "What Comes After General Motors", in *Annals of an Abiding Liberal*, p. 84.
50. "What Comes After General Motors", in *Annals of an Abiding Liberal*, p. 82.
51. *NIS*, p. 116.
52. *NIS*, p. 111.
53. *ED*, p. 97.
54. *ED*, pp. 93–4.
55. *ED*, p. 94.
56. *ED*, p. 93.
57. *ED*, p. 98.
58. "Tasks for the Democratic Left", p. 20.
59. "Tasks for the Democratic Left", p. 20.
60. "Tasks for the Democratic Left", p. 20.
61. *AC*, p. 185.
62. *AC*, p. 187.
63. *AC*, p. 189.
64. *AC*, p. 214.
65. "What Comes After General Motors", in *Annals of an Abiding Liberal*, p. 74.
66. J. K. Galbraith, "Perfecting the Corporation: What Comes After General Motors", *The New Republic*, 2 November 1974, p. 17. This passage was deleted when the essay was reprinted five years later in *Annals of an Abiding Liberal*. Note that nationalisation is one of only a small minority of subjects on which Galbraith has actually altered (as opposed to merely broadened) his position: despite his assertion in private conversation that "coherence in these matters shows an inability to change your mind", his work in fact demonstrates a remarkably high degree of consistency.
67. *Almost Everyone's Guide to Economics*, p. 50.
68. *NIS*, p. 389.
69. Quoted in *Playboy*, *loc. cit.*, p. 78.
70. J. K. Galbraith, *The American Left and Some British Comparisons* (Fabian Tract 405, 1971), p. 9.
71. *The American Left*, p. 35.
72. *EPP*, p. 306.
73. *Almost Everyone's Guide to Economics*, p. 142.
74. *EPP*, pp. 308–9.
75. *NIS*, p. 343.
76. *The Age of Uncertainty*, p. 322.
77. *NIS*, p. 346.
78. "Economics and Art", in *LH*, p. 59.

79. "Economics and Art", in *LH*, p. 59.
80. *NIS*, p. 345.
81. *NIS*, p. 354.
82. "Some Reflections on Public Architecture and Public Works", in *EPL*, p. 131.
83. "Some Reflections on Public Architecture and Public Works", in *EPL*, p. 131.
84. "Some Reflections on Public Architecture and Public Works", in *EPL*, p. 132.
85. "Economics as a System of Belief", in *EPL*, p. 58n.
86. *NIS*, p. 349.
87. "What Comes After General Motors", in *Annals of an Abiding Liberal*, p. 77.
88. *NIS*, pp. 349–50.
89. See, for example, J. Meade, "Is 'The New Industrial State' Inevitable?", *Economic Journal*, 1968.
90. *EPP*, p. 337.
91. "The Galbraith Plan to Promote the Minorities", *The New York Times Magazine*, 22 August 1971, p. 35.
92. *The Age of Uncertainty*, p. 167.
93. "Conversation with an Inconvenient Economist", in M. Sharpe, *John Kenneth Galbraith and the Lower Economics*, 2nd ed., (White Plains: International Arts and Sciences Press, Inc., 1973), p. 108.
94. A more extensive account of Galbraith's views on macroeconomic policy may be found in D. A. Reisman, "Social Justice and Macroeconomic Policy: The Case of J. K. Galbraith", in Aubrey Jones (ed.), *Economics and Equality* (Banbury: Philip Allan, 1976).

7. SUPPORT

1. "Economics and Art", in *LH*, p. 50.
2. M. S. Randhawa and J. K. Galbraith, *Indian Painting* (London: Hamish Hamilton, 1969).
3. "Economics and Art", in *LH*, p. 52.
4. "Economics and Art", in *LH*, p. 54.
5. J. K. Galbraith, *Made to Last* (London: Hamish Hamilton, 1964), p. 40.
6. "Economics and Art", in *LH*, pp. 54–5.
7. "Economics and Art", in *LH*, p. 57.
8. "Economics and Art", in *LH*, p. 57.
9. *EPP*, p. 79.
10. *EPP*, p. 79.
11. *EPP*, p. 83.
12. *EPP*, p. 83.
13. *NIS*, p. 344.
14. "Economics and the Quality of Life", in *EPL*, p. 20.
15. *EPP*, pp. 82–3.
16. *EPP*, p. 84.
17. "The Strategy of Peaceful Competition", in *LH*, p. 33.
18. "Economics as a System of Belief", in *EPL*, p. 66.
19. *EPP*, pp. 84–5.
20. "Some Reflections on Public Architecture and Public Works", in *EPL*, p. 129.
21. "Some Reflections on Public Architecture and Public Works", in *EPL*, p. 130.

22. "Some Reflections on Public Architecture and Public Works", in *EPL*, p. 131.
23. "The Strategy of Peaceful Competition", in *LH*, p. 33.
24. *ED*, p. 63.
25. *AS*, p. 283.
26. *EPP*, p. 172.
27. *NIS*, p. 233.
28. *NIS*, p. 310.
29. *NIS*, p. 235.
30. *EPP*, p. 162.
31. *AS*, p. 283.
32. *NIS*, pp. 337–8.
33. *EPP*, p. 313.
34. H. Demsetz, "Where Is The New Industrial State?", *Economic Inquiry* 1974, p. 12.
35. *AC*, p. 152.
36. *EPP*, p. 275n.
37. *Almost Everyone's Guide to Economics*, p. 38.
38. "Conversation with an Inconvenient Economist", *loc. cit.*, p. 116.
39. "Conversation with an Inconvenient Economist", *loc. cit.*, pp. 116–7.
40. *EPP*, p. 281.
41. *EPP*, p. 279.
42. *The American Left*, p. 33.
43. *The American Left*, p. 33.
44. For a lengthier treatment of this issue, see D. A. Reisman, "Galbraith and Social Welfare", in N. Timms (ed.), *Social Welfare: Why and How?* (London: Routledge & Kegan Paul Ltd., 1980).
45. *Almost Everyone's Guide to Economics*, p. 143.
46. Quoted in Playboy, *loc. cit.*, p. 70.

8. ADAM SMITH AND MARKET CAPITALISM

All works cited are by Adam Smith.

1. *The Wealth of Nations* (1776), ed. by Edwin Cannan (abbreviated to *WN*) (London: Methuen, 1961), vol. 1, p. 475.
2. *Lectures on Justice, Police, Revenue and Arms* (lectures given in 1763), ed. by Edwin Cannan (abbreviated to *LJ*) (Oxford: Clarendon Press, 1896), p. 169.
3. *WN*, II, pp. 49–50.
4. *The Theory of Moral Sentiments* (1759) (abbreviated to *MS*) (New York: Augustus M. Kelley, 1966), p. 343.
5. *MS*, p. 342.
6. *WN*, II, p. 208.
7. *WN*, I, p. 478.
8. *WN*, I, p. 63.
9. "The History of Astronomy" (abbreviated to "HA"), in *Essays on Philosophical Subjects* (1795), reprinted in J. Ralph Lindgren (ed.), *The Early Writings of Adam Smith* (New York: Augustus M. Kelley, 1967), p. 100.
10. *WN*, II, p. 208.

11. *MS*, p. 258.
12. *MS*, p. 126.
13. *MS*, p. 110.
14. *MS*, p. 235.
15. *MS*, p. 235.
16. *WN*, II, p. 208.
17. *MS*, p. 203.
18. *WN*, I, p. 67.
19. *WN*, I, p. 64.
20. *WN*, I, pp. 62–3.
21. *WN*, II, p. 401.
22. *WN*, I, p. 186.
23. *WN*, I, p. 161.
24. "An Early Draft of Part of *The Wealth of Nations*" (probably written about 1763), in W. R. Scott, *Adam Smith as Student and Professor* (Glasgow: University of Glasgow Press, 1937), p. 346.
25. *WN*, I, p. 36.
26. *WN*, II, pp. 114–16.
27. *WN*, I, p. 364.
28. *MS*, p. 230.
29. *WN*, I, p. 371.
30. *WN*, I, pp. 362–3.
31. *MS*, p. 170.
32. *MS*, p. 56.
33. *MS*, p. 445.
34. *MS*, p. 204.
35. *MS*, p. 289.
36. *MS*, pp. 121–2.
37. *MS*, p. 166.
38. *MS*, p. 23.
39. *MS*, p. 292.
40. *MS*, p. 224.
41. *MS*, p. 194.
42. *MS*, p. 292.
43. *MS*, p. 78.
44. *WN*, I, p. 468.
45. *MS*, p. 294.
46. *WN*, I, pp. 492–3.
47. *MS*, pp. 294–5.
48. *WN*, II, p. 431.
49. *WN*, II, p. 303.
50. *WN*, II, p. 304.
51. *WN*, II, p. 302.
52. *WN*, I, p. 433.
53. *MS*, p. 77.
54. *WN*, I, p. 519.
55. *WN*, II, p. 232.
56. *MS*, p. 77.
57. *MS*, p. 315.

58. *LJ*, p. 253.
59. *LJ*, p. 253.
60. *WN*, II, p. 272.
61. *WN*, I, p. 292.
62. *WN*, I, p. 375.
63. *WN*, II, p. 103.
64. *WN*, II, p. 188.
65. *WN*, II, p. 188.
66. *MS*, p. 293.
67. *WN*, I, p. 490.
68. *WN*, II, pp. 137–8.
69. *WN*, II, p. 357.
70. *WN*, II, p. 347.
71. *WN*, II, p. 241.
72. *WN*, II, p. 158.
73. *WN*, II, p. 269.
74. *WN*, II, p. 267.
75. *WN*, II, p. 264.
76. *WN*, II, pp. 276–8.
77. *WN*, II, p. 268.
78. *WN*, II, p. 264.
79. *WN*, II, p. 278.
80. *WN*, I, p. 295.
81. *WN*, I, p. 295.
82. *WN*, I, p. 494.
83. *WN*, II, p. 159.
84. "Early Draft", p. 344.
85. *WN*, I, p. 14.
86. *WN*, I, p. 144.
87. *WN*, II, p. 344.
88. *WN*, II, pp. 342, 344.
89. *WN*, II, p. 342.
90. *WN*, II, p. 342.
91. *WN*, I, p. 367.
92. *WN*, I, p. 358.
93. *MS*, p. 46.
94. *WN*, I, p. 468.
95. *WN*, II, p. 129.
96. *WN*, I, p. 519.
97. *WN*, I, p. 522.
98. *MS*, p. 502.
99. *LJ*, pp. 44–5.
100. *WN*, II, p. 306.
101. *WN*, II, p. 308.
102. *WN*, II, p. 250.
103. *WN*, II, p. 246.
104. *WN*, II, p. 246.
105. *WN*, II, p. 342.
106. *MS*, p. 367.

107. *WN*, II, pp. 233–4; *LJ*, p. 262.
108. *LJ*, p. 54.
109. *WN*, I, p. 449.
110. *LJ*, p. 130.
111. *WN*, I, p. 449.
112. *LJ*, pp. 159–60.
113. *WN*, I, pp. 82–3.
114. *WN*, I, p. 180.
115. *LJ*, p. 158.
116. "The Imitative Arts", in J. R. Lindgren, *op. cit.*, p. 148.
117. *WN*, I, p. 307. Italics mine.
118. *WN*, II, p. 400.
119. *MS*, p. 314.
120. *WN*, II, p. 405.
121. *MS*, p. 284.
122. *WN*, I, p. 132.
123. *Lectures on Rhetoric and Belles Lettres* (lectures given in 1762–3), ed. by John M. Lothian (London: Thomas Nelson & Sons Ltd., 1963), pp. 40–1.
124. *WN*, I, p. 192.
125. *WN*, I, p. 37.
126. *WN*, I, p. 368.
127. *MS*, p. 259.
128. *MS*, p. 263.
129. *WN*, I, p. 437.
130. *WN*, I, p. 439.
131. *WN*, II, p. 308.
132. *MS*, p. 265.
133. *WN*, II, p. 284.
134. *WN*, I, p. 113.
135. *WN*, II, p. 179.
136. *MS*, p. 263.
137. *WN*, II, p. 322.
138. *WN*, II, p. 319.
139. *WN*, II, p. 325.
140. *WN*, I, pp. 427–8.
141. *WN*, II, p. 326.
142. *WN*, II, p. 326.
143. *WN*, II, p. 331.
144. *WN*, II, p. 314.
145. *WN*, II, p. 315.
146. *WN*, II, p. 319.
147. *WN*, II, p. 325.
148. *MS*, p. 253.
149. *WN*, II, p. 483.
150. *WN*, I, p. 433.
151. "HA", p. 49.

Index